R 01085 87235

Margaret Wade Labarge was educated at Harvard and Oxford Universities and lives in Ottawa. She taught at Ottawa and Carleton Universities before becoming a full-time writer. A highly distinguished medieval historian, her previous books include *Simon de Montfort*, *Henry V*, and *Gascony: England's First Colony 1204–1453*.

BY MARGARET WADE LABARGE

Simon de Montfort

Henry V

St Louis

Gascony: England's First Colony, 1204–1453

Mistress, Maids and Men:
Baronial Life in the Thirteenth Century
(originally published as *A Baronial Household
of the Thirteenth Century*)

Medieval Travellers: The Rich and Restless

A Small Sound of the Trumpet: Women in Medieval Life

Medieval Travellers

The Rich and Restless

MARGARET WADE LABARGE

PHOENIX

A PHOENIX PAPERBACK

First published in Great Britain in 1982
by Hamish Hamilton Ltd
This paperback edition published in 2005
by Phoenix,
an imprint of Orion Books Ltd,
Orion House, 5 Upper St Martin's Lane,
London WC2H 9EA

A CIP catalogue record for this book
is available from the British Library.

ISBN 0 75382 041 2

Typeset by Butler and Tanner Ltd,
Frome and London

Printed and bound in Great Britain by
Clays Ltd, St Ives plc

www.orionbooks.co.uk

For Sarah, Monica and Emily,
Matthew, Jeremy and Regan –
another generation of travellers

CONTENTS

ACKNOWLEDGEMENTS

This description of the wanderings of some rich and restless medieval travellers has been much enhanced by the generous assistance of many scholarly friends and acquaintances who kindly pointed out useful sources of information or provided new light on attitudes, customs and conditions. I am particularly grateful to Dr William Voelkle, Pierpont Morgan Library, New York, for information about the early medieval maps in their collection; to Professor Michael Sheehan, Pontifical Institute of Medieval Studies, Toronto, for the use of his index of medieval English wills; to Professor R. H. C. Davis, for enlightenment about Compostela and its pilgrims; to Colonel B. Greenhous for material about the management and shipping of large quantities of horses and some insight into the nature of Central Asian caravans; and to Professor F. R. H. Du Boulay for the phrase which forms the sub-title of the book and so appositely describes its subject. Professor J. G. Bellamy read chapters 1–4, providing helpful comments, and Miss P. Blackstock most kindly read and criticised the complete text. For any errors that remain, I am totally responsible.

A medievalist working in Canada is always grateful for the range of institutional libraries which provide hospitality and assistance. In London, the British Library and the Institute of Historical Research; in Toronto, the Pontifical Institute of Medieval Studies and the Robarts Library of the University of Toronto; and in Ottawa, the National Library and the libraries of Carleton University, University of Ottawa and St Paul's University have all been most helpful.

Finally, the enthusiasm and interest in my medieval travellers expressed by my patient friends during the years of research and writing have been an invaluable stimulus and support.

Margaret Wade Labarge

INTRODUCTION

Harried modern tourists, shuffling through crowded airports hung round with flight bags and cameras, are inclined to feel that no previous generation ever travelled so widely or responded so enthusiastically to the lure of distant places. They are certainly convinced that no one in the remote Middle Ages ever went far from home or indulged themselves in foreign travel. The reality is quite different from this outdated stereotype, for even contemporary travel of the most luxurious kind would find it hard to compete with the elegance of the embassy of Thomas Becket to France in 1158. William Fitzstephen, one of Becket's biographers, details with enthusiasm the elaborate spectacle that the travels of an important member of the medieval establishment could provide.

On this occasion Becket's retinue as chancellor of England was made up of some two hundred members of his household – knights, clerks, officials and young nobles sent to him for training. All were on horseback and dressed in new clothes suitable to their station in society. There were large iron-bound chariots, each pulled by five horses, and each having its own driver, guardian and fierce watchdog. A groom walked beside each of the strong and shapely horses – more like chargers, Fitzstephen says proudly, than your usual rather broken down cart animals. Several of the chariots were earmarked for specific uses. One was set aside for transporting the requirements of the chapel, another for the chamber, one for the chancellor's exchequer and another for his kitchen. Two were required to transport iron-bound barrels of fine English ale, 'that most healthy drink the colour of wine but of better flavour', which was intended as a gift for the French. The remaining carts carried food and drink for the company, bags of bedclothes, other bags of tapestries and hangings to decorate Becket's bed and chamber when he received guests, as well as that miscellaneous baggage so truthfully described as impedimenta. At the head of the twelve packhorses was the one carrying the altar ornaments, sacred vessels and service books for the chancellor's chapel. The others were loaded with chests of gold and silver vessels as well as the more utilitarian plates and dishes, kettles and cauldrons. Other chests carried Becket's supply of money (in pennies as the only actual coins), sufficient for his daily expenses and the expected gifts. Among the remaining baggage were books and clothes, and the clothes at least must have taken considerable space for the chancellor was reported to have twenty-four complete changes with him, as well as the elegant robes destined to be given away and left overseas. The logistics of such a group would appal the most experienced modern travel agent.

As all this motley assembly passed through the French towns on its way to Paris it was carefully marshalled to produce the greatest effect on the bystanders. First came the foot servants in small groups, singing as they went, and followed by the greyhounds and other hunting dogs with their runners and attendants. At a reasonable distance behind came the chariots and the carts with their precious cargoes protected with tarpaulins of hides. Plodding after the carts came the sumpter, or pack, horses, ridden by their grooms with a monkey chattering from each saddle. By this time the curious inhabitants were certain to have emerged from their doors to discover what this procession meant and were informed that the English chancellor was sent on a message to the king of France. The men and women gaped at the sight of the squires, carrying their knights' shields and leading their chargers, then the young nobles of the household on horseback and the falconers with their birds. There were still others to come, the household officials, the knights and clerks riding two by two and finally, the glittering focus of this elaborate cavalcade, the Chancellor himself, surrounded by a few close companions. No wonder the French exclaimed: 'Marvellous is the English king whose chancellor journeys in such state.'[1] Fitzstephen's conviction of the suitability of such magnificence was generally shared and specifically echoed by John Mirk, a popular fourteenth-century preacher. Mirk perceived Becket as a patriot and a proper lord, particularly 'manful' in his luxurious maintenance of his household and his ostentation in clothes, horses and retinue.[2]

It was this stunning effect of magnificence, privilege and carefully calculated display that distinguished the travels of the medieval upper class and is so foreign to. us. Medieval society had a strong sense of 'estate', a belief that each person had a special place in society – usually through birth, sometimes by function – which he was bound to uphold and make clear to those around him. Thus it was the pleasant duty of the rich and powerful to wear fine clothes and jewellery, to ride a spirited horse, to set a generous table and to scatter largess among the less fortunate. From an early period kings and nobles found it imperative to tour their territories or lordships, both to assert the reality of their power at a time when rule resided in the person of the lord and, since freight was difficult and expensive, to consume on the spot the produce of the neighbouring manors. Because kings, nobles, leading churchmen and important officials held so many of the levers of power in their own hands, and were frequently linked by ties of kinship and marriage, they were constantly in touch with one another, even across national barriers which only slowly became important. Since they travelled a great deal with a large retinue and many belongings they found it reasonable to maintain the same pattern of life wherever they went, and considered it equally important that strangers and acquaintances alike could recognise at a glance their place in the social hierarchy. Display and elegance were necessary; comfort, though desired, was secondary. To our minds medieval travellers of all classes had very minimal standards of comfort and ranked it low as a matter of importance but then the conditions of everyday life did not make even moderate comfort easy to attain.

Looking at the medieval travellers of the upper classes between the thirteenth and the mid-fifteenth centuries, especially in England and France, we find a wide range of reasons for travel as well as a variety of travellers. All through this period kings moved their courts and nobles their households with monotonous frequency, urged on by reasons of state, a passion for pilgrimages, the desire to visit their favourite hunting spots or merely boredom. Many upper-class men were accustomed to farflung, even incessant travel as crusaders, diplomats or because they were young restless adventurers for whom there was no settled niche in the social hierarchy who must journey in search of fortune. Important ecclesiastics visited their dioceses, shared in church councils and secular parliaments and often had to make their way to the papal curia on matters of urgent business. The travels of upper-class women were more restricted but they too were mobile. Queens and their attendant ladies generally shared in the many royal progresses and the moves of the royal household from one palace or hunting lodge to another. Wives of important nobles took part in the transport of their households between castles and manors. Social occasions such as weddings, great feasts and especially tournaments, attracted not only the lords and ambitious knights who took part but also their wives and marriageable daughters. Royal wives often accompanied their husbands on crusade to the Holy Land in the thirteenth century and were accompanied by other noble ladies. The widow took advantage of her favoured position in medieval society and its accompanying freedom of action to visit relatives or friends, or to go on pilgrimage where she might well be joined by a highly-born nun looking for a legitimate diversion from the monotonous routine of convent life.

Despite the number of such noble travellers the amount of actual travel writing is very limited until the mid-fourteenth century. The descriptions we do have of earlier travels tend to be bald and factual, with little personal response to the new wonders they saw or the difficulties they faced. Such exceptions as the gossipy archdeacon, Gerald of Wales, at the end of the twelfth century and the Sire de Joinville, friend and biographer of Louis IX of France, in the thirteenth, delight us with their unusually human and personal note. By the end of the fourteenth century, and even more in the fifteenth, travellers' reports developed a more personal flavour. The reader can begin to know something of the individual and not merely judge the accuracy of the observer. It may seem surprising

1. Emperor Frederick II with his falconers

to emphasise the accuracy of medieval reports but, in fact, many medieval men provided excellent descriptions of places and matters of which they had firsthand knowledge, particularly where it was only necessary to record surface phenomena without searching for hidden causes or abstract principles. On the other hand, when they reported secondhand stories the fabulous easily crept in, since for many parts of the world they relied on wild scraps of other travellers' tales and had no standards against which to judge. Under such circumstances it is not really surprising that someone who had just seen a giraffe or a rhinoceros for the first time should find the description of a unicorn equally plausible.

Few medieval travellers were very interested in the hidden processes which lay behind the visible natural world, although there were, of course, exceptions. Frederick II, that extraordinary thirteenth-century ruler of Sicily and the Holy Roman Empire, was a close observer of nature. He wrote the definitive treatise on the care and training of falcons and had sufficient scientific curiosity to send off messengers to investigate for him the habits of the barnacle goose. In the Middle Ages this bird was generally believed to develop from a growth common on timbers or dead trees. Frederick's messengers were commissioned to bring him back samples of wood with such growths which the pragmatic emperor then examined but could find no corroborating evidence that any bird had ever sprung from them. He suggested that the superstition arose from the fact that barnacle geese bred in such remote latitudes that men, in ignorance of their real nesting places, invented this explanation.[3] Two centuries later Aeneas Silvius, the indefatigable, curious and practical humanist who became Pope Pius II, used a diplomatic visit to Scotland to do his own research into the tenacious legend. He, like Frederick, could find no real evidence and reported with obvious scepticism that the story of the remarkable tree which was supposed to hatch the goose was always told of a further shore unvisited by the narrator.[4] A fifteenth-century Bohemian traveller to England suggests a more practical reason for the continued acceptance of the legend. Entertained at an official banquet given by the duke of Clarence on a meatless day, he and his retinue were surprised to be offered barnacle goose. Their English hosts assured them that, although it tasted like a bird, it was truly a fish and could be eaten on fish days since it was produced in the sea.[5] Such casuistical reasoning could be most useful given the number of meatless days in the medieval calendar.

Where firsthand reports of travellers are lacking there are other possible sources of information. Chronicles and literary works provide useful hints and observations and a surprising amount of factual information is to be found in the various accounts. The wardrobe accounts of royalty, like the less complicated household accounts of nobles and distinguished churchmen, are full of details about the ways such people travelled and the expenses incurred on their journeys. Equally informative are the expense accounts of noble diplomats and officials, as they had to submit an itemised list of expenditures to the exchequer before they were reimbursed. Such accounts also help in estimating the length of a day's journey by detailing where each night was spent. Some of their entries can seem remarkably modern, as when a thirteenth-century official carefully included in his claim for the expenses of travelling from England to Bordeaux and back on royal business the cost of his losses on foreign exchange.[6] From such sources we can learn a great deal about where and how such upper-class people travelled and how conditions and attitudes changed in the course of these three centuries.

There is no suggestion that the important people were the only, or the most far-ranging, medieval travellers. Such friars as John of Plano Carpini, William of Rubruck and Orderic of Pordenone, who provided the first factual accounts of the Mongol Empire at its height; Marco Polo, Nicolo Conti, and all those other merchants, known and unknown, who criss-crossed the Mediterranean, the Black Sea and many parts of Asia in search of trade; the humble soldiers, pilgrims and vagabonds to be met on many medieval roads: all added considerably to the general fund of knowledge and the sense of ease in confronting the unfamiliar. Nevertheless, their travels were utilitarian, their style spartan compared to the voyages of the great and powerful. Because the medieval upper classes set policy and controlled events to a greater degree than we find easy to recognise they served as patrons and models of culture and behaviour. Travel not only educated them but also broadened the horizons of their accompanying retinues which were drawn from all levels of the social scale. Since the ways of kings and nobles were eagerly imitated by their inferiors, the knowledge and experience gained abroad and the growing interest in the strange and remote were gradually disseminated throughout society. The late fifteenth and the early sixteenth centuries were the age of discovery. The princes of Europe encouraged their sailors and explorers to go in search of the new worlds of whose existence and possible profit-ability their diplomats and noble adventurers, as well as their merchants and sailors, had begun to convince them. That expansion of the known world could not have happened without the technical and intellectual foundations gradually built up by so many gen-erations of individual travellers.

A voyage backward in time to look at the travels of some of these medieval men and women, seeing through their eyes the conditions which shaped their voyaging, and sharing their experiences and reactions as they went to the boundaries of their known world, provides an illuminating tour of unfamiliar territory.

CHAPTER ONE

THE SHAPE OF THEIR WORLD

The serious modern traveller about to set off for some strange and unknown place expects to prepare for his travels by the careful study of maps and the consultation of a number of easily available guidebooks. Normally he also has a reasonable amount of practical information about the problems of long-distance travel in general and of his destination in particular. The situation of his medieval counterpart was quite different. The store of available knowledge, either in written form or on maps, was at first very limited and often marked by a fascinating jumble of the real and the mythical. In addition, the rather fortuitous survival of manuscripts makes it difficult to estimate who might have had the opportunity to consult what authorities. There is no question that all through the Middle Ages much information was gained from personal contact with ambassadors from near and far and ecclesiastics from remote places. Kings' courts, noble households and the more important abbeys were the normal places of entertainment for such distinguished guests and their hosts listened to them with interest, but it is impossible to know how widely the information they gained was disseminated. By the end of the twelfth century, however, a considerable amount of practical topographical knowledge of the main countries of Europe and the Middle East had already been accumulated and was quite widely known. The great crusading waves of the late eleventh and twelfth centuries took great numbers of men and women on the difficult land journey to Constantinople or on the voyage through the islands of the Mediterranean and the Aegean. The passion for long-range pilgrimages to Jerusalem,

Compostela and Rome, the constantly expanding network of long-distance trade and the creation of European trading posts all through the Mediterranean and up into the Black Sea meant that few localities in Europe lacked direct contact with individuals who had personally travelled considerable distances. Naturally not all the information they brought back was equally trustworthy for the calibre of travellers' reports in any age varies with the abilities of the observer. Much legend heard at secondhand was frequently related as fact and then further enhanced by subsequent narrators, but there was also much sharp observation of detail and a real concern for accuracy. The important travellers with whom we are particularly concerned could also be informed by the literate and highly trained clerks who were in touch with the growing body of knowledge. As well, the highly born were more likely to meet such an extraordinary traveller as John of Plano Carpini, the fat and elderly Franciscan sent by Innocent IV in 1245 as an ambassador to the conquering Mongols. In two years the friar and his companion rode from Poland thousands of miles across the steppes of Asia to the headquarters of the Great Khan at Karakorum, south of Lake Baikal in Outer Mongolia, and returned safely to report to the pope and the French king.[1] The Italian Franciscan Salimbene, who was at Sens when Brother John passed through the town after narrating his travels to the French court, suggests the importance of the network of personal communication when he remarked on how the friar was constantly invited out as a most prized guest to dinner and supper.[2] Those who listened to his almost incredible adventures, which brought remote Asia and the dreaded Mongols to vivid life, were given sober fact to confront the legends already rife about such lands.

Such personal contacts continued to increase and multiply but by the fourteenth century there is also proof in the contemporary inventories of royal and noble households of collections of maps or books touching on distant lands. Books might well be read aloud to the assembled household, a common amusement all through the Middle Ages, but by the fourteenth and fifteenth centuries there is evidence that private reading had become a more frequent pleasure and was encouraged by the wealthy nobles' acquisition of beautifully illuminated books of hours and romances. This enjoyment was made easier for the older, more sedentary lord or lady by the development of spectacles at the end of the thirteenth century. A century later Philip the Bold, duke of Burgundy, even had his glasses in their silver case attached to his reading desk so that they would not be broken or mislaid.[3] A practical work described as 'a paper book of diverse words in diverse languages', which certainly sounds like an inexpensive traveller's dictionary, was included in the inventory of books of Sir Simon Burley, tutor of the young Richard II at the end of the fourteenth century.[4] The library lists of royalty and nobles, incomplete and fragmentary as they are, suggest that the lay lords, as well as the ecclesiastics and university scholars, had the basic reference works on which the geographical knowledge of the Middle Ages was based. The thirteenth century *Speculum*, or Mirror, compiled by Vincent of Beauvais, a learned Dominican closely linked to the court of Louis IX, summarised the best general knowledge of his time and was later to be found in most important libraries. The section on nature was generally borrowed from earlier scholars but that on history was sufficiently contemporary to include a summary of John of Plano Carpini's report on the Mongols, thus bringing the Franciscan's account to a much wider audience.

Even more popular was Bartholomew the Englishman's useful compendium, *On the Properties of Things*, which stands in relation to Vincent's *Speculum* as the one volume quick reference to a full-length encyclopedia. Written in Latin in the mid-thirteenth century by an English Franciscan teaching at Paris, it was soon translated into several languages and was even one of the texts rented by Paris booksellers to the local students. It represents the general knowledge which the cultured person of the later Middle Ages might be expected to have and turns up in many quite small or unexpected libraries. The lords of Berkeley in distant Gloucestershire, for example, encouraged their chaplain, John Trevisa, at the end of the fourteenth century to make an English translation for the castle library.[5] Bartholomew's range was wide, from the nature of God to domestic minutiae, but he devoted three books of his great work to geography, two describing the features of the earth and of the various bodies of water and one listing, more or less alphabetically, regions and provinces with their outstanding characteristics. In the accepted medieval tradition he borrowed much of his geographical lore from the encyclopedists who had preceded him, especially Isidore of Seville whose seventh century *Etymologies* had transmitted to the Middle Ages most of its classical heritage and whose work was a veritable storehouse consistently plundered by later writers. However, Bartholomew was not content merely to copy. He recognised the feudal world of his own time and frequently added his own contemporary description of places he knew or had heard about. Like most medieval travellers his appreciation of landscape was tied to the fertility of land and useful streams – a natural concern when the successful cultivation of land was the basic need. He was a reasonably even tempered authority and he obviously enjoyed writing about the polar bears in Iceland with their habit of making holes in the ice and fishing through them but he reserves his warmest praise for England, 'the plenteuouseste corner of the world'. A typical medieval English prejudice against the Scots is evident in his comment that they are sufficiently good-looking in face and figure but their native costume deforms their appearance, although he recognises that they are brave and fierce fighters, used to a sparse living.[6]

The brief and generally sober information provided by Bartholomew was exceeded in popularity among the upper classes by two books of travellers' tales, those of Marco Polo and of Sir John Mandeville – one mainly true, one mainly fabulous. Seventeen-year-old Marco Polo travelled across Asia to China in the company of his father and uncle, both Venetian merchants. His description of that trip, their long stay in China, their return journey through the China Sea and the Indian Ocean to Persia and their final return to Venice after an absence of twenty-five years has become an accepted classic. We owe its existence to the fact that Marco Polo fought with the Venetian navy against the Genoese soon after his return and was captured in the battle. While in prison in 1298 he dictated to a fellow prisoner with some reputation as a poet the tales which had beguiled their captivity. The book was a great success, being translated almost immediately into several languages and Italian dialects of which a remarkable number of manuscripts survive. Marco Polo's travels had taken him to such extraordinary places, and life at the court of Kublai Khan was so remote from that of thirteenth-century Europe, that the truth of his stories was generally doubted, though his book was widely read for its fascination. More modern explorers have demonstrated that Polo was a remarkably accurate observer with very few mentions of the purely legendary. He provided for a growing audience an entrancing picture of China just before the break-up of the Mongol empire shut for further centuries the overland route between Europe and the Far East. Certainly, Polo's travels and the wonders he saw sparked great interest in the riches which might be found there and it is known that the account of his travels was one of the books read with interest and attention by Christopher Columbus.[7]

The travels of Sir John Mandeville were quite another matter. Although the author begins his book by introducing himself as an English knight, born at St Albans, who went to the Holy Land in 1322 and then travelled most of the known – and a good deal of the unknown – world, Sir John's existence as a real traveller has been proved as fabulous as some of his stories, though the actual author has never been firmly identified. The book was written in the mid-fourteenth century and is a patchwork from a wide collection of authorities, some truthful, others fictional. The compilation was written first in French, then translated into Latin and later into English and spread rapidly through western Europe.[8] Its author was blessed with a racy style and an engaging ability to combine his various sources which, in the accepted medieval tradition, he does not acknowledge. They ranged from serious works like Vincent of Beauvais' *Speculum*, and the reports of the travels in Asia of such friars as William of Rubruck, who was sent to the Mongols by Louis IX soon after Plano Carpini's return, and Orderic of Pordenone, who travelled to China in the early fourteenth century, to the forged letter of Prester John, that extraordinary apocryphal Christian ruler whose kingdom was gradually transferred from Asia to Africa, but was always a place of riches and power and, it was hoped, of possible help against the Saracens or the pagans. Since the Holy Land had attracted a great number of pilgrims, some of whom were serious students and others interested observers, Mandeville found a fair number of earlier descriptions of the country and the Holy Places on which to build when he came to write about Palestine. He borrowed from the histories of Jacques de Vitry, bishop of Acre at the beginning of the thirteenth century, and the Armenian historian Hayton, who died at the beginning of the fourteenth century. The author of Mandeville's *Travels* also found useful material in a report produced by William of Boldensele for Cardinal Talleyrand-Perigord, a friend of Petrarch who was very curious about overseas territories. Boldensele was a Dominican from Minden in Westphalia who claimed relationship to a celebrated German noble family through his mother. His pilgrimage to the Holy Land was imposed as a penance by John XXII for some undefined 'apostasy' and took place in 1334-5. The Dominican visited Constantinople, Egypt and Syria as well as the Holy Places and the detailed report he drew up for the cardinal in 1336 was very popular. It was translated into French within fifteen years and both the original and the translations survive in many fourteenth-and fifteenth-century manuscripts, often combined with other reports less accurate than his. Boldensele had an unusually scientific spirit for his time and was capable of giving a map-like description of a country without a personal point of view or any addition of the miraculous.[9] His sober report was a more useful source than many of the others on which the author of Mandeville drew. Not surprisingly, much of the charm of Mandeville's book for its medieval readers lay in its more fabulous portions – the miraculous stories borrowed from the *Golden Legend* and the romances of Alexander, as well as the remarkable animals whose descriptions were taken from the early bestiaries. Mandeville had something to interest everybody, and there is little doubt that he interested a great many, reinforcing their credulity with his mythical animals and human monsters. However, to make the distinction between the 'truth' of Marco Polo and the 'fiction' of Mandeville is easier done with the benefit of several centuries' hindsight. Given the inaccessibility of central Asia and China after the mid-fourteenth century and the practical impossibility of discovering the sober truth, it is not surprising that medieval visions of the Far East were a fine mix of fact

2. Fifteenth-century pictorial map of the Holy Land

and fiction uncritically accepted. The 'marvels' described by Polo and Mandeville bore for the medieval reader their original meaning of astonishment and wonder. They nourished their imagination and ultimately helped to encourage serious exploration.

Descriptive writing about the Holy Land abounded, inspired by devotion and the momentous experience of crusade or pilgrimage, but few of the authors insisted so vigorously on their excellent qualifications as the German Ludolph von Suchem who was overseas from 1336 to 1341. He remarked condescendingly that many people wrote about the Holy Land and the other lands beyond the sea after a single quick passage while he had lived there for five continuous years 'being both by day and by night in the company of kings and princes, chiefs, nobles and lords'. Ludolph was convinced that he was well equipped to write a 'compendious history' built on what he heard from 'truthful men' or 'happily extracted' from previous histories such as that of William of Boldensele who was in fact far more acute about geography than his self-satisfied compatriot.[10] Unfortunately few people were interested in providing adequate and accurate descriptions of lands closer to home so we are grateful to the occasional individual who displayed such a geographical interest. Gerald of Wales, the loquacious archdeacon,

made use of his travels on church or royal business to gather material for his assorted treatises. He wrote a careful and most informative description of his native Wales as well as a topography of
Ireland, both countries practically unknown to the English of his
day. *The Topography of Ireland* and its companion, the *Conquest of
Ireland*, were inspired by his trip to Ireland in 1185 with Prince
John, the youngest son of Henry II. Neither is as judicious as his
description of his beloved Wales, for Gerald looked on Ireland
with the prejudices of its Anglo-Norman conquerors and had few
compliments for the Irish clergy. The way in which he proposed to
bring the *Topography* to public attention is an interesting comment
on the customs of his time. Gerald was as vain as most authors and
certainly craved personal fame so he decided to read his corrected
work aloud at Oxford where he could count on a learned audience.
Since the book was divided into three parts he read one part each
day and – perhaps to encourage attendance – entertained generously on each of the three days. His method of attracting public
attention vaguely suggests the modern launching of favoured books
but he drew from different publics. The archdeacon's guests on one
day were the doctors of the various faculties of the university and
their best students and on another the knights of the town and the
leading citizens, suggesting that he was not aiming solely for a
clerical audience. Even more medieval in concept was the provision
on the first day of a feast for all the poor of the town whom
Gerald had gathered together to share a dinner which they probably
enjoyed a great deal more than the reading.[11]

Gerald of Wales and Gilles Le Bouvier, herald of Charles VII of
France and Berry king-at-arms, were separated by very different
personalities as well as two and a half centuries. Le Bouvier was a
man of noble family from Berry who had originally followed the
great duke of Berry and after his death moved to the service of the
dauphin at Bourges. Beginning as an unimportant messenger in
the dauphin's stable, he was first used on minor missions, then
promoted to herald in 1420 and given the title of Berry king-at-
arms, that is, the king's leading herald. During the following years
he was sent on many major missions and appears to have been
present at many of the campaigns for the recovery of France. We

catch a glimpse of him in 1437, wearing his herald's rich coat-of-arms of blue velvet with three fleurs-de-lis embroidered in gold and edged with large pearls, and leading the procession when Charles VII re-entered Paris.[12] His experience enabled him to write a chronicle as well as the *Description of Countries* but it is his introduction to the latter that suggests both his interests and the changes that had come about since the days of Gerald of Wales. The elderly herald who had decided at sixteen that he wanted to travel and see the world had by the age of sixty covered much of Europe, the Middle East, Constantinople, Armenia and the Black Sea area around Trebizond. When he came to write up his notes and impressions of the places and people he had seen his interest in travel was still unquenched for his youthful enthusiasm is echoed in his explanation of why he wrote:

> So that many men of various nations and countries can delight themselves and take pleasure as I have done in time past to see the world and the various things which are therein, and also for many who wish to know without going there and the others who wish to go, see and travel, I have begun this little book, according to my small understanding, so that those who see it can truly know the manner, form and characteristics of the things which are in all the Christian kingdoms and the other kingdoms where I have found myself.[13]

He promises to describe the size of kingdoms, their mountains and rivers, and the characteristics of countries and their inhabitants, writing only about where he himself had been.

His work is fascinating and remarkably accurate despite certain expected preferences. He considered France 'the most beautiful, most pleasant, most gracious and best proportioned' of all kingdoms, with six months of summer and six of winter, neither of which were too hot or too cold. He gave its size – twenty-two days' journey from Ecluse (Sluis) in the north to St-Jean-Pied-du-Port at the foot of the Pyrenees, and sixteen from St-Matthieu-fin-des-terres (Brittany) to Lyon on the Rhone – and naturally lauded the beauties of Paris and the royal palace there.[14] But mere national chauvinism was not the herald's most striking characteristic. He was interested in the nature of the soil and its products, whether wine was made or drunk and what goods were manufactured, mentioning, for example, that Tournai was famous for mercery and war harness. His care in listing such thermal stations as St-Laurent-les-Bains, Vichy, Bagnères and Dax suggests that Frenchmen's concern with their liver and the favoured curative spas has a long and popular history. Naturally the nations closest to France attracted most of his attention and were most carefully described, providing such useful pieces of information as the method of evaporating the salt from the salt well at Salins in the county of Burgundy. The herald's eye was sharp for in Savoy, Dauphiné, Piedmont and Switzerland he remarked on the number of people with enlarged throats, though he did not understand the cause of such goitres.[15] In Italy he emphasised the sad state of Rome, devastated by wars, with wild animals living in caves within the city, contrasting it to the commercial prosperity of Milan, adding that in Lombardy they shoe their oxen as they do horses in other countries. Another source of fascination was the stoves used in Bavaria in winter, for 'they are so warm in their rooms craftsmen can do their work and keep their wives and children . . . nobles, soldiers and other men of leisure do likewise in playing, singing, eating and drinking to pass the time.'[16] His description of the islands on the way to the East is clear and specific, as is his account of the Venetian and Genoese trading posts of Tana and Caffa on the Black Sea, adding that the sea voyage from Flanders to Tana is 'half the world', while few westerners go there by land because of the dangers of the trip, for the oncoming Turks now controlled much of this territory. He has little to mention east of Armenia though, like other commentators, he praises the Turks as the most honest and the best warriors of all the Saracens. The tone of his comments on Constantinople and Armenia make it evident that he wrote before the final fall of Constantinople and the old Byzantine empire in 1453. Le Bouvier refers to Jerusalem only to dismiss any need for him to describe it, saying specifically that there were so many pilgrims who had learned enough to discuss it sufficiently.[17]

His information on the eastern and northern countries was scanty for he had little to say about the Scandinavian or Baltic countries, though he mentioned the periods of total sunlight and total darkness, the cold and the warlike nature of the men who 'are always ready to battle even against their lord'. Le Bouvier, in another very French comment, considered that this was probably due to the fact that they drank beer and mead instead of wine, 'for such men fight more easily than those nourished with wine'. His remarks about Prussia were restricted to the description of the nature of the expeditions which used to be conducted there by the Teutonic Knights against the northern marches in which they were assisted 'before the French wars' by noble knights and squires from the borders of France. The Spanish peninsula, England, Scotland and Ireland also received summary treatment though Le Bouvier estimated the length of England at eight days' journey and reluctantly admitted that the English were good men of war and archers. He commented on the effect of the longstanding war between the English and the Scots which resulted in ravaged land between them requiring three days' travel so that it was necessary to carry all supplies, especially when going to Scotland.[18] Ireland was notable only for the pilgrimage spot of St Patrick's Purgatory and the fact that it was the poorest country in the world. Nevertheless one casual sentence shows how far Europe had moved from the twelfth-century topography of Gerald of Wales and its totally closed world:

> Beyond this land of Ireland are to be found neither lands nor other islands towards the setting sun. And some say that if a ship was steered in a direct line for a long distance the ship would find itself in the land of Prester John. And others say that it is the edge of the lands of the western coast.[19]

The fifteenth-century herald marks the change in tone, in interests and in openness to new worlds that was rapidly coming to Europe, although his conditions of travel and the maps he would have known were still medieval.

Medieval maps, like their travellers' tales, tended to be of two varieties, the symbolic and the practical. The original world maps, which graced the halls and later the libraries of kings and a few nobles, were seen almost as illustrated romances rather than matter-of-fact guides to lead travellers from one place to another.

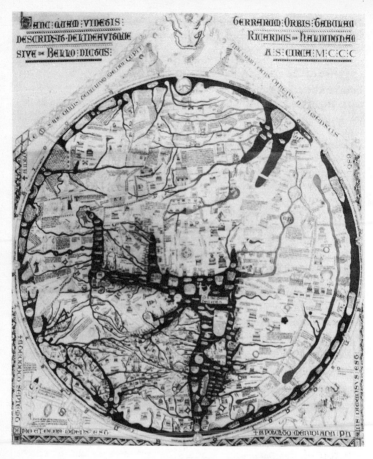

3. Mappa mundi from Hereford Cathedral

The World Map of c. 1300 displayed in Hereford Cathedral suggests the usual pattern and illustrates how medieval thinkers visualised their world. That map portrays a circular flat world surmounted by a portrayal of the Day of Judgment. Jerusalem is at the centre and east at the top. The eye descends from the Garden of Eden to the great city of Babylon, the Tower of Babel and then to Calvary and the cross as the central event of human history. The Mediterranean is the map's most obvious feature and it is closed at the bottom of the map by the Pillars of Hercules, for at this time the Straits of Gibraltar were considered by abstract thinkers, if not by sailors, to be the boundary of the known world. It requires an active exercise of the imagination to recognise France, much less England, Scotland and Ireland which are squeezed almost unrecognisably into the map's lower lefthand quarter. The Red Sea and Persian Gulf are vividly red with a large, amorphous island of Ceylon at the foot of the Arabian peninsula. Occasional real features are illustrated on the map, such as the famous lighthouse at Alexandria, but much of its depiction of the unknown countries of Asia and Africa is filled with charming sketches of real and fantastic beasts and legendary men, as well as such highlights of biblical history as Noah's ark.[20] Such a map was of little practical use to real travellers, much as they might enjoy its fantasies.

At the same time, however, new types of working maps were being devised. The thirteenth-century chronicler Matthew Paris provided useful drawings of England and Scotland which were less maps than illustrated itineraries, showing the line of travel from Dover to the north. He also drew a similar itinerary from London to Apulia.[21] Many travellers, especially merchants and pilgrims, relied heavily on the numerous unillustrated itineraries available, which listed the intermediate towns between two distant points, usually giving some estimate of distances along the way and putting special emphasis on major towns and places of pilgrimage. By 1360 the Gough Map of England, Scotland and Wales suggests how much progress had been made in drawing a real map. East is still at the top of the map and Scotland is remarkably elongated, but the general features and delineation of the main roads would be exceedingly helpful for someone seeking specific information. It appears, both from its large size and the nail holes around its edge, that the Gough map was designed to give practical help to actual travellers and that it was probably nailed up in some central place where it could be easily consulted.[22]

Maps were occasionally created to accompany the presentation copy of books, as was the case in Marino Sanudo's *Secrets for Crusaders*, written at the beginning of the fourteenth century. Sanudo came from a noble and wealthy Venetian family with extensive

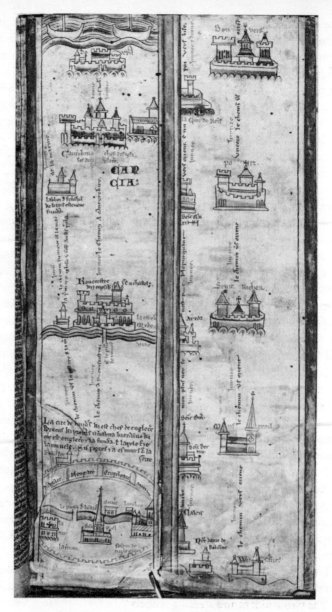

4. *Matthew Paris's Itinerary from London to Dover*

interests in the Greek islands, was part Greek himself and had travelled extensively in the eastern Mediterranean. Although he started his discussion of the Holy Land with Adam and Eve his book dealt primarily with the history of the crusades and put forward still another plan for reconquest. It is best known for the maps with which it was generously illustrated when Sanudo presented a copy to Pope John XXII in 1321 for they marked a major step forward in serious mapmaking. They were created by Pietro Vesconte, a Genoese who worked in Venice. His careful map of Palestine was distinguished by an identifying grid of squares over the whole surface, making it perhaps 'the earliest map to portray with conscientious accuracy the geography of a particular country'.[23]

Vesconte was undoubtedly one of the greatest cartographers of his day and was also active in improving the charts used by mariners. Medieval seamen had originally guided themselves by crude coastal charts which identified the shores along which they sailed, but new conditions meant they now needed something better. The extension of trade and shipping by the Catalans, Genoese and Venetians, not only throughout the Mediterranean but into the Black Sea and the Atlantic where they encountered the Castilian, Breton, and English sailors used to that coast, had been made possible by such technical improvements as the compass, the attached rudder and the better methods of rigging sails. The charts also had to be improved for men who were now sailing out of sight of land and to much more remote places. The result was the creation of portolans, sailing charts made primarily for seamen and originally only for the Mediterranean and the Black Sea. There was still almost no ability to compute longitude, while latitudes were not yet exact, but the refined and improved portolans can be recognised by their complex network of straight lines in the direction of the various winds connecting the main points of importance, brought up to date with log and compass readings. Many of the portolans were in atlas form, combining four to twelve charts, which may account for the ordinance of the king of Aragon in 1354 that every ship's captain should carry on board at least two copies of the marine charts as well as two rudders and steering wheels.[24]

By the end of the fourteenth century such charts were of interest to others besides mariners and merchants. By 1375, for example, a Catalan world map had been composed for Charles V of France. Made of parchment, brilliantly coloured and mounted on leaves so as to fold like a screen, it was up-to-the-minute in its details, for the western part was a portolan while the eastern was based on the work of the great geographer of antiquity, Ptolemy, with additions from the travels of Marco Polo. Such elegant gifts might also be used as presents to rulers to smooth the way to easier trading. A Florentine jewel merchant and ivoryworker travelled to Spain, Bordeaux, England and Ireland in 1399 carrying jewels for sale. While he was in Barcelona, then famous for its cartography, he ordered some fine maps from two expert Jewish cartographers and had them carefully wrapped in the secrecy of his Barcelona warehouse. He proposed to present them to the kings of Navarre, Aragon and England in gratitude for their allowing him free passage across their lands without tolls or duties. Maps appear to have been welcome presents to others besides kings for the duke of Berry was given several by his officials as New Year's presents and kept them in his library.[25] By the middle of the fifteenth century royal courts and important households had considerable access to the new maps which were changing the look of the world, leading such maritime princes as Henry the Navigator of Portugal to encourage the explorations which heralded the age of discovery and changed man's perception of the known world.

CHAPTER TWO

POINT OF DEPARTURE

The upper-class medieval traveller set off on his journey with different expectations and preconceptions than those of his modern counterpart. His ideas of time and distance were controlled by the level of medieval technology and his matter of fact acceptance of contemporary conditions often needs some elucidation to make it intelligible to a later age. Ordinary trips to frequent destinations would provide few problems for the experienced officials in charge of the itinerant court or travelling household. Memory and capable servants would take the place of maps and signposts for signposts were not common – or very useful in a generally illiterate society – while maps, as we have seen, were often unavailable or merely ornamental. The reasons for such short journeys might include visits to other landholdings, castles or manors; a series of local pilgrimages; such matters of business as meetings of parliament or convocation or council, coronations or important weddings; and, of course, the two most favoured social excuses, a hunting expedition or a tournament. Distant travels, requiring passage by ship or the crossing of the Alpine passes, were likely to have as their goal a crusading expedition or overseas pilgrimage, or a diplomatic embassy to another country. These required much more extensive preparation for in such cases it was essential to settle current affairs, acquire the necessary safe-conducts and be sure of a full purse. Travel has always been expensive when conducted in the grand style. Despite the attendant difficulties far-flung travels, for religious as well as secular reasons, were remarkably common among the medieval upper classes. Men's motives were as mixed in the Middle

Ages as in any other period and it is not surprising that a real religious sentiment was often reinforced by a series of secular considerations – the desire for escape from an unfortunate political or legal situation, wanderlust, or even as a remedy for boredom.

To a degree which we now find incomprehensible the lord or lady setting off on a trip in this period had little responsibility for anything but the actual decision which put the wheels in motion, and their reasons for their moves were manifold and sometimes surprising. Queen Eleanor of Provence, for example, explained to her son Edward I that her sudden departure from Gillingham in September 1291 and consequent move to Marlborough was caused by the inferior quality of the air. The queen felt that Gillingham was polluted by an excess of smoke in the evenings and did not propose to put up with it.[1] The average number of accompanying servants for such a person has no current parallel since during the Middle Ages the size of a traveller's retinue was designed to reflect the importance of its central figure, and solitary travel was something to be avoided. A king's court in passage was an awe-inspiring sight, and the surrounding countryside might well tremble at its appearance, dreading the arrival of royal retainers insistent on finding food and lodging for such hordes of people. Even a country bishop or a minor noble or his lady would travel with a retinue of thirty to forty and great nobles might have many more. In such a cavalcade the servants' functions were minutely laid down. House servants packed the clothes, household goods and equipment which always followed the lord, grooms saddled the horses and helped to pack the carts and sumpter animals with the chests and coffers and bags. Retainers acting as harbingers were dispatched ahead of the unwieldy cavalcade to make sure of the night's lodging or to acquire necessary provisions. Cushioned by constant service, the member of the establishment travelled with considerable ease and, never having known anything but the limitations of medieval travel, was not intimidated by the difficulties which he took as a matter of course.

The fact that all travel for the rich, and even the middle class, was achieved by horse, by small boats on navigable rivers, or by not much larger boats in the Mediterranean, the Channel or along the

Atlantic coast naturally determined its speed. This was still further affected by the size of the company and the difficulties of the particular route. Speed of travel was normally of little concern to the king or the noble, though royal messengers or important officials might push themselves to cover the greatest distance as quickly as possible. A large retinue could generally only go as fast as the walking servants or the laden carts could move. Queens or noble ladies usually rode but also travelled in chariots or litters, and these too were slow paced. Generally a reasonable speed for a large and elegant retinue might be fifteen to twenty miles a day, though this too depended on numbers and formality. For example, Edward III was stated to have been constantly attended by twenty-four foot archers, known as the king's bodyguard, whenever he moved about the country and thus could only ride ten to twelve miles a day, while Richard II at a time of crisis once rode the seventy miles from Daventry to Westminster overnight, only pausing at St Albans to change horses. In 1393 an impatient Henry of Derby, when returning to England accompanied by only a few members of his household, averaged thirty miles a day between Paris and Calais. Duke Philip the Bold of Burgundy was even more impetuous for he was constantly on the road and changed his residence as many as one hundred times a year. Travelling primarily in his own lands where post horses and prearranged food and lodging were easy to achieve, he might make as much as thirty-seven miles a day.[2] However, such speed was the exception rather than the rule for the highly placed.

Medieval man's attitude to time was originally more flexible than ours. He had inherited through the church the antique system of measuring time, counting twelve day hours from sunrise to sunset and twelve night hours from sunset to sunrise. Outside the church most men relied on sun dials for a rough sense of time and some sun dials were small enough to be carried about with ease, like the portable sun dial preserved at Canterbury which proudly claims to be the earliest pocket-watch. In the later Middle Ages a different type known as the 'chilinder' by its cylindrical shape, was apparently taken over from Islam and remained in use into the seventeenth century. Usually made of wood and known as 'the traveller's dial' it was possessed by such varying types as the monk in Chaucer's

'Shipman's Tale' and Holbein's ambassadors to England.[3] The church bells sounded the main divisions every three hours, marking the hours of divine office to be said by religious at each period. Such bells, from abbey tower or town church, would guide and inform the traveller when the sun was overcast. Under this system, however, the length of the hours was constantly shifting with the seasons and the geographic location – a winter daylight hour would not be the same length in Scotland as in Rome. Although mechanical clocks began to appear at the beginning of the fourteenth century, replacing the old, inaccurate water clocks, they were originally very large and very rare. It was not till the end of the century that the general adoption of such clocks began to alter medieval perceptions of time. The mechanical clock marked a day of twenty-four hours of equal length at any season of the year, which suited the entrepreneurs of the towns wanting to regularise working hours, though rulers too soon saw the advantage of such rationalised time and extended its use. For example, in 1370 King Charles V ordered all the bells of Paris to regulate themselves by the clock of the royal palace which struck the hour and the quarters. By the middle of the fifteenth century a large mechanical clock was the pride of a rich town and its place in the belfry marked the town's importance. Smaller clocks had also become an expected luxury at courts and in the homes of the greatest nobles. When King John of France was a prisoner in England after the battle of Poitiers (1356) he even had a new clock made for his use by his king of minstrels, who must have been a multi-talented servant. In 1423 Margaret of Bavaria, the widow of Duke John the Fearless of Burgundy, had a small gilded clock, decorated in silver-gilt, in her chamber – it sounds attractively feminine.[4] Despite general acceptance of the new pattern by the upper classes and the towns, time in the country paid more attention to the working hours of daylight than to any artificial reckoning, a fact which persisted long after the Middle Ages and continues to be reflected in rural dissatisfaction with Daylight Saving.

If the medieval reckoning of time seems unfamiliar so too do their hours of meals. The general practice was to rise early and in all large households a chaplain said the morning mass. At court or in important establishments the king or the great lord would attend

5. Fifteenth-century clocks in Horologium Sapientiae

mass in his own private chapel or oratory, while the service for the less distinguished members of the household would be said elsewhere. Breakfast was usually just that – a hunk of bread and a drink of wine or beer – before the typical early start on the road but on special occasions this snack could be remarkably robust. A memo of the supplies provided for the breakfast of the chancellor, the treasurer, Master William of Wykeham and many other magnates of King Edward III's council at Westminster in 1366 suggests a singularly hearty prelude to their labours. The list included beef, two calves, two sheep, fifteen capons, twelve goslings, ten bitterns, twenty-four doves, eighteen rabbits, one lamb, sixteen chickens, two codfish, three pickerel, eight plaice, one turbot, a conger eel, three dories, smoked salmon, sea shrimps, all with assorted sauces and washed down with thirty gallons of beer and 'various kinds of drinks'.[5]

On the road a pause would be made for dinner between ten and eleven, after which the company would travel on till about four, or a little later in summer, when the household would stop for the night and arrange for their supper. In good weather the midday meal was often taken outdoors and both romances and the descriptions of days of hunting strongly suggest that medieval people were very fond of picnics. On very hot journeys, such as the trip of the archbishop of Bordeaux from Avignon to Gascony in July and August 1357, extra stops were required for drinks for both men and horses. Food was occasionally purchased at inns but often such large groups carried with them or bought their own provisions and merely sought cooking facilities. The same pattern might also apply to supper if the travelling household had to stay at an inn. It was very common on such occasions to supplement the common fare with such luxuries as a lord took for granted for himself. A rather lively book of French dialogue drawn up (probably at Bury St Edmunds) for the benefit of strangers travelling in France at the end of the fourteenth century suggests that the lord's forerunner not only had to make sure of the necessary food and drink but was encouraged to find some young and attractive girls to add their attractions to an evening of singing, dancing and drinking too much. The unfortunate lord complains of a headache the following morning as a result of his various indulgences, but sets off on his journey nevertheless.[6]

Whatever the speed of his travel or the divisions of his day the first concern of the traveller had to be the roads on which he travelled. The medieval traveller undoubtedly complained about the roads, like many travellers of many centuries and probably with more justification than most, but at least a sufficient network for his needs existed in most parts of medieval Europe. In both England and France the roads ranged in width and importance from the narrow trackways which might connect manor to manor or village to village for those on foot, up through the roads accommodating single cart traffic and beasts on their way to market, to the main highways which in England and France were some thirty to thirty-four feet in width. The old Roman roads, some of which were still in use, might be as wide as sixty-four feet. Obviously the large retinues which accompanied the noble travellers necessarily kept when possible to the main roads to allow the passage of the extensive cavalcade. Even on such roads mud in winter, dust in summer, the perils of wild animals or brigands in the many forested sections of the country, broken bridges or unfordable streams were all expected hazards.

Their travels would often direct them to the most important cities of their time. Considerable mental effort is required to visualise the reality of medieval towns and cities. The first thing that strikes us when we look at the population figures is how small the political and commercial centres were. Paris, for example, the greatest capital of northern Europe, was considered of giant size with a population of around 100,000 at the beginning of the four-teenth century. This status was shared by the most important Italian towns, for Venice, Genoa, Milan and Florence appear to have ranged from perhaps 200,000 for Venice to over 50,000 for the others. A city with a population of more than 25,000 was considered very large. London with 40,000 was far and away the most populous city in England while York and Bristol, perhaps a third that size, were the only others even considered as cities by foreigners. Ghent, Bruges, Toulouse and Bordeaux all hovered between the 40,000 to 30,000 mark. Unlike England, however, France had a large number of cities of about 10,000 inhabitants, especially in the south with its longer tradition of a Roman urban past.[7] Such figures, though merely an approximation and ferociously debated, help to flesh out the rather idyllic picture which medieval illustrations of cities so often evoke. Medieval cities were small in size, packing their population within the necessary but expensive walls. Despite this restriction, there were open spaces near at hand and even in the most flourishing towns, where suburbs were developing rapidly outside the walls, no medieval man or woman was ever very far from country sights, sounds, or smells.

The towns to which medieval travellers came provided both excitement and difficulties. There was an air of raw vitality and riches in such prosperous and growing centres as Paris, London, Venice, or even provincial Bordeaux, shown by their network of parish churches and a great cathedral, usually at this period in some stage of building or repair. The vigorous commercial life provided the opportunity of buying fine cloths, spices, and other luxuries which were almost impossible to find elsewhere. Richness and

6. An idealised picture of Paris in the Middle Ages used by Jean Fouquet for
a vision of the Holy Ghost

beauty were everywhere but so were the problems of jampacked humanity. Medieval streets tended to be smelly and filthy since it was a regular practice to throw refuse in the streets (and often to empty chamber pots out of upper windows) thus adding to the droppings of the scores of animals passing by. It normally required the ceremonial arrival of a prince or a major procession to enforce a general clean-up. Drainage was seldom adequate and the small streams, and even the wider rivers, became polluted by butcher's offal, tanner's waste and the continuous debris of living crowds. Not all city streets were paved, though the market and the main squares normally had cobbles pounded into a sand base. Smaller streets and lanes, even those carrying heavy traffic, were often merely covered with gravel and sand. Many of the traffic problems of medieval cities sound exceedingly familiar for horsemen and carts were often subject to long delays at the fortified town gate or wherever tolls were taken. Heavy traffic was ordered to use only certain gates and streets but often evaded the requirement while large carts with iron-shod wheels helped to break down the paved surfaces. It was important to reach a town or city before nightfall or curfew closed its gates for night-time travel was always hazardous, the city streets generally unlit and the curfew enforced for fear of crime. Many London inns, like the Tabard made famous by Chaucer, clustered in Southwark, just south of London Bridge, to provide easy access for those travellers coming up from Dover or Canterbury who arrived late and had to wait till the following morning to cross London Bridge.

Even to mention London Bridge is to remind ourselves that medieval roads were only as useful as the bridges which allowed the traveller to cross the main streams. Towns were often strategically located on a major river and the bridge which led to it was often both built and repaired with the proceeds of pontage, or bridge tolls, as well as pious gifts. It is a vivid commentary on the normal state of medieval roads and bridges that pious gifts and bequests for their improvement were such a notable feature of medieval wills. Richard Whittington, the famous mayor of London, left £100 in 1423 for the repair and improvement of 'vile roads where it will be most necessary' and William Chichele, brother of the archbishop, provided £10 in his will for the 'sustentacion' of London Bridge, with special concern for the piles to be driven there. Even a well-maintained bridge was not always a guarantee of safety as the sad tale of Richard Lamberd attests. He had been leading a hackney to King Edward I over the bridge of Rochester when the horse was hurled by the wind into the Medway, and drowned, a considerable financial loss.[8] London Bridge no longer recalls its exciting past when it was the one active thoroughfare into London and was packed with houses, stalls and even a chapel and hermitage. England was fortunate that its rivers were not particularly wide or swift for the difficulties of bridging the Rhone, the Garonne or the Rhine were much more acute. Most of the great medieval bridges have disappeared but some reminders of the past remain. The familiar fragment of the Pont-St-Bénézet at Avignon with its ruined chapel still echoes in the children's song while the three graceful towers of the Pont Valentré over the Tarn at Cahors exemplify the

7. A typical scene of the crowded life on an important bridge such as this one in Paris

pattern of the most impressive medieval bridges. Not far away at Albi a more modest stone bridge suggests the common medieval construction and continues to serve twentieth-century traffic. The important pilgrimage route of the road to Santiago de Compostela, crossing northern Spain and its many rivers, continues to make use of the results of medieval piety and generosity. The town of Puente la Reina in Navarre, where the routes coming from France converged with the Spanish track, takes its name from the still-used hump-backed bridge provided by Queen Urraca in the eleventh century. Further west Domingo, an eleventh-century hermit, gained sanctity and the nickname of 'de la Calzada' for his work in constructing a road, a bridge and finally a hospice in the wilds between Logroño and Burgos. Medieval travellers often commented on bridges or noted their absence. They detailed the horrors of wide or swift rivers which had to be crossed by inadequate ferries, particularly difficult for travellers on horseback who often had to swim their horse behind the tiny tipsy craft. Even such a major city as Bordeaux, facing the wide Garonne, had to be reached by ferry if one came directly from the north for the nearest bridge over the river was some ninety miles upstream at Agen.

Rivers were, however, not only obstacles to be crossed but also a useful part of the network of communication. Rivers had been used to transport heavy and bulky freight since ancient times, but they also carried travellers, especially those of importance who could easily afford to hire boats for themselves and perhaps part of their retinue. The problem of choosing the best itinerary in unfamiliar country was somewhat alleviated by the very common practice of hiring local guides, for to act as a guide was generally considered a duty of the reasonable man towards his neighbour, which Christians certainly should interpret generously. Raymond d'Aguilers, chronicling the passage of Count Raymond of Toulouse through Slavonia on the First Crusade, remarked with utter astonishment that the inhabitants 'would neither trade with us *nor provide guides*' (my italics). Obviously knowledgeable guides were the most useful but perhaps not as frequent as travellers might hope, since, according to the author of the first guidebook of France in the sixteenth century, a reliable guide sure of the way to the next stopping place might be enthusiastically greeted as 'an angel from heaven'.[9]

After the day's journey the noble traveller could look for his night's lodging in several places. It was often possible for those of adequate social standing to seek accommodation at a friendly castle where hospitality was an accepted tradition. Strange faces might be welcome as providing a change from the usual routine, perhaps news of happenings elsewhere and the possibility of entertainment by the minstrels and musicians of the cavalcade. Some hosts took this duty of hospitality very seriously. Philip de Barri, brother of Gerald of Wales, was a most generous host and a popular one, for his castle of Manorbier was halfway between a port in Devon and that of Milford Haven, both much frequented by voyagers. Gerald wrote warmly of his much-loved brother and how he welcomed all guests, both rich and poor, without discrimination. Philip suffered, however, from an unusual scruple. Since so many rich lords came to stay with him, and of course had to be suitably entertained, he was unable to give as much to the poor as he wished and decided to consult the papal curia on the tricky problem of whether alms given to the rich were of as much merit as those given to the poor. The cardinal who responded encouraged him to continue giving hospitality to the rich without question, citing the example of Abraham who might never have received the visiting angels in his home if he had enquired about their status. Hospitality and charity, the cardinal concluded, should be given to rich and poor alike.[10]

Monasteries had a special duty of hospitality towards the poor, but the great were particularly willing to insist on its application to themselves, especially if there were any family or local connection. Unfortunately such neighbouring patrons could be extraordinarily critical if they thought they were not being received with sufficient enthusiasm and elegance. Large monastic houses like Cluny, St Albans, Bury St Edmunds or St-Denis frequently entertained kings and nobles on their travels. Both St Albans and St-Denis were especially popular since they were only a day's journey from the capitals. Kings and lords recognised the obligation of offering gifts to the monasteries at which they stayed but the expense of providing suitable hospitality could be a devastating drain on monastic revenues, while the crush of people following the court was distracting to the monks. Few monastic houses were like Cluny where Salimbene could report in astonishment that its multitude of buildings was so great that the pope with his cardinals and all his court as well as the emperor with all his could lodge there simultaneously without requiring any monk to leave his cell or suffer any discomfort.[11]

The special problems of the lay or ecclesiastical lord who was frequently called to London or Paris and needed accommodation there were often solved by the owning or renting of a house. In the thirteenth century Eudes Rigaud, archbishop of Rouen and adviser to Louis IX, stayed in Paris at a manor belonging to his diocese and Simon de Montfort, earl of Leicester, seems to have made use of the London houses of such prelates as the bishops of Winchester and Durham. In both Paris and London those close to the royal family developed elegant town houses. In London Henry of Lancaster built his great palace of the Savoy from the spoils he acquired from his capture of Bergerac in 1346 and his son-in-law John of Gaunt enjoyed it until it was burnt by the angry mobs during the Peasants' Revolt. In Paris the same pattern was to be found among the royal relations. In other less frequently visited cities, the lord's harbingers, or what a more recent generation would describe as billeting officers, when seeking accommodation would quite frequently take over whole houses, having come to some more or less agreeable settlement with the owner. Once lodging was found it had to be prepared. The duties of the forerunner of such a large establishment as that of Philip the Good of Burgundy were carefully laid down. This burdened official headed a staff whose duties included airing, cleaning, throwing out the old bedstraw and restuffing the mattresses with fresh, shaking the dust out of the old hangings and arranging the screens. Then wood had to be supplied for the kitchens and, in bad weather, for the rooms as well. Candles and torches had to be provided and at least one placed in an iron lantern at the front door to mark the entry. Even on a more modest scale the process had difficulties, as Henry of Lancaster suggested in his *Livre de Seyntz Medicines*. He described how in such cases the poor man must clean his house, scrub it to kill the fleas and evict his cat. His efforts might be aided by the insistence of the lord's servants in preparing the place properly, clearing away all the old furniture and putting the lord's standard on all the doors to mark his occupancy.[12]

8. *A fifteenth-century inn primarily for pilgrims rather than nobles*

When travelling outside their own countries even lords were not always able to find a friendly castle or monastery and had to put more reliance on inns or hospices, especially if their party was small. Hospices were particularly in evidence around places of pilgrimage and on the main routes leading to them. Founded and funded as charitable works they existed to aid all those who had taken on the religious obligation of a pilgrimage and to sustain and care for those who fell sick by the way. Inns of course were to be found in all cities, especially in popular centres like Rome and Venice. Toulouse too, with its important location on the main pilgrimage route to Compostela, had a large number of inns. These establishments tended to be reasonably small. The required stabling for horses and mules would take up most of the ground floor, while just above was the hall where travellers could take their meals, whether they stayed the night or not. The upper floors would have the bedrooms with several beds in each room. Each bed was about seven feet wide and six feet long, and was designed to hold two or three at a time. Such crowded conditions would be the last resort for proud nobles but were often endured by busy officials and less important members of the retinue as well as merchants. There was a range of inns in the largest centres and some of them certainly aimed to provide for the comfort and convenience of the most important. In the fifteenth century the doge and councillors of Venice conceded to Roland Verardo the right to keep a hostel for princes and ambassadors going to the Holy Land so that they could be 'commodiously and properly entertained'.[13] Venice drew enormous profits from its voyages to the Holy Land so that every possible attempt was made to satisfy travellers of all ranks and to smooth their path.

Travel outside one's own country posed another set of problems from the more normal round at home. For the English going to the continent it meant a Channel crossing, a prospect looked at with some concern by travellers on both side of the Channel. For all those going to Italy, whether to Rome on ecclesiastical business or pilgrimage or to Venice as the launching spot for an expedition overseas, it also meant the perils of the Alpine passes. During the fourteenth and fifteenth centuries, with the increase in endemic warfare, it was important for the traveller to have a safe-conduct while the cautious man had a separate one from the lord of each place through which he passed. It served as a useful, though not unchallengeable, bulwark against being captured and held to ransom.

The English upper-class traveller probably viewed the Channel crossing with more equanimity than men from the continent since it was an inevitable beginning to many of his travels. Nevertheless a popular snatch of fifteenth-century English verse insisted that a landsman, no matter how brave, shall 'quwake by the berde' before he got as far as the Lizard, the constant landmark for sailors as they leave the south-west coast of England.[14] The most popular crossing, because it was the shortest, was originally between Dover and Wissant, just south of Calais. After Calais had been captured by Edward III in 1347 and became the home of the wool staple it served as the most usual cross-Channel port for the English. Many small boats were available to travellers for it was relatively easy to hire your own ship at a reasonable cost if you had a large retinue to transport or had to make special speed. It is almost impossible to give an idea of the size and pattern of these boats, but their capacity must have been larger than we tend to think. After all, the elephant given to Henry III by Louis IX in 1254 was shipped across the Channel in February of the following year. One hopes, both for the sake of the no doubt terrified sailors and of the unhappy elephant, that the Channel was calm that day. Large numbers of horses were also continuously shipped across the Channel, in times of peace as well as of war. When Edward I went to Gascony in 1286 but paid a preliminary visit to the court of Philip the Fair in Paris he took 1,000 horses with him and arranged for their cross-Channel transportation in groups of twenty-four.[15] In the mid-fifteenth century the Bohemian noble, Leo of Rozmital, who was on a grand tour of Europe, crossed from Calais to Dover with his entourage. His companions wrote eloquently of the horrors of the whole performance. First of all, there was the problem of waiting for a favourable wind, then the first ship they had hired and loaded with sixteen horses sprang a leak. The horses were in water up to their bellies so that the ship had to return to Calais. On the second attempt Rozmital had to be rowed out to the ship in a small boat but storm winds came up and he nearly drowned. They reached their ship with great difficulty and 'my lord and his attendants were so distressed by the waves that they lay on the ship as if they had been dead'. Their return trip, sailing from Poole to Brittany, was equally discouraging. After waiting eight days for a favourable wind they were attacked by armed pirates once they got to sea in the belief that they were French. They were allowed to go free after showing the safe-conduct prudently acquired from Edward IV, but they continued to be driven by a contrary wind. Finally they arrived at Guernsey where they had to wait another eleven days, even though the pirates had obligingly shown the captain of their ship how to set his course and which stars to steer by. The favourable wind which allowed them to leave Guernsey was followed by a sudden storm in which the ship nearly foundered. Even over the centuries

one can almost hear the great sigh of relief with which they chronicle their final landing at St-Malo, formidable behind its encircling
walls and guarded at night by free-running watchdogs.[16]

Once safely across the Channel and headed for Italy, crossing the
Alps had to be considered the next major stumbling block, although
some traffic went down the Rhone and then sailed to Genoa. The
old Roman road along the Provençal coast had ceased to be maintained by the sixth century and Moslem attacks had menaced traffic
as far inland as Mont-Cenis. When the Moslem pirates had finally
been driven off there remained the danger of the Corsican and
Sardinian buccaneers in the Gulf of Genoa, raiding along the coastal
roads and terrifying travellers. Dante even used 'the most desolate,
the most solitary' road between Lerici and Turbia in mountainous
Liguria as a realistic basis for comparison when he wished to emphasise the unparalleled horrors of the road up the mountain of Purgatory.[17] The traveller from the north tended to choose the Alpine
pass best suited to his purposes. The most popular passes for travellers coming through France in the early Middle Ages were the
Mont-Cenis and the Great St Bernard. These were rivalled in the
thirteenth century by the Simplon, somewhat east of the Great
St Bernard, and the St Gotthard in the central Alps, often more
convenient for travellers coming from England and the Low Countries. Furthest to the east was the Brenner Pass, the lowest and by
far the easiest crossing but really only practical for the Germans.
Imperial armies almost always marched that way since its fertile
surroundings made provisioning of soldiers an easier task.

Because the Alps were crossed so frequently many of the voyagers paid little attention to the difficulties of transit, regarding
them matter-of-factly as normal hazards. Archbishop Rigaud, crossing the Alps at the beginning of February 1254 found himself held
up at Salins in the Jura mountains for three days by the depth of
the snow but then pushed on to cross the Simplon pass and reach
the river Adige. His laconic comment on the nature of the trip was
'but not without danger'. Adam of Usk, on the other hand, at the
beginning of the fifteenth century was far more emotional about
crossing the St Gotthard in mid-March. He wrote that he was
drawn in an ox-wagon 'half-dead with cold and with mine eyes

blindfold lest I should see the dangers of the pass'. Pero Tafur, a Spanish traveller who followed Adam's route in the 1430s, obviously kept his eyes open, for his description is much more complete. An ox was harnessed by a very long rope to a trailer 'like a Castilian threshing machine'. The passenger sat on the trailer holding the reins of his horse who walked behind him and thus they crossed safely for only the ox was in danger if the road failed. Tafur observed the mountaineers discharging their firearms to dislodge snow and forestall avalanches which might bury travellers. Since he crossed in August when the thaws were at their peak he also noted that the streams and rivers were much swollen by the melting snow.[18]

Once across the Alps those bound for the Holy Land or the eastern Mediterranean were faced by the voyage that awaited them. Navigation there posed other problems than those which beset ships in the Channel and on the Atlantic coast and Mediterranean sailors used differently designed ships. Venice and Genoa, the great sea-going republics which monopolised much of the carrying trade in the Mediterranean and up into the Black Sea, relied on oared galleys as well as large transport and sailing vessels which were carvel built, that is, with flush planks, rather than the clinker-built ships of the Atlantic and North Sea which had planks overlapping downward and fastened with copper nails. The oared galleys were usually outfitted with a sail but could be handled more easily than current sailing ships when close to shore or if the winds were unfavourable. Noble travellers did not look at the Genoese or Venetian ships with the practiced eye of the merchants who used them constantly. Such recent technical improvements as the boxed compass, the attached rudder and the growing accuracy of the portolan charts did not really interest them. They relied on local information to tell them who was the best owner with whom to ship or, for the most important, with whom to contract for the use of an entire vessel.

Seasickness, terror of storms and boredom while waiting for favourable winds have always loomed large in all accounts of sea voyages, long or short. Given the small size and primitive nature of these early ships it is not surprising that a common and striking element of all medieval travellers' tales – true of all centuries and all classes – was a colourful account of a terrible storm at sea. The preacher Jacques de Vitry at the beginning of the thirteenth century found in men's behaviour at such times excellent morals to be used in his sermons. Joinville, returning from crusade with Louis IX, sympathised with the desperate Queen Marguerite when their drowning seemed imminent. He himself had just vowed a pilgrimage to the shrine of St-Nicholas-de-Port near Nancy, for St Nicholas was considered a patron of those at sea, and promised the queen that he would take the silver ship she had just promised to St Nicholas if the king would not allow her to make a pilgrimage. In the fifteenth century the Gascon noble, Nompar de Caumont, vividly describes the difficulties he encountered sailing from Rhodes to Sicily in October. His ship was struck by lightning in the gulf of Crete and then, off the shore of Sicily near Syracuse, was driven

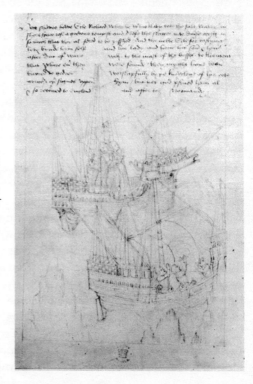

9. *The Earl of Warwick and his family lashed to the mast in a great storm at sea so that in case of shipwreck they could at least be buried together*

back to Messina by a great wind which came up so suddenly that the ship's master and sailors had no time to lower the sail. The vessel rolled so heavily that the sails of the mainmast touched the sea, the mast broke and the terrified passengers, tied to planks to avoid being swept overboard by the high waves, took to their prayers and the confession of their sins.[19] Erasmus's sixteenth-century satire on the sudden and emotional devotion of passengers faced with shipwreck, their superstition and the excessive promises, which they did not really propose to keep, shows little human sympathy with the overwhelming terror and the emotional impact produced by uncontrollable natural forces. Christians were not alone in their terror for the very same fear of storms at sea was shared by the Moors who were active in conveying their own pilgrims to Mecca and also as pirates. Abd-er-Razzak, sent as an ambassador to India in the mid-fifteenth century by the Shah of Persia, encountered a great storm when returning to Arabia. He describes the general terror and panicky behaviour, emphasising all the terrors with which the ocean could threaten voyagers. He gave himself up for lost and took to prayer but firmly decided that if he ever got safely home he would never set out on another voyage, 'not even in the company of a king'.[20]

Apart from the nightmares experienced at sea the medieval traveller paid little attention to the vagaries of the weather. Much of his life was normally spent outdoors, constantly exposed to the elements, so it was rare that wind or storm, mud or dust, snow or heat were allowed to influence his plans. Gerald of Wales remarked rather smugly that it was unmanly to watch for a breeze or a calm before setting out on the day's business on land, only those crossing the sea should pay such attention to the weather. Not everyone found it easy to be quite so objective. When Pope John XXII, in mid-July 1327, found it necessary to send Hugh of Angoulême, his nuncio in England, a bracing letter exhorting him to continue his mission despite his sufferings from the English climate, one suspects a worse than usual English summer and perhaps a very homesick ecclesiastic.[21] Colin Muset, a thirteenth-century lyric poet from Lorraine who seems to have thoroughly enjoyed the comforts of life, put into pathetic verse the reluctance with which the hangers-on of the great travelling households might view their journeys in bad weather. He sang of the joys of staying inside when winter arrived, if only he could find a host generous enough to entertain him comfortably so that he could avoid the muddy ride behind a bad-tempered lord on whom he had to rely for largess.[22]

The medieval traveller of the upper class set out on his journeys sharing the general conceptions and conditions of his day. The specific style of his travel would depend primarily on his rank and then on the purpose of his journey, for there were many different reasons which impelled such upper-class travellers to take to the road.

CHAPTER THREE

ITINERANT KINGS AND QUEENS

Glimpses of medieval royal households on the move give some idea of the various reasons for their travel and provide an illuminating commentary on certain unfamiliar patterns of medieval life which required the proper marshalling of whole echelons of officials and servants. The fact that the king was constantly travelling was taken for granted during the Middle Ages. The person of the ruler was so important that to maintain his power the king had to be visible to his subjects and accessible to his barons and nobles. In medieval terms this meant appearances in many parts of the realm, especially where dissatisfaction, revolt or the imposition of a particular policy required the actual presence of the king with his visible aura of power and lordship. Mobility was encouraged by the royal possession of scores of castles, manors and favourite hunting lodges, some more favoured than others, as well as by the problem of feeding such an unwieldy group and cleaning up behind them. In consequence the king was frequently in the saddle. The classic description of the horrors of an itinerant court is that of Peter of Blois, the acerbic archdeacon whose letters enlivened the end of the twelfth century. His vivid evocation of the appalling discomforts of travelling with the court of Henry II, an admittedly impetuous and strenuous king, may be particularly bitter because it was written when Peter was a jaundiced convalescent. In any case, he found sufficient strength to belabour in elegant Latin the horrors of the food and drink, the extortionate royal stewards always expecting to have their palms greased with continuing largess but nevertheless evicting unfortunate courtiers from their beds, and the hodgepodge of hangers-on who made up the king's train. Peter records the strain of following such a wilful king but also recognised that many men in the cumbersome entourage were not there for ambition's sake but as part of their daily employment.[1]

The size and complexity of the organisation of the king's household in both England and France developed enormously from the thirteenth to the fifteenth century. Although certain of the great officials and their staffs, who had originally perambulated with the king, gradually set up permanent quarters in their respective capitals, the indispensable core of the household surrounding the king continued to expand to meet the changing needs. We know much more about this process in England than in France. The first English ordinance regarding the royal household, the *Constitutio Domus Regis* in the mid-twelfth century, antedates by a century Louis IX's first regulation of the comparable French establishment. There was naturally considerable similarity between the French and English royal households since they, like the households of other important personages, were designed to provide protection and companionship as well as necessary personal and domestic services at home or on the road. Nevertheless, the development of a more complex and elaborate organisation surrounding the ruler of the realm did not move in tandem in the two kingdoms.

We can learn the make-up, duties and privileges of the members of the king's household from a series of ordinances in both England and France. There were also satellite households of the queen and the royal children which are best known through occasional surviving accounts. Our knowledge of the French royal household suffers from the large gaps in medieval French accounts for, unlike the generous store of wardrobe and household accounts preserved in the Public Record Office, the French records have suffered from fire and sword. Only scraps of the archives of the *Chambre des Comptes* escaped two eighteenth-century disasters – the fire in its building in 1739 and the enthusiasm of the revolutionaries who sent the remaining parchments to the arsenals to be used in cartridges. The records of the *Chambre aux Deniers*, which handled the early household finances, were captured at the battle of Poitiers in 1356 along with King John and have disappeared. Nevertheless the

10. *Formal entry into Paris in 1389 of Queen Isabeau of Bavaria, wife of Charles VI*

available accounts with their careful itemisation of the myriad and sometimes surprising expenses help to lend vitality and a sense of real life to our effort to follow the king and queen and the court as they set forth on still another of their innumerable journeys, making the generalities of the chroniclers' descriptions more intelligible to modern minds.

The size of the large establishment which followed the king is almost beyond our comprehension. Its complexity and the diffi-culties of moving it from place to place are described in the House-hold Ordinance of 1318 in which Edward II and his officials attempted to regularise and improve household administration and tried to alleviate the most obvious problems of lodging the royal household on the move. The household was broken up into thirty-nine separate categories, each with its own harbinger responsible for finding lodging and food. A common, and detested, abuse which the ordinance tried to remedy was to order that none of the royal household were to seize foodstuffs against the will of the owner if they could be bought elsewhere. In cases of necessity they could take them politely but must pay the rightful cost.[2] The diversity of the retinue is astounding – knights and sergeants, clerks and chaplains, the steward, the treasurer, the heads of the various household offices such as the chamber, the hall, the kitchen and the pantry with their array of subordinate servants and clerks, the roster of messengers, minstrels and trumpeters – the variety seems endless.

The crucially important department for the success of the king's journeys was that of the marshal of the household who shouldered the ultimate responsibility for all matters regarding horses and transport. He needed to be a most efficient and able man, for his duties were manifold. His responsibility for the horses ranged from the king's great charger to the meanest pack-horse. Although lists are often given and the horses distinguished by colour and type it is almost impossible to draw accurate deductions from the very fragmentary surviving lists. Generally there was a rough relationship between price and function, that is, the most expensive were the warhorses or chargers of the king and the knights, followed by the palfreys (the riding horse of the upper classes), the rounceys ridden by the ordinary men-at-arms and finally the hackneys and carthorses which were primarily beasts of burden. The marshal had to arrange that these animals were cared for when sick, replaced when necessary and, above all, in the right place at the right time, for without an adequate supply of horses the travelling household would grind to a stop. Availability could be a real problem if the monarch was impetuous or changeable. The logistics and expense involved are suggested by an entry on the wardrobe account in April 1300 detailing the expenses of John de Riston. He was required to lead eight warhorses, ten palfreys and two sumpterhorses, destined for the use of Edward I and his son, from Stamford to York, where it turned out they were not required, so the horses were put to graze. From there John and an accompanying groom had to lead them on to Carlisle to await the king's arrival. The wages of the servants and the smith who had to shoe the horses in the course of their two hundred mile journey as well as the necessary provisions for the horses and their stabling came to over £13.[3] The number of animals required also startles us. In the English household ordinance of 1445, for example, sixty horses are listed for the king's own stable plus a further 186 for chariots, carts,

11. The Queen's chariot from the Luttrell Psalter

for servants allowed a horse for their own transport as well as all the packhorses. It was a formidable number. Perhaps the modern reader should also be reminded that a medieval king or lord would have the same liking for an especially fine horse that the present generation has for a Rolls-Royce or a Mercedes. For the medieval man, as for the modern, there were easily recognised and carefully maintained social differences in the style of transportation.

The king rode unless illness forced him to use a litter, but the queen might often use a chariot. A queen's chariot was originally a large, rather lumbering vehicle of wood and iron, which is best illustrated by the familiar drawing in the Luttrell Psalter. Since these early coaches had no springs they must have been dreadfully uncomfortable as well as desperately slow. However, by the late fourteenth century 'rocking' chariots, on which the body was suspended by chains, were known in France where they began to replace the old-fashioned model where the box rested directly on the axles. Naturally such chariots were a luxury, generally restricted to royalty and people of distinction though a great lady of the

fourteenth century considered one her rightful perquisite. As the heavy chariot moved slowly along the bumpy roads the painting and gilding of its sides and of the arches that supported its cover proclaimed to the countryside the importance of its occupants. The interiors were usually decorated with luxurious cloths and gilt rosettes while efforts were always made to soften the ride by the provision of elegant cushions. Queen Isabella, wife of Edward II of England, and her ladies were supported by ones covered with gold and silver tissue and flame-coloured silk.[4] Ladies, or the sick, also used litters which were suspended between two horses. They were equipped with mattresses and cushions and were somewhat more comfortable than the chariots. Access to both these conveyances was provided by a small stepladder, rather reminiscent of a gipsy caravan, until almost the sixteenth century.

The very size of the baggage train which followed the king and queen can only be suggested by the many accounts which give a fluctuating and bewildering number of chariots with their drivers, carts and carters, sumpterhorses and sumptermen, all with their attendant rooms. For example, in 1286 Edward I had with him in France twelve carters, each with his own groom, and twenty-five sumpters, three of whom carried the king's bed and one his breakfast, apart from such normal loads as the king's treasure, the robes and armour and the kitchen bags. The same year the queen's household included among her permanent servants eight carters, fourteen outriders for the carts and the chariots and twenty-four sumptermen.[5] Fortunately whenever the household's baggage exceeded the available carrying capacity it was usually easy and inexpensive to hire carts and carters for temporary service. Occasionally personal details bear witness to a reasonable system of promotion and replacement, and even the provision of pensions for at least some servants. Christian Page was the coachman of Queen Eleanor of England and part of her household at least by 1285, although he was ill in the latter part of the year. He served as her coachman in 1286 but then began to lose his sight. As his blindness increased he was given an assistant, Michael, who had been in charge of the chariot of the royal princesses. By July 1290 Christian had been sent back to his native county of Ponthieu with his expenses paid by the queen. After Eleanor's death in November 1290 the king did not forget her old coachman for in February 1291 he ordered the seneschal of Ponthieu (the French county which Eleanor had inherited from her mother) to provide Page with a daily pension of 4½d and 33s 4d yearly for his robes because of his long daily service to the queen. Michael, who had replaced Page as queen's coachman in 1289, was left a legacy by the queen which her executors actually increased. He too was later pensioned for in 1296 the king ordered the abbot and convent of Waverley to provide him with the necessary victuals for his lifetime, again because of his service to the queen.[6]

Resort was frequently made to boats to transport the household baggage when roads were bad or non-existent. When Queen Isabella in 1311–12 had difficulty in making the journey from York to Howden, a journey of some twenty-five to thirty miles, four boats were hired to take the queen, her damsels, squires and the equipment of the small wardrobe down the Ouse, a trip which took the masters and their assistant boatmen two days. On another occasion two of the queen's servants were detailed to stand guard in a boat at Berwick in which the queen's belongings had been placed because of the lack of carriage and were then responsible for taking them all to London. The trip took thirty days, spent partly at sea and partly in various ports because of adverse winds.[7]

12. *The travelling chest of Lady Margaret Beaufort, late fifteenth-century, but characteristic of a constant pattern*

To fill all the carts and pack the sumpterhorses required great numbers of boxes, barrels, coffers, chests, bags and sacks, as well as the necessary trussing cord. The containers came in all sizes and shapes. In many cases the most precious items each had its own box which was then placed in a larger coffer and perhaps in still another box in a manner reminiscent of Russian toys. Chests were made of iron and wood but many of the boxes exposed to the weather were made of *cuir bouilli*, the leather soaked in oil which thus became both pliable and waterproof. Sometimes such leather boxes were reinforced with iron fittings and most had locks and complex keys which were always being replaced. Rawhide covers for the carts which carried valuables or expensive robes were common. By the fifteenth century at least the chests which carried clothes were lined with linen as a means to protect their contents from the dust. The shape of some of these chests, often described as *bahuts*, was marked by a curved top, encouraging the rapid run-off of rain, a design which survived into this century in old-fashioned trunks.

The size of the royal household's baggage train was often extended by the belongings of members of the household who had the privilege of having their bulkiest goods carried in one of the royal carts. For example, Sir Peter de Colingeburn had been accustomed to have a sack with his bed and all its equipment carried in one of the carts used by the wardrobe. This particular privilege had been cancelled so the compiler of the wardrobe account noted that

13. Royal portable bed of the twelfth century

Sir Peter was now allowed extra costs for the carriage of these items which required a horse and the wages of its groom at 4½d a day.[8] The whole cumbersome baggage train must have always been a tremendous temptation to thieves and the light-fingered, since the precious contents of the coffers included costly objects far beyond the average man's dreams. The most lively description of what might happen if a royal baggage train was attacked is to be found in a report on the return of the French army from its disastrous invasion of Aragon in 1285, carrying with it the corpse of King Philip III. The king of Aragon, to mark his respect for a fellow monarch, held his army back from attacking either the king's corpse or the oriflame, the sacred French banner, but he let them loose on the pack train. The Spanish chronicler catches our attention with a vivid simile as he describes the Aragonese attack on the French flanks, killing men and seizing coffers: 'you would have heard a greater cracking from the breaking of coffers than if you had been in a wood in which a thousand men did nothing else but split wood.'[9]

Fortunately royal households were often on the move for more cheerful reasons and with happier results. In the thirteenth century both Louis IX of France and Henry III of England were itinerant kings. In the earlier days of their long reigns they clashed over the control of the English lands in Poitou which Philip Augustus had confiscated from John Lackland and which Henry tried unsuccessfully to regain. Louis took great care to invest his younger brother Alphonse with the disputed title of count of Poitiers as soon as he was old enough. In order to emphasise the French presence in the lands of Eleanor of Aquitaine King Louis held a great court at Saumur in June 1241 where he knighted his young brother and several companions. To celebrate the occasion a two-day feast was held where the chronicler Joinville, then about sixteen, carved before his lord Thibault, king of Navarre and count of Champagne. The feast made a profound impression on the young squire who recounted gleefully its splendours. He asserted that many folk said that there were more than three thousand knights there and that they had never seen so many garments of cloth of gold and silk at one feast. The accounts lend some credence to Joinville's naive satisfaction with the size and splendour of the feast, for 50,000 loaves of bread were paid for during the two days, though this included the king's bread and that given as alms. Valuable cloths were bought, especially for the robes of the new knights, while other cloths were taken from the king's own supply. The expense of the baggage train was particularly heavy. Five carts, requiring seventeen horses and taking thirty-two days on the road, were needed to carry the tents destined to shelter the members of the court. The necessary money for the costly festivities was brought from Paris by five horses. At this time in France and England pennies were the only money in general circulation and they were bulky and heavy to transport.[10] The feast at Saumur underlines one reason for the travels of the court – the need to display magnificence, and thus power, in an uneasy part of the realm, in fact, the medieval version of 'showing the flag'.

These glittering royal progresses were not viewed in the same light by lower classes and a few of their complaints about the problems caused by such a massive invasion of demanding strangers have fortunately been preserved. A poor widow of Chinon declared that her quilt and pillow had been commandeered by a royal official. They were carried to the castle for the king's use and she had never been able to get them back, although she had been trying for six years. On another occasion an inhabitant of Hesdin complained that the queen's cooks had been lodged in his house, which was worth thirty *livres*, and had burnt it down. The queen had paid him only ten *livres* and he wanted the balance. Another man's rouncey had been appropriated by a royal official for the use of one of the subordinate royal servants. The official had promised to pay him twelve *sous* daily for its use, according to the king's custom, but had kept the horse seven weeks and paid him nothing. Louis IX, during the later years of his reign after his return from his first crusade, continued to visit his kingdom and has recently been described as a 'middle-aged but restless peripatetic'.[11] However, by this time Louis had begun to recognise the abuses which often accompanied the exercise of the royal right of *gîte*, the revenues paid to provide hospitality on the visit of a superior and his retinue, and made some effort to ease the burden.

Edward I, nephew of Louis IX, also spent much of his thirty-five-year reign on the move. Not only his wars against the Welsh and the Scots, but his efforts to bring order to the English possession of Gascony with an inevitable concomitant of continued negotiations with a more and more intransigent French court, meant constant travel for the energetic king. The records of the royal wardrobe and household for 1285–6 cover the period when Edward, Queen

Eleanor and all the household went to Gascony by way of Paris and throw unexpected gleams of light on everyday life in such an itinerant court. The queen's washerwoman had her weekly wages increased to 12d because her labours overseas were greater than they had been in England. There were frequent payments for the little boats that ferried the king, and occasionally the queen, across the Seine from their quarters in the abbey of Saint-Germain-des-Près to the French king's palace at the Louvre. The constant traffic between the abbey and the river obviously overtaxed the path, for Walter the doorkeeper was reimbursed for cleaning the pathway between two pairs of gates at Saint-Germain 'where men make haste because that way stinks'. By the end of July 1286 the whole cavalcade (including ten messengers, the king of the heralds and five royal trumpeters) was again on the move on its way south to Gascony. The keeper of the king's palfreys was detached from the court for three months to act as harbinger, by which time the court had only got as far south as Sainte-Foy-la-Grande on the Dordogne. It seems obvious that the king was engaged in a methodical royal visit of the whole of his tempestuous duchy. Not till 5 January 1287 did Edward and his queen settle down in Bordeaux in relative comfort to wait out the wettest part of the winter. By mid-March they were off again. Not surprisingly men and horses fell sick on the way, for such long-drawn-out travels must have put considerable strain on all those involved in the logistics of the operation.[12]

King Edward's travels in 1286 were unusually far-ranging but the affairs of Gascony, Scotland and Wales kept him constantly on the move during most of his reign. Edward's visit to Lanercost Priory, a house of Augustinian canons in the valley of the Irthing east of Carlisle, illustrates the financial difficulties that could ensue for the unhappy host when the king and his household not only stopped but stayed on.[13] The king arrived at Lanercost for a brief stay at Michaelmas 1306 but because of illness he was forced to remain there till the beginning of March 1307. Edward had come north because of the current trouble in Scotland and despite his age and failing health had set forth in the summer to enforce Scottish subordination. His spirit was stronger than his body for the chroniclers report that by this time the king could no longer ride but had to travel by litter in short stages and with frequent stops. Edward certainly had no intention of spending a long period at Lanercost, for his forerunners were already making provision for the accommodation of the king's household at Hulme Cultram, a Cistercian abbey some seventeen miles west of Carlisle. Nevertheless the state of the king's health made him unable to continue and the whole household settled at Lanercost Priory. The company included the king and queen, some of the officers of the household, chaplains, doctors, trumpeters and the usual large body of personal servants, porters and sumpters – probably about 200 people in all.

The strain on the priory must have been great. Lanercost was not a large house and its canons could be forced to squeeze into the smallest possible space but an influx of these proportions, not for just a few days but for over five months, posed enormous problems. The king and queen could be given the guesthouse while the more important members of the household were probably accommodated in the prior's house, but there were all the servants as well as the large number of horses who needed protection from the cold north country winter. The shortage of housing seems to have been solved by building a large number of wooden huts and even putting up the occasional tent. When it became obvious that the stay would be lengthy a number of carpenters were put to work improving the chambers of the king and queen, fitting several new glass windows as well as roofing them with lead.

A much greater problem must have been how to feed this large and hungry company, accustomed to luxuries of diet which were not part of the normal bill of fare for their hosts the canons. Foodstuffs seem to have been stockpiled in depots at Carlisle and Newcastle and sent on as needed to the priory. Although nearby Inglewood Forest had the reputation of being rich in deer, those captured by the royal huntsmen could merely provide a welcome change from the more usual pigs and oxen driven on from Carlisle. Because of the unusual nature of this particular visit record has come down of certain unexpected items. Edward's illness meant the constant attention of his physicians and the wardrobe accounts therefore give details of the frequent purchase of drugs and medicines for the royal patient. On one occasion Richard of Montpellier –

from a town well known for its medical expertise – was paid £164 14s 9d for 2196½ pounds of assorted medicines at a standard rate of 18d a pound. The account encourages the suspicion that over-medication was a medieval problem too. Master Nicholas of Tyngewyk later ordered another consignment of drugs and spices from London for his royal patient. The list suggests that hope of the king's recovery had been abandoned since it included some of the spices necessary for embalming the king's corpse. The range of medicines and equipment is extraordinary, ranging from thirty-eight enema syringes to pomegranate wine, various ointments and a 'comforting' electuary (a powdered medicine to be mixed with honey or syrup) made from amber, musk, pearl, jacinth, gold and silver at a mark (13s 6d) a pound. Other items included four ounces

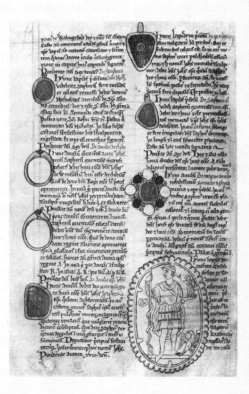

14. *An inventory of rings provided by Matthew Paris in his* Vitae Offarum *suggests the royal supply of jewellery*

of sugar rosettes and various plasters, including one for the king's neck made with laudanum and amber.[14]

A couple of inventories, one made at Lanercost in January 1307 of the royal plate, and a much more detailed list drawn up at Burgh-on-Sands ten days after the king's death, give an idea of what the king usually carried with him. Besides such expected items as gold buckles and fifty-nine gold rings (often given as presents to favoured visitors), a gold cup given him by young Queen Margaret three years before and a pair of table knives with crystal handles, there were two chests with relics of all kinds. These included the usual fragments of bone of a number of saints, especially English saints such as St Richard of Chichester and St William of York, an arm of St David (probably acquired during the conquest of Wales), a reliquary with some milk of the Virgin Mary, a thorn from Christ's crown of thorns and, more unexpectedly, 'a saint's tooth which acts as a protection against thunderstorms'.[15]

It must have been with politely disguised relief that the canons of Lanercost watched the departure of the king and queen and their household at the beginning of March 1307. Lanercost had been a prosperous house during much of the thirteenth century but the combination of the king's visit and the effects of the border war, during which the priory was invaded four times by Scottish troops, burned down twice and pillaged twice, overburdened it. The king recognised that the priory had been impoverished and gave the canons the revenues of a couple of churches as some recompense for their expenses, made offerings in the church and paid for certain repairs and improvements to their property, but the weight of hospitality had been too much. The unfortunate priory, further harassed by the Scots during the early fourteenth century, declined into the shadows of monastic history.

Reasons of policy were often responsible for the travels of a king and his court and one issue which often took the kings of England to France until the beginning of the Hundred Years War was the need of the king as duke of Aquitaine to do homage to the French king for his lands in Gascony. English rulers detested this obligation, since it put them in a subordinate position to the French king and much ill feeling resulted. This was particularly true of Edward II whose twenty-year reign saw him treating with no less than four French kings and faced with the unpalatable requirement of doing homage to each. Philip the Fair was Edward's father-in-law and, although the trip of the king, Queen Isabella and the court to Paris was delayed until 1313, the swearing of homage was made somewhat less offensive by treating it as a gala social occasion which included the knighting of Philip's sons, a great feast and the taking of crusading vows by both kings at Notre Dame. Louis X's brief reign of only two years allowed Edward to sidestep the ceremony of homage but when Philip V came to the throne in 1316 the French began to apply pressure. In the summer of 1320 Edward finally ran out of reasons for delay. He slipped over to Amiens for a brief, almost secretive, stay and performed homage for his duchy. Even for such an unceremonial occasion the wardrobe account provides an interesting light on the absolute minimum required when the king and a small household had to be lodged, and the costs of clearing up behind them.[16]

The king, his men and the necessary offices were distributed among the houses of some of the inhabitants of Amiens. The king paid Peter du Garde £6 13s 4d as a gift for all the damages caused to his dwelling where Edward had lodged. John le Mouner's house was preempted for the king's chapel, while the house of William le Mouner served as the passageway between the king's chamber and the chapel. Two women provided space for the more domestic offices – Sanxia's house had the kitchen, the offices and the servants' halls, while Margaret only had to provide space for the storeroom of the king's kitchen. The royal officials saw to it that a master carpenter was hired at the cost of £4 to restore and repair all the damages caused by the carpenters and others who had made changes in the state rooms, the halls for the superior members of the household and their other apartments. Workmen were also hired to take down the hangings in the various rooms and carry them to the river where they were to be shipped to the place where they were to be repaired. This small item suggests how very hard on perishable materials this constant hanging and rehanging must have been. The local painter, who was called upon to paint the shields of the king's arms in the streets of Amiens so that all could know where the king's offices were, was obviously a very ordinary member of his craft for he was paid only 1s 6d. The serjeant of the town, who had been appointed by the major to accompany the royal harbingers – and no doubt to mollify local sensibilities – received 20s.

The effects of the Hundred Years War precluded much of the more extensive peacetime travel indulged in by the courts. During the periods of hostilities both French and English kings tended to act as military commanders at the head of their armies and such expeditions cannot properly be called travel. However, the Hundred Years War was also notable for the long periods of time in which the main battlefield was diplomatic and during such lulls the normal pattern of royal courts moving frequently from one of their own palaces or manors to another naturally continued. War might also provide unusual travel for a king, as was the case for King John II of France who spent three and a half years as a prisoner in England after his capture at the battle of Poitiers (1356) while negotiations dragged on over his ransom and a peace treaty. Even in such an unprecedented situation the mechanism of keeping accounts continued, although the royal expenses were naturally confined to his immediate entourage. Despite his enforced stay in England King John did not lack for servants or the luxuries of life and the harsh reality of his captivity was glossed over by a series of social occasions at which he was an honoured guest. His captor, the Black Prince, continued to treat him with great courtesy and also provided considerable companionship to Philip, the king's youngest son who remained with him in England. The story is told by a later Burgundian chronicler that Philip got his nickname of 'the Bold' at the English court both because of his bravery and his high temper. On one occasion, when the fifteen-year-old prisoner was playing chess with the twenty-seven-year-old prince, they quarrelled over the taking of a piece and, as often happened in such a case, angrily pulled their daggers. They were separated by the English lords present, although King Edward III is said to have regretted that two such valiant king's sons had not been allowed to carry through the contest.[17]

Certain of King John's concerns, such as his fondness for music, seem to have been amply met. There is reference to the king's organs, the leather needed for repairing them, and the pay for the man who pumped the bellows for three days. These were probably not the smallest portative organs but the slightly larger instrument known as the 'positive', which could be transported from place to place and King John paid for their move when he was transferred from Somerton Castle in Lincolnshire to London. John's king of minstrels also went to Chichester to see some instruments the king had heard about and was repaid for the purchase of a harp.[18]

Even the household of a captive king was sometimes on the move and the problems such travel might occasion are illustrated in the journal of the king's expenses. At the end of March 1360, when John and his retinue moved from Somerton to the Tower of London at King Edward's command, Messire Aymart, the paymaster for John's household, rented five carts – one each for the king's chamber, the chamber of Philip his son, the chapel, the pantry and kitchen, and – more surprisingly – for 'Master Jehan the fool'. The widowed countess of Pembroke, Marie de Saint-Pol, who had both French and English ties, loaned the king three carts and carters who helped in transporting the royal baggage. In addition another twelve carts had to be rented for these belongings and, since it was impossible to find that many willing to go directly to London, the journey had to be accomplished in stages. Carts were emptied and others hired at the main stopping points of Stamford, Huntingdon and Royston. Apparently this was not an easy task as both at Huntingdon and Royston space had to be rented where the loads could be stored and guarded until the necessary carts were procured. While the royal equipment, surprisingly bulky for one officially a prisoner, was moving slowly towards London, King John and his son, guarded by twenty-four bowmen and twenty men-at-arms, travelled by way of Grantham and the abbey of St Albans, where they both made an offering at the martyr's shrine.[19]

By the end of May the tempo of King John's activities had picked up for news of the treaty of Bretigny had arrived in London within a week of its conclusion. The king began to prepare for his longed-for return to France. Servants were paid off, the owners of the houses near the Tower of London where the king's men and horses had been lodged were paid the final instalment of rent, generous tips were handed out to King Edward's huntsmen and chamber servants, various pious donations were made and young Philip was given 100 nobles 'to use at will'. The king's spicer bought two new locks for the precious royal spice chests and cord to tie them on their trip from London to Calais. On 10 June the king and his retinue went down the Thames by boat to Eltham to stay overnight with Queen Philippa and the following day after dinner the procession started off on the road to Dover at the dignified pace that befitted the retinue of a king. They spent Saturday at Canterbury visiting the cathedral and Becket's shrine and then went on to Dover where King John dined once more with the Black Prince. In a final exchange of gifts the French king was given King Edward's personal drinking cup, a gesture he reciprocated by presenting his own cup which had belonged to Louis IX. Finally on 8 July the French king was taken across the Channel in Edward's own ship, while five other ships paid for by the English king, carried his household and baggage.[20] King John still had to wait in Calais for over three months until the first instalment of his ransom was paid over to the English but he was finally returned to Boulogne and French soil by the Black Prince who had captured him. It was a luxurious ending to a silk-lined captivity, for the sufferings caused by the royal imprisonment were borne chiefly by the people of France, heavily taxed for his huge ransom.

By the end of the fourteenth century the ceremonial side of kingship had become increasingly important. Kings had always showed themselves to their people to reinforce their position as rulers and to express some sense of the necessary relationship between the ruler and the ruled. Beginning with the last quarter of the fourteenth century every artifice of magnificence, ceremonial and pageantry was utilised to enhance the glory of the king. France specialised in solemn ceremonial entries of the king the first time he visited a town, and their protocol grew increasingly complex. Solemn processions greeted the arrival of a queen for her marriage and her coronation was only subordinate in panoply to that of the king. As well there were the triumphal processions organised to meet a conquering ruler after a military success. The courts of

France and England led the way, closely followed by Burgundy which by the mid-fifteenth century was demonstrably the most elegant and luxurious court in Christendom.

Certain celebrations were of special splendour, particularly when both policy and prestige demanded a sumptuous display. Such an occasion was the visit to Paris in 1378 of Charles IV, Holy Roman Emperor and king of Bohemia. Son of the chivalrous and blind King John of Bohemia, who had been killed at Crécy, Charles had been brought up at the French court, his sister had married King John the Good and his own first wife was Blanche of Valois. The French king saw his uncle's visit as an ideal opportunity for making his case against the English with the utmost publicity and inflicted a long and carefully presented speech on the emperor and his associates. The whole visit was not consumed by speeches and business, however. The feast of 6 January 1378 held in the great hall of the Palais de la Cité was a most elaborate affair worthy of such a solemn occasion. At the famous marble table at the head of the hall, backed by resplendent hangings, sat the king, the emperor, his son Wenceslas, the archbishop of Reims and three other important bishops. The other most noble guests were divided among five other large tables, each with its own dais. Separated from them by barriers were other tables for the more than 800 knights who shared in the elaborate three-course meal, with ten different dishes provided for each course. In addition, as both a diversion and an exercise in crusading propaganda, the king provided a most elegant and complex dinnertime entertainment representing the successful siege of Jerusalem during the First Crusade. A good-sized ship, complete with mast, sail, and castles fore and aft was moved into place in the centre of the hall by hidden men working it from inside. It contained men representing Peter the Hermit, Godfrey de Bouillon and eleven of the other important knights accompanying him, all identified heraldically. The chronicler was enraptured by the success of the illusion that this really was a ship floating on the water. Then appeared the city of Jerusalem, with walls, the temple, and a high tower that nearly touched the ceiling from which costumed Saracens called the muezzin in Arabic. An enjoyable mock battle ensued with the crusaders swarming up scaling ladders, occasionally being repulsed and falling off but in the end entering the city, planting their banner and throwing the defeated Saracens over the walls.[21] This elaborate presentation on such an emotional subject, at the moment close to the heart of Charles IV and his adviser, Philippe de Mezières, underlines how important spectacle had become as a propaganda tool for royalty and how the travels of monarchs could be used as an occasion to heighten prestige among a wider audience and to put forward policy.

The height of elegance and minute etiquette to which a medieval travelling court could attain is perhaps best mirrored in the visit by Frederick, archduke of Austria and king of the Romans (later Emperor Frederick III), to Duke Philip the Good of Burgundy at Besançon in November 1442. Philip was not only duke of Burgundy, he was also count of Burgundy, that separate territory later known as Franche-Comté which owed fealty to the Empire. Olivier de La Marche, chivalrous courtier and panegyrist of Philip and his son, Charles the Rash, provided the details of this occasion for he delighted in eloquent descriptions of the magnificence of the Burgundian court and the punctiliousness of its etiquette. This visit gave him ample scope.[22] Duke Philip himself lodged in the house of the Franciscans at Besançon and had the archbishop's palace prepared for Frederick with rich chambers of silk, embroidery and tapestry. When the day came for the arrival of the imperial party the duke rode out to meet them, accompanied by his nobles and relations. Among the cavalcade was the Seigneur de Créqui, a knight of Picardy who was also a member of the duke's own order of the Golden Fleece and was considered 'a very honorable knight, valiant in arms and a great traveller'. The duke of Brunswick, who had been visiting Philip in Dijon while returning from a pilgrimage to Compostela, joined the welcoming party. He was a reassuring companion for Philip because he knew German and the proper behaviour with the lords of the empire for, as La Marche wisely remarks, 'each nation has its own way of behaving'.[23] They went out one-half league from the city to meet King Frederick and his retinue who made an impressive sight, since they were all carrying lances and shields, crannequins (foot crossbows) or other arms. The great standard of the imperial eagle lent an exotic note as did the blond hair of the Germans and Bohemians, shining in the sun.

It is obvious that by the mid-fifteenth century the smallest niceties of etiquette were given supreme importance at court. Just how far you went to meet someone, for example, was strictly governed by rules of relative status, as was your posture when greeting him. Any variation aroused comment among the skilled courtiers. La Marche sounds a little surprised that Philip did not get off his horse when he met the king but only did proper reverence. Perhaps, the puzzled protocol expert suggests, it was because Frederick was not yet crowned emperor or because Duke Philip was himself of royal blood. In any case no major diplomatic imbroglio seems to have resulted. The citizens of Besançon met the cavalcade at the city gate with a pall of cloth of gold carried by the most important bourgeois under which the king entered the city. He had politely asked the duke to join him but Philip refused, obeying etiquette by riding at the king's left side with the head of his horse at the rear flank of the king's. The procession was headed by the archbishop of Besançon on foot followed by all the prelates and clerics of the city carrying the relics, while behind the king and duke came the nobles of the empire and the duchy in proper order. When they had arrived at the archiepiscopal palace the king and duke dismounted, visited the church, and then the duke led the king to his chamber and left him. Since the hereditary marshal of the emperor at Besançon had been in the procession he was able to claim Frederick's horse as his rightful perquisite. Etiquette again ruled when Philip gave a splendid dinner for King Frederick and the lords of his company on the following Sunday for the king ate alone, attended only by the duke who carved for him and served his dinner in the proper manner.

Protocol was put aside for the next few days as Philip and Frederick discussed the matters of business which had prompted the visit, but by the end of the week the ceremonial aspect again came to the fore with the arrival of the duchess, Philip's third wife Isabel of Portugal. Once more everyone demonstrated the most fastidious manners. Thus, the king and his knights went a full quarter of a league outside the city to welcome her, a most condescending gesture towards one of lower status. The duchess arrived in a litter covered with crimson cloth of gold, which was followed by two white hackneys with trappings of the same cloth, each led by a groom on foot. Behind them rode twelve damsels on hackneys trapped with cloth of gold and they in turn were followed by four chariots full of ladies, on whose standard of beauty La Marche reported with approval. As this gorgeous cavalcade rode towards Besançon King Frederick rode to the right of the duchess's litter as if, reported La Marche with amazement, he was only a simple count.[24] The state visit wore on, punctuated by assemblies, banquets, dances, masquerades and diversions planned to honour the king of the Romans. La Marche was particularly fascinated by one detail from all these festivities and draws a charmingly vivid picture. Whenever the king danced, as he often did with the duchess, two distinguished knights danced before him, each carrying a torch and linking hands.[25] At the end of the ten-day visit there was the usual exchange of presents, the duke providing tapestries, for which the Flemish part of his lands were famous, while the Germans presented mail jackets and crannequins from Nuremberg, noted for its fine armour and weapons.

So came to an end a typical fifteenth-century example of a court visit. The elaborate courtesies, the minute details of precedence seem unreal if not foolish to our more casual age, but they truly served political ends. Behind the glittering façade, and supporting it, was an extremely complex and carefully detailed structure. Trained officials and hordes of specialised servants made such a wandering life possible and ensured the passage of the court and all its belongings from place to place.

CHAPTER FOUR

TRAVELLING HOUSEHOLDS

The households of the barons and nobles of England and France differed only in their size from those of the king for they too were self-supporting units. From the thirteenth to the fifteenth century the royal court was both a constant focus of interest and a school of financial and administrative practice for such magnates. There was a continuing thrust during these three centuries towards further elaboration, both in the regulations covering the make-up of the expanding household and in the complexity of the resulting accounting. Royal etiquette had become more and more refined by the fifteenth century, more and more minute in its regulations, with an increasing emphasis on elegance, the proper recognition of rank and the need to impress. These developments at court were mirror-ed, somewhat distorted and simplified, in the imitative practices of the upper classes. Like their king, the medieval nobles were used to living in a crowd and they also travelled in one, while the officials of their households maintained the day to day routine wherever they might be. Although originally noble households were much smaller than the enormous royal establishment, they too expanded over the years, adding to the original solid core of senior officials, clerks, chaplains, general servants and such indispensable specialists as the tailor who often had to make or mend elaborate robes while on the road. The presence of men-at-arms in these retinues often varied according to the political circumstances or the more or less disturbed state of the country through which they had to travel. Gradually more and more specialised members were added to the original complement. Nobles also began to have their accompanying heralds, harbingers, minstrels, fools and private physicians. Examples of certain of these households over the passage of time illustrate the changes and sharply delineate the progression by which the social pattern developed into ever greater ostentation and display. From the thirteenth century on all such households had their own household accounts, although unfortunately very few of the earlier ones have survived. It needs to be remembered that the lists of people in these accounts to whom wages were paid do not necessarily give a totally accurate picture of the numbers involved since many officials of some status would probably have had more than the one servant for whom the lord's household account was responsible. However, despite the gaps in our knowledge it is still possible to draw a generally truthful picture of how these households led their itinerant lives and their inevitable emphasis on the mechanics of travel and transport.

The household of Eleanor, countess of Leicester, is a good beginning to such a quick survey. Her household account for six and a half months of 1265 is the earliest surviving private account in England,[1] and happens to deal with the eventful months when her brothers, King Henry III and Earl Richard of Cornwall, and their sons Edward and Henry of Almaine, were the prisoners of her husband, Simon de Montfort, after the battle of Lewes. It covers the period of Edward's escape, the revival of royal power under his command, the battle of Evesham and Simon's death, and ends not long before the countess and her only daughter left England for exile in France. Compared to the far more complex royal accounting it is a very simple affair. The various expenses for the day, as dictated to the clerk responsible for writing it, are on the face of the membrane, while on the dorse is a running list of wages and incidental expenses, more or less concurrent with the daily accounting on the other side. Because the period between 19 February and 1 October 1265 was one both of triumph and disaster the sober entries reflect the changing situation.

The accepted pattern of the frequent movement of such important baronial households is obvious from the beginning. The account opens with the countess at Wallingford, where Prince Edward and Henry of Almaine were then confined. On Saturday she travelled to Reading and on Sunday 22 February had reached Odiham, a castle given to Simon and Eleanor some thirty years before. She and her retinue, using some fifty-five horses, travelled at a reasonable speed of some fifteen miles a day. Once settled at Odiham, the countess seems to have sent back some of the horses – perhaps with members of the conducting retinue – for the number of horses in the stable, carefully registered by the clerk every day, drops to around thirty.[2] During the middle of March Eleanor was hostess to a number of guests, including her son Guy with his retinue and Prince Edward and Henry of Almaine whom Henry de Montfort brought to Odiham to await his father's arrival on 19 March. The increase in the company, with the resultant complications in running the household, is suggested by the rise in the number of horses in the stables, from the original thirty to the extraordinary 334 when the earl arrived. Simon stayed at Odiham two weeks and during this time there is no record of the numbers involved, their guests or the quality of the food as the expenses of the whole household were entered on the earl's roll which has not survived. When Easter approached the countess ordered the dispatch of some special luxuries for her brothers, King Henry and Earl Richard, who were still kept comfortably but firmly under guard. The king received two barrels of sturgeon and 6s worth of whale while Earl Richard was more generously treated with a supply of twenty pounds of almonds, five pounds of rice, two pounds each of cinnamon, pepper and sugar, one pound of galingale and one of ginger, and twenty pieces of whale.[3]

After the departure of her husband, whom she was never to see again, Countess Eleanor remained at Odiham until the end of May. She must have received news there of Prince Edward's escape from Hereford on 28 May and realised the danger implied for on the afternoon of 1 June she and her household travelled hurriedly to Portchester, some forty miles away, where the strongly fortified castle was controlled by her son Simon. One of her servants acted as guide on this journey which must have lasted well into the night. The next few days at Portchester were obviously taken up by a discussion of possible baronial strategy with young Simon as well as Amaury, her youngest son, who had arrived at the castle with his retinue and one or two other baronial supporters. Within ten days Countess Eleanor and her household were again on their way, strengthened by some of young Simon's men-at-arms, Amaury and various baronial sympathisers. The group was a sizeable one, requiring eighty-four horses, and there had been much bustle in renting and borrowing horses for the extra carts and the poorly mounted members of the household. The assorted company travelled to Dover at a rapid clip, going by way of Bramber, Wilmington and Winchelsea and covering some thirty miles a day. They bought their dinner at Chichester on Friday, while on Sunday at Winchelsea the countess, and young Simon who had joined her, endeavoured to reinforce local support by entertaining all the burgesses at dinner. The safety of Dover Castle, held by the baronial forces with Henry de Montfort as its constable, was reached on 15 June when the extra horses and carts were paid off or returned to their owners.[4]

The accounts, if read in the light of the fateful events of July and

15. Dover Castle, temporary home of the Countess of Leicester in the summer of 1265

August, suggest some of the problems that faced the countess after the disastrous defeat at Evesham, where both her husband and her eldest son Henry died. Her own household had to be broken up, for the countess and her daughter were ordered to leave England, though Prince Edward agreed to receive and pardon those of her household who wished to remain in England. It is not surprising that a household roll which covers such a traumatic period should become increasingly sombre – at the end of June for example, the countess dismissed the keeper of her greyhounds, for such pastimes as hunting were no longer possible. Generally the various expenses detailed on the back of the membrane were totally utilitarian – the common repairs, the small purchases for men and horses, with frequent payments to messengers, the most necessary of all servants during those confused days. Unlike other almost contemporary accounts there is no mention of music, no harper, no minstrels and very few special luxuries, although parchment was bought at London for a book of hours for the countess's daughter which was quickly written at Oxford and paid for before they left Odiham. It would appear to have been a relatively unadorned prayer book since the total cost was only 24s. The need to mend six of the silver spoons with six silver pennies also suggests rather quick and rough repairs.[5] The accounts demonstrate that the countess of Leicester's household could be on the move, could function efficiently even under the extraordinary conditions of the summer of 1265, but it was a household geared for survival in civil war, not for high culture.

A very different household, also headed by a woman though in much happier conditions, was that of Mahaut of Artois. Although Mahaut was not a king's daughter like Eleanor, she was the granddaughter of Count Robert of Artois who was a younger brother of Louis IX of France, cousin of Philip the Fair, mother-in-law of Philip V and Charles IV, and grandmother of a count of Flanders and a duke of Burgundy. As such she was the type of great lady who moved comfortably in the very highest circles in the realm and vividly illustrates the privileged position of the wealthy widow of medieval society and her remarkable freedom of movement. The death of both her husband, Count Othon of Burgundy, and her father at the battle of Courtrai in 1303 left Mahaut both a widow and the heiress of the county of Artois. Her need to make frequent tours of Artois and her continuing concern with the county of Burgundy meant that she needed to abandon the Hôtel d'Artois in Paris to travel either north or south-east. The countess took her household of about forty with her on most of her moves and there is evidence of something of a family feeling towards them, for Mahaut even made sure that four of her grooms of the stable were given extra money to help them buy winter cloaks.[6]

The countess's travels usually included a couple of trips a year to Artois, less frequent expeditions to the county of Burgundy and various short journeys around Paris to such popular places as Fontainebleau, Vincennes, Conflans, Pontoise and the abbey of Maubuisson where her father was buried. Her admiring biographer suggests that she was a typical representative of the medieval noble on the move undeterred by bad weather, poor roads or the fatigue of age.[7] It is revealing to compare her accounts with the more spartan travels of the countess of Leicester. Both countesses obviously indulged in judicious political entertaining though Mahaut found it very expensive when she felt bound to show proper courtesy to the leaders of the French army which made its headquarters at Arras in 1328. What immediately strikes the eye is how much more pleasant and luxurious the countess of Artois' travels were. There are records of many gifts brought her, ranging from the usual game and wine to the unexpected heavy cream carefully brought over by the chambermaid of a neighbouring lady. There were other more exotic presents too. Queen Jeanne gave her mother a parrot in a painted birdcage, the abbess of Maubuisson sent a magpie and the bishop of Therouanne a leather case containing carving knives. A Cistercian monk brought her the most unusual gift, a mandrake, a plant highly prized in the Middle Ages as a sovereign remedy for many complaints since the juice of its root was in fact a useful narcotic.[8]

The arrangements for the transport of the Countess Mahaut's household were in the accepted pattern. Since her usual retinue was only made up of some forty people it was not very large and probably only required some sixty horses. Count Robert II of

16. Fourteenth-century rocking chariot, perhaps more comfortable than that used by Mahaut of Artois

Artois, Mahaut's father, had established a stud at Domfront to make sure of the availability of good horses, but this had been left to his grandson, not his daughter. Nevertheless, the countess was well equipped with the necessary horses and many highly decorated saddles. These must have been extremely elegant as many were worked in silk velvet with flowers of gold, others with pearls. Not surprisingly leather covers were provided for the safe transport of such precious objects. Mahaut and her ladies also had side-saddles, although many medieval ladies continued to ride astride as the Countess Eleanor had done, wearing what appears to have been some kind of protective breeches made by her tailor.[9] The implication of Mahaut's accounts is that she was not an enthusiastic horsewoman since she made much use of a large four-wheeled chariot which was constantly being repaired or replaced. Not only was it provided when necessary with new wheels, well shod with iron, but there might also be a new cover of tan cloth, lined on the inside with samite. The interior was adorned with velvet curtains sprinkled with silver rosettes, striped hangings of perse (a fine, usually dark blue, woollen cloth), with the chains and rings to hang them, a carpet of seven and a half ells, and eighteen decorative silver knobs. The size and elegance of this conveyance, as well as the special harness of its horses, must have alerted the villages along its route to the passage of the countess as it creaked across the flat northern plains on its way to Arras or Hesdin. As Mahaut grew older she relied more and more on another litter. The one she used in 1321 was covered in scarlet, had a well-stuffed mattress with three cushions and two pillows covered with luxurious silk, striped with gold and silver, and filled with down. Its horses had saddle pads of velvet and housings of azure perse. For access there was a folding stool and a small ladder.[10]

It would appear that Mahaut arranged to have certain pieces of furniture left in the houses where she most frequently stayed, such as Paris, Arras or Hesdin. Large beds thus remained stationary but the countess carried a small one on her travels. The various elements which made up a 'chamber', such as the canopy over the bed, curtains, covers, quilts, etc., required a good deal of special care, a situation undoubtedly aggravated by the constant packing and repacking caused by the many moves. At Arras or Hesdin, where Mahaut had a large number of visitors, she often had to supplement her 'chambers' by renting extras in the town, while on some occasions beds were merely sheltered by pavilions or small tents. The countess carried with her the most valuable tapestries and cushions, but her walls were still painted, not completely hung with tapestries. In striking contrast to the English account of some fifty years before, Mahaut had many more luxuries to accompany her on her journeys, including a silver basin for washing her hands and a deeper one for shampoos, for which not only soap but 'ashes for washing Madame's head' were purchased. Bath tubs were in her residences in Paris and Hesdin and she had *chaises percées* with covers that opened and closed.[11]

The accounts also contain hints that Mahaut benefited from her long stays in Paris with its greater culture and more advanced technology. She already had a clock at Hesdin whose repairs figure in her accounts. It appears, rather surprisingly, that there were no minstrels actually attached to her household but they appeared at all her feasts and were generously rewarded. Upon special occasions, such as her solemn entry to Artois in 1319, ceremonial trumpeters were borrowed from Hugues de Chalons and two little drummers were also pressed into service. Minstrels, musicians, acrobats, fools, jugglers and tumblers all helped to provide amusement on the great occasions when the countess entertained her royal relatives and members of the high nobility.[12] In quieter moments Mahaut gained pleasure from her books and continually extended her library. An interest in books was already obvious in her family a century before the English poet Hoccleve admonished Sir John Oldcastle to put aside his Lollard reading of the Bible and, like other nobles, restrict his reading to the stories of the siege of Troy or Thebes, the treatise of Vegetius, or the romance of Lancelot of the Lake. The only Bible reading Hoccleve considered pertinent to chivalry was to be concentrated on such war-like books of the Old Testament as Kings, Joshua or Judith.[13] French nobles had a more relaxed outlook. Mahaut's father had taken an interest in Adam de la Halle, the Arras poet, had paid for two books of astronomy and arranged to have the hours of St Louis, his newly canonised uncle, written for him. Her husband had been accompanied on the Aragonese campaign in 1285 by Jean de Priorat, who translated into French Vegetius' *De re militari*, the most popular military treatise of the Middle Ages. With such a background it is not surprising that the countess's own tastes were remarkably wide-ranging. In her young days she acquired a number of romances in French on Percival, Tristan and 'the matter of Troy', and had a copy of the *Croniques des rois de France* written and illuminated for her. The range of her interests was further emphasised by her paying writers in Hesdin in 13123 to copy the 'romance of the Great Cham', i.e. Marco Polo's story. The book had been completed in Genoa in 1298 and in 1307 Marco Polo himself presented the first copy taken from the original to Thibault de Cepoy, an ambassador for Charles de Valois, brother of the French king, who appears to have made Polo's acquaintance in Venice in that year. The note on the manuscript explains that Polo wanted what he had seen to be known throughout the world and that he had special reverence for Charles of Valois. The copy brought home to France by Cepoy was copied again for Charles of Valois and also for friends who asked for it. Mahaut must have heard of it at the French court and been anxious to own a copy for herself. The process continued for Mahaut's chancellor, Thierry d'Hireçon who was to become bishop of Arras, then had the countess's book transcribed for himself. After the death of her only son in 1316 Mahaut restricted her purchases to works of piety and philosophy, including a Boethius in French. Her books were a normal part of her life, carried around with her in great leather bags and subject to the usual and unusual hazards of such a peripatetic existence. In fact, the surprising detail available about the contents of the countess's library comes from the fact that a number of her books, valued at 200 *livres*, were looted in 1316 when adherents of the revolutionary league of Artois broke into her estate at Hesdin and stole the jewels and books they found there. The aggrieved countess carefully listed her losses when complaining to the *parlement* of Paris.[14] The picture of the Countess Mahaut to be gained from her accounts is that of a great lady leading an active, busy and independent life almost to her death in 1329.

As the fourteenth century wore on some noble households, particularly those of John of Gaunt in England and of the brothers of Charles V in France, developed such splendour that they became almost royal courts. This tendency was accelerated by the extreme youth of Richard II in England and the spells of madness of Charles VI in France. In both kingdoms the royal uncles vied for influence, a share in the royal riches and an increase in their prestige, using their growing magnificence as a tool. By 1398, for example, the household of the duke of Berry was composed of some 280 people, without counting the various men-at-arms. There were the duke's essential functionaries – the officers of the chamber and of the traditional divisions of pantry, butlery, kitchen, fruitery, stable and what perhaps can best be described as the quartermaster's department. All these had their subordinate personnel. In the kitchen, for example, apart from the regular cooks, there were such categories as carving servants, turnspits, water-carriers, butchers, sauce-makers and young errand runners. The ducal chapel, like the royal chapel on which it was modelled, also had its own hierarchical organisation with ten chaplains under the orders of the duke's chief chaplain and confessor. In addition there were the men responsible for the other activities which had now been recognised as a necessary part of such a major household – nine secretaries, two doctors, a barber for bloodletting, ushers of the hall, minstrels and messengers. Not surprisingly, with such a vast group of officials and servants the problem of lodging was always difficult and became almost insoluble when on the move for even the duke's own major establishments did not have room for all his household. At this time the castle of Bourges was not totally inhabitable so that some of the duke's household took over the archbishop's palace. When even that overflowed the rest took refuge in three of the local inns. It is worth noting that the lowest members of the household, who must have been the ones most frequently installed elsewhere, did not necessarily have the luxury of a bed to themselves since the accounts record payment for ten horses and six beds in one inn and five horses and two beds in another. The difficulties were even greater at Berry's favourite castle of Mehun-sur-Yèvre, lovingly illustrated in the duke's *Très Riches Heures*, where not only innkeepers were pressed into service but even the local parish priest had to take in the overflow. Supplies in Berry provided less of a problem. It was a rich and fertile district where the necessary foodstuffs could easily be gathered from the duke's own supplies or purchased, though the difficulties of their necessary transportation to the appropriate spot remained.[15] Fortunately, the duke of Berry was a great deal less restless than many of his contemporaries. He was quite happy to spend several months at a time in one of his establishments – in the Hôtel de Nesle at Paris, at Poitiers or at Bourges – with only short excursions to neighbouring localities.

The household of Philip the Bold, younger brother of the duke of Berry, shows a similar pattern of growth. In 1371 when the duke was at Rouvres, the ducal castle just outside Dijon, he was only accompanied by 100 persons and some seventy-six horses, but when Flanders came into his hands on the death of his wife's father in 1383 there was a rapid increase in the size and elegance of their household. The duke and duchess arrived in Ypres in January 1386 accompanied by 353 persons and 405 horses.[16] Philip was always a much more constant traveller than his older brother and also made use of all sorts of transportation. For example in mid-January 1371 he embarked at Chalon in a flotilla of six ships to travel down the Sâone and the Rhone to greet the newly elected pope at Avignon. Gregory XI was the nephew of Clement VI and had many relations among the nobility and high ecclesiastics of the south of France and Aquitaine. The pope was interested in achieving at least a truce between the French and English fighting in Aquitaine so Duke Philip, with his brother, Louis of Anjou, who was already at Ville-neuve just across the river from Avignon, were anxious to impress on the papal court the righteousness of the French claims. Philip's trip down river was speedy. Taking advantage of the current, the flat-bottomed boats could make about forty miles a day with the company dining aboard but sleeping on shore. It must have been a cold, unpleasant trip in January and the two fiddlers who enter-tained the company as they passed Lyon would have provided a welcome diversion. Philip arrived at Villeneuve five days after his departure from Chalon and he and his brother were the guests of

17. Mid fourteenth-century musicians always happy to entertain a noble household

the pope at dinner the next day. The occasion was marked by the usual exchange of presents but had no other results of substance. After further discussions with his brother Philip rode back to Dijon. The boats in which he had travelled would have a long slow trip upstream, pulled by teams of horses and taking three weeks to a month to complete the return trip. Five years later Philip retraced his route down-river, hoping to persuade Pope Gregory not to leave Avignon for Rome. His flotilla on this occasion was more impressive – ten of his own ships, led by the royal craft prepared for Charles V who had hoped to lead the mission himself. It appears to have resembled an elegant houseboat for it had a hall with two glass windows. The passage from Tournus to Avignon at the end of August took seven days, probably because the current of the river was considerably slower than in the winter rainy season. No doubt the trip was pleasant in the summer weather but Philip could not alter Gregory's decision. The pope had already left Avignon before the duke could report back to the king on his return.[17]

Another function which often moved a noble household was a politic appearance at a royal coronation. Amadeus Monseigneur, as the son of Count Amadeus VI of Savoy was called during his father's lifetime, represented Savoy at the coronation of Charles VI in 1380. The accounts of the treasurer of Amadeus' household dealing with the expenses of his master, the accompanying nobles and household during the two month trip give a good picture of the travelling style of a less wealthy lord than the dukes of Berry or Burgundy.[18] The retinue of Amadeus Monseigneur had to be sufficiently impressive to represent Savoy properly and consisted of nobles, officials – including a herald king-at-arms and a chaplain – and household servants. John of Sion, the cook, was much in evidence since he made his master's favourite soup almost every night and remembered to put the mushrooms and garlic in the salad. Because the group was travelling with 102 horses and was outside of its own territory, guides were occasionally needed for the harbingers sent ahead to arrange lodging in various inns on the way to Paris. Savoy no longer had its own establishment in the French capital yet a stay there was essential to buy the fine cloths, furs and jewels which would allow them to cut a proper figure at the

coronation festivities. Amadeus' officials went ahead to find sufficient lodging for the company who had to be spread out among six
inns. Amadeus himself, after having dinner with King Charles at
Melun, stayed at an inn known as Château de la Palée during the
last week of October. Unfortunately he fell ill and two of the royal
doctors were dispatched to visit him. The stay in Paris allowed for
all the necessary purchases, although the fine cloths had to be made
up by Amadeus' own tailor, brought along for this purpose. He
seems to have been overburdened for he had to speed after his
master at the last moment to get the elegant new coronation robes
to Reims in time. Meanwhile the rest of the company had slowly
ambled towards Reims and managed their arrival – perhaps by
design – to coincide with the entry of the young king to a fanfare
of thirty trumpets. The king's solemn anointing and coronation
took place in the cathedral on Sunday 4 November, attended by
all the important lords of the realm, while the great feast and
entertainment which followed was all at the king's expense. Young
Amadeus merely had to provide considerable largess to the many
minstrels who had flocked to such a profitable occasion. Before
leaving Reims on Tuesday Amadeus paid off some of his retinue
and left generous expense money for two sick servants who had to
be left behind. The return journey was much faster and by the
evening of 17 November the company was back at Bourg which
they had left seven and a half weeks before.[19]

One of the most widely travelled of all these households of the
late fourteenth century was that of Henry of Derby, oldest son of
John of Gaunt and the future King Henry IV. Like so many other
young men of his class he was very rich but insufficiently occupied,
for so long as his father lived his own political influence and inde-
pendence of action was limited. Strong and active, Henry yearned
to apply his energies to some suitable cause, to see something of
the world and to escape from his irritating position at his cousin
Richard's court. John of Gaunt was happy to finance his son's
expensive travels. For such restless young nobles, when a pause in
the conduct of wars allowed no physical outlet for their enormous
animal energies and their passion to practise their knightly skills,
there were two honourable routes by which to attack such

boredom – crusades and tournaments. Henry became involved in both, as will be seen, but in describing his travelling household it is worth mentioning that he passed two full years of the period 1390–3 out of England and that the household which accompanied him in his non-military endeavours varied between forty and eighty people. Such a large establishment underlines just how thoroughly insulated a lord could be from the rigours or the difficulties of foreign travel. Comfortably cushioned by familiar friends and officials, the lord's view of foreign places was essentially superficial and singularly untouched by any real contact with foreigners. The members of the military class whom he would meet essentially shared an international culture of wars, tournaments and hunting. It was almost a totally masculine world too, except for the occasional ladies who might ornament a court dinner or decorate the stands at a tournament and, it has been suggested, had much of the

18. *The Earl of Derby embarks for France*

atmosphere, the comradeship and the luxuries of an officers' mess.[20] They enjoyed themselves while their officials or hired experts could tackle such inconvenient problems as currency, language and the difficulties of dealing with the local inhabitants.

Henry spent from November 1390 to March 1391 wintering at Konigsberg (Kaliningrad) and Danzig (Gdansk) after his partici- pation in a crusading expedition with the Teutonic Knights into Lithuania. The following year he again led an expedition to Prussia but for some unknown reason there had been a change in plan. Henry then decided on a pilgrimage to the Holy Land which involved him in a long land journey from Danzig to Venice. The young man visited the Bohemian court of King Wenceslas at Prague where the English company was given a warm welcome, since Richard's queen was Wenceslas's sister. From there they went on to Vienna and arrived in Venice at the end of November, and had returned from the voyage to the Holy Land by 20 March. After a couple of weeks in Venice he and his retinue of about forty travelled across Italy to Turin, crossed the Alps through the Mont-Cenis pass to Chambéry, Macon, Troyes and Paris where he arrived 22 June. By this time he may have been feeling eager to return to England for it only took him five days to get from Paris to London.[21] It was a period of his life to which Henry always looked back with pleasure and almost nostalgia. Although a married man – at the age of twenty-three he already had three sons – the long absence from England seems to have bothered him not at all and it is interesting to note that his closest friends were always those who had shared the wandering years with him in that extraordinarily widely travelled household.

The last example of such wandering households is that of Baron Leo of Rozmital, a Bohemian noble whose travels in 1465–7 have been faithfully described by two members of his retinue.[22] A com- parison of his excursions through much of Europe and England with those of Henry of Derby some seventy-five years before show a number of differences. Because our knowledge of Henry's travels is almost entirely based on very full, financial accounts rather than on any personal record there is bound to be a dissimilar point of view but there also seems to have been a real divergence of outlook.

Henry of Derby was genuinely enthusiastic about participation in the crusading expedition of the Teutonic Knights, a natural development from his fascination with tournaments, while his pilgrimage to the Holy Land appears to have been a rather rapid, formalistic affair, primarily inspired by the sense of doing the proper and expected thing. Rozmital's long journey through Europe suggests much more of a genuine traveller's curiosity. His pilgrimages to Compostela, Guadalupe, Canterbury and other smaller shrines do not bulk large in his whole itinerary although he was a devout Catholic and duly records the relics he was shown at the various courts. The secular enjoyments of Bruges, for example, seem to have been much more to the taste of both the baron and his retinue. His visits to so many of the major courts of Christendom suggest some unmentioned diplomatic purpose for he was a brother-in-law of the Bohemian king who supported the Hussites and needed some diplomatic support from European rulers against papal antagonism for these heretics.

The retinue of the travelling Bohemian was a moderately large and distinguished one. It included some forty people, fifty-two horses and a supply wagon. Leo was accompanied by his uncle, a tall man still much interested in jousting and wrestling, five other nobles, two Germans from well-known Nuremberg families (one of whom wrote one of the reports of their travels), his standard-bearer (who also wrote his story of their wanderings), the comptroller of the Queen of Bohemia's household, a herald, jesters, three noble pages, the steward, the cook and the essential grooms and personal servants. They must have been a striking cavalcade with the gentlemen of the retinue clad in red, embroidered with gold and velvet, ornamented with pearls sewn on the sleeves, and with their long blond hair flowing down their back according to the Bohemian custom. The descriptive nature of the reports of their travels means that we know a great deal more about the individuals who travelled with Rozmital and the happenings along the way. The comptroller, for example, was apparently captured by pirates near Barcelona and completely disappears. One of the pages caused the company considerable trouble by accidentally wounding a local inhabitant with his catapult as the company travelled the thirty miles north from Ponte Vedra to Compostela. On their return his fellows were lying in wait for them though the threatening situation was fortunately defused by Rozmital's herald who was able to talk to them in Galician. The rigours of the journey to remote Compostela had been heightened by the disappearance of their cook at Braga, apparently accompanied by some of the other servants as well. They only returned after the party had reached Compostela and it is clear that a servantless existence had few charms for their chronicler:

> We suffered great hardship and had to do our own cooking, and at times came to such a pass that we had to make our lodging under a tree and tie up the horses near us like gipsies. One ran to fetch a sheep, another had to skin it, others made a fire and cooked it. Some fed the horses, my lord helping like any other. We had a hard and miserable life until we were three days from St James.[23]

Despite such setbacks it is obvious from both chroniclers that their travels with the baron gave the whole company much excitement and pleasure.

They were good observers, providing a very careful eye-witness account of the court of Edward IV of England and the extremely rigid etiquette enforced by his Woodville queen. Like so many other medieval travellers their descriptions of sea travel with its storms and discomforts are vivid with remembered hardship and terror.

The travelling noble household with its large and sprawling company was a common sight on the roads of medieval Europe, though its head had few of the problems that afflicted less favoured travellers. His journeyings were often undertaken on his own initiative and large staffs cushioned their lord from many of the inevitable discomforts and insulated him from strange sights and unintelligible foreigners. The joy of travelling for the sake of discovery was not originally part of the medieval cast of thought. The king of Portugal emphasised the harshness of a traveller's life when he welcomed Rozmital to his court at Evora, describing the weariness, the over-ridden horses and the inevitably empty purse. The royal offer of financial assistance was tactfully spurned though the king maintained the tradition of royal largess by presenting the Bohemian with two Moors and two apes as a souvenir of his stay. It appears that by the middle of the fifteenth century the noble as traveller had become a familiar figure and perhaps the cheerful baron of Rozmital can sum up the appearance of a newer attitude

19. *The landing of Dame de Coucy and the unloading of her luggage*

among such travellers. When asked by the duke of Milan what present he would like Rozmital returned a polite answer:

> Most illustrious Prince, I return you grateful thanks for your highness's kindness and bounty. But I cannot bring myself to consider asking for a present from your highness, for it was not for this that I set out from my home, but rather to pass through the courts of kings and princes and to see with my own eyes as becomes a nobleman.[24]

79

'To see with my own eyes' – it is this growing element of active curiosity which helps to mark the coming change from the Middle Ages to the age of discovery.

CHAPTER FIVE

NOBLE PILGRIMS

To talk of medieval travellers without acknowledging that many of their travels were pilgrimages and that pilgrims were drawn from every social class would be an impossibility. Kings and queens generally restricted their pilgrimages to favourite shrines within their own realms but lords, and occasionally ladies, were to be found on the galleys bound for the Holy Land or on the roads that led to Compostela. Upper-class pilgrims travelled in far greater comfort, even with elegance, and generally continued to be surrounded by at least the core of their protective retinue, but they shared with their fellow Christians along the way the desire to see for themselves the scenes of Christ's life as well as the impulse to seek favours or to give thanks at the shrine of a powerful saint. During the Middle Ages it was a pious commonplace that pilgrimage was in itself a meritorious act, closely allied with and symbolic of every man's journey towards the heavenly kingdom. This belief, with its accompanying promise of measurable spiritual rewards through the growing attachment of indulgences to the visit of such shrines, certainly served as an incentive. Most upper-class pilgrims, eminently satisfied with their place in the social order, were not likely to question the excesses, superstition and credulity bound up with so many pilgrimage shrines, though the stinging satire of Erasmus in the sixteenth century had been anticipated by Lollard denunciations in the fourteenth. Despite the fact that knights sympathetic to John Wycliffe's Lollard beliefs were a small but influential group at the English court at the end of the fourteenth century, they had little effect on the more traditional religious patterns of most of

20. *Fifteenth-century view of Jerusalem*

their social equals. For these men and women the religious motive which prompted their pilgrimages was genuine though not necessarily profound. It was certainly heightened in many cases by a natural curiosity and desire to see the world as well as a wish to escape from a too familiar routine. An incorrigible wanderlust and unassuaged restlessness is evident in at least some of the noble pilgrims whose journeys we know. Ghillebert de Lannoy was one of the most tireless. A prominent Burgundian noble who led a busy life of military activity as well as official and diplomatic service for Duke Philip the Good, he also made no less than three pilgrimages to Jerusalem, two to Santiago de Compostela and one to St Patrick's Purgatory in remote Donegal. The last of his recorded travels was a pilgrimage to Rome in the jubilee year of 1450 when he was sixty-four.[1]

The three great pilgrimages of the Middle Ages were those to Jerusalem, Compostela and Rome, although there were many other popular pilgrimage spots of second rank much closer to home. No Englishman could be ignorant of the magnificent shrine of Thomas Becket at Canterbury, nor the northern French fail to seek spiritual help from St Michael at his towering abbey off the Norman coast. These, and a host of other more local shrines, all enjoyed a stream of visitors, though certain localities attracted more of the upper class than others, and their relative popularity might wax and wane over the years.

Pilgrimages could also be made by proxy and the rich and important often ordered such substitute spirituality. A vow of pilgrimage was frequently made at a time of great devotion, or perhaps in a case of serious illness, and the fulfilment of such a vow might well seem excessively onerous once the crisis had passed. Thus ecclesiastical provision was made for pilgrimages to be discharged by proxy or by a gift of money. Blanche of Castile, desperately homesick after her marriage to the heir of the throne of France, had vowed a pilgrimage to Compostela but was urged by the bishop of Paris to fulfil her promise by giving the money it would have cost to St-Jacques in Paris, and Blanche regretfully obeyed.[2] At the beginning of the fourteenth century when the church of St-Jacques-aux-Pèlerins was founded in Paris Countess Mahaut of Artois accompanied her daughter, Queen Jeanne, to the laying of the foundation stone. Mahaut continued to be generous in her gifts to the church, donating windows and 80 *livres* for the confraternity fund, for devotion to St James was a strong element in her piety. In 1304 she paid for a pilgrim to visit Compostela to pray for the cure of her daughter and in 1317 after her son had died a servant, Yvon le Breton, was dispatched to Compostela with his expenses paid, carrying an offering of 4s of silver for the salvation of her son's soul. It would appear that Yvon took some time to complete this project for the letter of the treasurer of Compostela, attesting that he had visited the shrine of St James for the countess, had laid the silver on the altar of the apostle and fully completed his pilgrimage, is dated 1 May 1321.[3] Gifts as substitutions for pilgrimages could also prove a useful source of funds for ambitious ecclesiastics anxious to beautify their churches. In the mid-fourteenth century Archbishop Thoresby of York persuaded Agnes de Hulme to bequeath to his new building at the cathedral a sum of money that would have been sufficient to hire a person to make a proxy pilgrimage to the shrine of St James at Compostela. Agnes remained anxious to display her devotion to St James and specified that her money should be used for a window in the church with St James in one of the lights.[4]

This passion for subsidising vicarious pilgrimages as a means of acquiring spiritual merit was widespread, as is attested by a number of wills both in France and England. Bernard-Ezi II, lord of Albret in south-west Aquitaine, dealt with a number of unachieved pilgrimages in his first will of 1341. There were pilgrimages to St James and to other lesser shrines, including that of another royal saint, Louis of Anjou, a great-nephew of St Louis IX, who had become a Franciscan and was venerated at Marseilles. Bernard-Ezi had also vowed a pilgrimage to the Holy Land when his wife fell sick and he wanted to be sure that if he did not succeed in making it himself one of his sons would carry out the obligation. The rather petulant phrase with which he substitutes charitable donations 'if it should happen that my children are ungrateful enough not to wish to accomplish this pilgrimage for my soul' may have had its foundation in the fact that he himself had failed to make the journey to St James which his mother had requested be made by one of her sons, merely passing that obligation on to the next generation.[5] The same pattern is to be seen in the English wills as well. An early glimpse in the thirteenth century reveals Bartholomew de Leigh commanding his executors and friends to enable his nephew to complete the pilgrimage to St James honourably if Bartholomew himself had not made the promised journey. When so many more wills are recorded after the beginning of the fifteenth century such provisions are reasonably common, although the pilgrimages are frequently local ones within England to such shrines as Canterbury or Walsingham, or to the shrines of native saints like William of Norwich, John of Beverley or Richard of Chichester. For example, the earl of Arundel, when invalided home after the siege of Harfleur in 1415, requested in his will that a pilgrimage on foot be made on his behalf to Canterbury and that two other men go on foot to the nearby shrine of St Richard of Chichester. The earl instructed his executors to pay these proxy pilgrims not only the offerings they were to make on his behalf but also generous expenses 'as if he had made the pilgrimages himself in his estate'. A more unusual bequest for a pilgrimage, suggesting a nostalgia for the scenes of much of his working life as Henry V's representative to the papal curia, was made by Master Thomas Polton, bishop of Worcester. In 1433 he left £20 to find a suitable chaplain to go to Rome and stay for two years continuously, doing the stations and visiting various holy places and the relics of the saints. The priest was to celebrate mass for the bishop's soul in the more devotional places and to distribute 100s to poor recluses of either sex and 'other miserable persons'. To make sure that his soul had his chaplain's full attention Polton ordered that the man was to swear an oath to his executors before leaving England that he would not adopt any other occupation while in Rome.[6] Despite such examples many of the great during these centuries did not wait for a proxy or approaching death to become interested in pilgrimages, they went at all stages of their lives, often in considerable splendour.

THE HOLY LAND

The greatest pilgrimage of all, that to the Holy Land, was a major undertaking even for the well-to-do, and, in this case, their wealth could usually only provide rather minor improvements on the general conditions, since it was unwise to appear too wealthy in Moslem territory. There had always been a constant trickle of pilgrims to the Holy Land from the early Christian era and this continued in the thirteenth century. However, until the final fall of Acre and the disappearance of the Christian kingdom in 1291 the primary focus of kings and knights was the crusade, which was regarded as a military pilgrimage and attempted to reinforce the dwindling Christian strength in Palestine. However, Christian pilgrimage to the holy places continued after their military defeat and the Moslem conquerors soon realised that it was to their commercial advantage to take advantage of this pious tourist traffic. Originally the most popular route to Jerusalem had been overland, through the Balkans to Constantinople and then south, but the Moslem successes and the threatening advances of the Turks in Asia Minor made such a trip far more difficult. By this time too, the Venetians and Genoese had gained control of the Mediterranean and found the increasing numbers of pilgrims taking passage in their ships an ideal balance to their other commercial interests. From the early thirteenth to the end of the fifteenth century the Venetian rulers found it advisable to legislate the conditions of this pilgrim traffic since it was essential for Venice's commercial reputation to have reasonably satisfied customers. The doge and his council insisted on the proper state of the ships, their equipment, the required number of mariners and the fulfilment of contracts made. Originally there were two voyages for pilgrim ships, one in the spring and one in the summer, since it was important to sail when the Mediterranean winds and weather were most favourable. Gradually the traffic was consolidated in one fleet, the spring voyage, although the rich and important whom the signoria of Venice wished to favour might be granted the right to hire a galley for themselves and to leave at any time.

Most pilgrims came to Venice over the Alps, sometimes taking to river boats on the Po or the Adige for the last stage of their journey. On arrival in Venice they stayed in one of its many inns, which catered to specific national groups and social classes, and then booked their passage with one of the captains who had

21. Marco Polo setting out from Venice

obtained the official licence to sail that year and had been allowed
to set up his standard in the Piazza San Marco. To simplify this
process and to ensure that the foreigners were well treated the
Venetian government licensed special guides who were stationed
in the Piazza or on the Rialto. They were expected to serve as
interpreters and honest middlemen in the pilgrim's efforts to book
the best passage, change his money into Venetian ducats (generally
accepted throughout the Mediterranean) and acquire the necessary
bedding and provisions. Guidebooks for pilgrims proliferated with
each subsequent text copying extensively from its predecessors but
adding whatever new information the author had found practical.
In the fifteenth century William Wey's careful listing of provisions
required by the pilgrim included the admonition to purchase con-
fections, cordials, laxatives and restoratives as well as the more
usual luxuries of spices and dried fruit.[7] Pilgrim narratives also
abound, though most were written by clerics, sometimes primarily

pious accounts, sometimes providing valuable geographical information. Several of the reports of important laymen like Ghillebert de Lannoy and Bertrandon de la Broquière in the early fifteenth century appear to reflect reconnaissance for a possible crusade rather than an actual pilgrimage, though they carefully list the pilgrimage sites and describe some of them. Henry of Derby's accounts in 1392–3 give the details of his travel expenses on his pilgrimage to the Holy Land, but they are more explicit about provisioning the galley in Venice than they are about the Holy Land itself where Henry and his retinue spent just over a week on shore. Henry made the usual visit to the Holy Sepulchre and hung a representation of his arms there but we have no record of his reaction to his journey.[8]

A most unusual record of a noble pilgrimage in the early fifteenth century is to be found in an English manuscript entitled the *Pageant of the Birth, Life and Death of Richard Beauchamp, earl of Warwick*, a collection of fifty-three line drawings by an English artist, probably

22. *The Earl of Warwick going on pilgrimage*

done about fifty years after the earl's death.[9] The drawings have captions explaining the particular event illustrated and provide an unparalleled series of pictures of the stages of such a great noble's pilgrimage as well as of other notable events of his life. Warwick is shown leaving England in 1408 in his pilgrim's gown and hat, carrying a pilgrim's staff. The earl crossed the Channel to France, where he met a French cousin, the duke of Bar, with whom he travelled to the king's court in Paris and shared the impressive Whitsun feast. When he left the French court Warwick was provided with a herald to attend him and conduct him safely through the realm, a courteous gesture of assistance and also a common precautionary method of supervising foreigners. The earl was met on his entrance into Lombardy by an Italian lord's challenge to joust and distinguished himself against his challenger at Verona. From there he went on to Venice to the inn of St George where his fame had preceded him. Warwick and his retinue obtained a special licence from the doge allowing them to take passage in a galley which agreed to take them to Jaffa, wait ten days in Acre where the harbour was safer, and then return to Jaffa to re-embark them. The normal time allowed pilgrims in the Holy Land seems to have been two or three weeks, but nobles were generally in more of a hurry, or perhaps able to complete their circuit more quickly because they were a smaller company. The artist seems to have been uninterested in the stages of this journey for his next picture shows the earl arriving at Jerusalem and being received by the Christian Patriarch's deputy. Another highly conventional drawing shows the earl in his pilgrim's garb making his offering at the altar of the Church of the Holy Sepulchre and having his arms hung on the north side as evidence of his visit. From the description of a Spanish pilgrim some forty years later, it appears that there was a great hall in the church of the Holy Sepulchre which was hung with the pennons and banners of many Christian kings and princes and where, too, knights were allowed to hang the representation of their arms.[10]

Warwick's pilgrimage was concluded by two unusual social occasions. The sultan's lieutenant invited the earl and his retinue to dinner, greeting them with great honour and generosity, and the earl then served as host at a return feast, also with gifts, while 'after dyner they hadden greet communycacion togedre'.[II] It is surprising to note that one of the reasons given for the Moslem invitation to the earl was that he was descended from Guy of Warwick, the hero of popular romance, whose life his hosts had read in books of their own language. Such knowledge would suggest considerable intermingling between Moslems and Christians at the higher levels. His pilgrimage completed, the earl returned to Venice and travelled on to Prussia for a crusading expedition before returning to England. He also enjoyed many tournaments along the way which his illustrator depicts in great detail and with obvious enjoyment. It is unusual to have such a consecutive pictorial account, especially in line drawings, but Warwick's mixture of pilgrimage, crusade and tournament was a common pattern of travel for the upper classes in the late fourteenth and early fifteenth centuries.

23. The Earl of Warwick's feast for the Sultan's lieutenant at Jerusalem

Henry of Derby and the earl of Warwick made the basic Jerusalem pilgrimage but some nobles did the longer complete circuit, which included not only Jerusalem but Sinai, Cairo, Damietta and Alexandria and sometimes Damascus and Beirut. Thomas Swinburne, an English knight who was castellan of Guines near Calais and later mayor of Bordeaux and castellan of Fronsac, made this circuit in 1392–3. A report of their pilgrimage with a sketchy account of its expenses was made by Thomas Brygg, one of his retainers.[12] On leaving Guines Swinburne and his companions joined a group which included two knights and seven squires from Germany and Bohemia with their retinues. When they arrived in Venice they were fortunate enough to be able to sail the following day, 2 September, on a merchant galley to Alexandria where they arrived 20 October. They stayed in the great merchant city for ten days and then took boats up the Nile to Cairo, fascinated by the crocodiles they saw along the way. Their five days in Cairo were occupied by some pious sightseeing and Brygg was anxious to record their first encounter with an elephant and a giraffe. Before setting off across the desert to Sinai they were taken to Matariya with its famous garden of balsam, carefully described in many of the medieval accounts of Egypt. The resin secreted by this tree was so highly prized that its first running was preserved for the use of the sultan who distributed small quantities to his leading officials. When Ghillebert de Lannoy was in Egypt twenty-five years later he was given a vial by the Patriarch of the Jacobite Christians who was part lord of the enclosed garden where it grew. The gift was a special favour and in recognition of his important status as ambassador of King Henry V.[13]

Swinburne and his company took ten days for their journey to Sinai and the renowned monastery of St Catherine of Mount Sinai, crossing the desert on camels. The general reaction of the European pilgrims who first made the acquaintance of camels under the harsh desert conditions was that they were very remarkable but bad-tempered beasts. Few western travellers had any conception of the importance of these animals to the nomads and traders of Africa and Arabia, and on the silk road to China, nor of the numbers involved. In the sixteenth century it was said that the pilgrim caravans from Damascus to Mecca, the pilgrimage centre and holy place of the Moslems, included 35,000 camels for the 40,000 to 50,000 pilgrims as well as horses and asses. The camel's ability to carry heavy loads – as much as 550 pounds for a pack camel – and to travel for three days without water in hot weather made them the preferred form of transport, while specially bred running camels provided a network of fast communication throughout the Moslem empire.[14]

The monastery of St Catherine sits on a wild rocky plateau under the looming peaks of Djebel Mousa, where Moses was believed to have received the tables of the law, and Djebel Katrin, where St Catherine's body was believed to have been left by an angel. The site is far down the Sinai peninsula and is still remote and difficult of access. A feeling of accomplishment must have sustained the pilgrims as they plodded across the wild and unfamiliar desert and climbed the steep and rocky mountains to make their visit to the holy places. From the peak of Djebel Katrin (8,667 ft) they could see both the gulf of Suez and the gulf of Aqaba leading to the Red Sea – a world very remote from Europe. It is not surprising that after all these exertions they felt that basic human urge to leave their mark and scratched their coats of arms and names on the monastery walls, where they can still be seen. Swinburne and his companions were single-minded pilgrims since Brygg's report only mentions their arduous climbs and the relics they visited in the monastery, with no suggestion of the wealth of icons and treasures that also rested in that ancient house.[15] After three days at St Catherine's, they set off on 22 November for a further two-week march to Gaza. From there the rest of their trip was less strenuous and they moved more rapidly, spending three days in Bethlehem, a week in Jerusalem and arriving in Damascus for Christmas. Leaving there on 31 December they were in Beirut by 3 January but had to wait twelve days for a ship to take them to Rhodes. Brygg finished his brief pedestrian report with a small flourish, very suitable for Englishmen, saying that they completed their pilgrimage to the honour of Almighty God at a chapel a mile outside Beirut, where St George had killed the dragon. The trip appears to have been an expensive one, as it has been estimated that Swinburne had to pay 477½ Venetian ducats for passage, wine, dragomans, camels, entry fees 'as well as other diverse expenses on victuals and many very small oddities' incurred by himself and his retinue.[16] One hopes they were satisfied with their exhausting journey.

Another noble pilgrim was Nompar de Caumont from the Agenais, who actively served the English in Aquitaine. He went to the Holy Land in 1419 and appears to have dictated the story of his pilgrimage to one of his clerks. The personal element in this somewhat fuller narrative hints at the nature of the man, a genuine pilgrim, truly pious and devoted to his wife whom he describes as *'ma tres chiere et ma tres bien amee m'amie et m'amour vraye'*.[17] As a prologue to the account of the voyage he describes the arrangements made for the safeguarding of his lands and people while he was away, the prayers that were to be said for his safety and the contract made with his squires and others of his company for the voyage to Outremer, swearing that neither side would abandon the other except in case of death. Nompar left Caumont on his pilgrimage on 17 February, going up the Garonne as far as Toulouse and then on to meet the count of Foix near Castelnaudary. The count counselled him to avoid Venice because of the unsettled state of the roads due to war and to sail from Barcelona. Nompar took his advice, crossing the Pyrenees by the pass of Puymorens and on to Puigcerda. The travelling was slow and difficult and undoubtedly the passes were heavy with snow in early March. Nompar comments one day that the travelling was so difficult that they only went one league (about three miles). He and his company paused to visit the shrine at Montserrat and arrived in Barcelona on 21 March. They stayed there about six weeks, finally sailing at the beginning of May. Both going and returning, the ships on which he took passage had trouble avoiding the Barbary coast, much feared because of its Moslem pirates, but they finally arrived safely in Majorca. From there they sailed to Sardinia, Sicily, Crete and Rhodes where they arrived 1 June. Nompar, only in his twenties, proposed to crown his pilgrimage by being knighted in the church of the Holy Sepulchre but in order to be allowed this privilege he had to have another knight with him. While in Rhodes he picked from among the Knights of St John a noble knight from Navarre – chosen, Nompar says, for his good manners, behaviour and good name – who agreed to accompany him for this purpose.[18] They finally arrived at Jaffa on 28 June. It had taken them eight weeks from Barcelona; the trip from Venice, considerably shorter, normally took four to six weeks, depending on weather and the number of stops. At Jaffa, their ship, like other pilgrim ships, could not discharge its passengers until the formalities of entry required by the Moslems had been accomplished, and the Franciscan from the convent on Mt Olivet, who would be their guide and responsible for their behaviour while in the Holy Land, had arrived. The normal itinerary was from Jaffa to Ramla, with a side trip to Lydda, considered to be the spot most sacred to St George, and of special interest to Nompar who claimed the saint as his patron. The heat was so oppressive in high summer that the pilgrims were urged to ride their donkeys – except in very exceptional circumstances Christians in the Holy Land were not allowed to ride horses – and to take the road to Jerusalem during the night. There they stayed at a great hostel, probably the hospital of St John, and began at once on their pilgrim round which, with all its many stops and indulgences, was carefully outlined in most of the guidebooks. On one night the pilgrims were locked into the church of the Holy Sepulchre by its Moslem guardians and allowed to spend the night at their devotions. Nompar describes with great care how on 8 July he made his confession, heard the mass of St George said on the altar of the Holy Sepulchre, went to communion and, in an elaborate ceremonial, was knighted by the good knight he had brought from Rhodes. With undisguised pleasure he reports how he placed his unfurled banner of arms beside the arms of the king of England (Henry of Derby), knowing that he had achieved what he most desired.[19] This practice of receiving knighthood at the Holy Sepulchre continued throughout the fifteenth century. When Brother Felix Fabri, the loquacious German Dominican, was there in 1483 a Prussian noble, who lived with the Franciscans and was highly respected by all in Jerusalem, would confer knighthood on those who deserved it and were 'proved to be noble of four descents: of sufficient substance, just, of good report, and not disgraced by any infamous misdemeanour'. Fabri was longwindedly lyrical on the special virtues of such knighthood, detailing its superiority in no less than forty different ways.[20]

Caumont then continued his round of the holy places – Bethlehem, Capharnum, Jericho and the River Jordan where he bathed. By 17 July he had managed to spend an unusual four nights in the Holy Sepulchre, a feat which he records with pious pride, and could

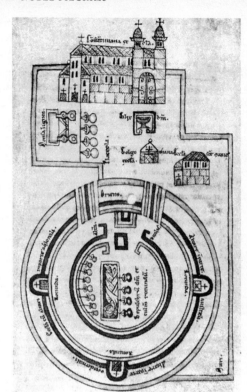

24. *Drawing of the precincts of the Church of the Holy Sepulchre from a thirteenth-century pilgrim's guide*

view with equanimity the need to return. By 21 July the ship raised anchor and set sail for Cyprus. On his return journey, having satisfactorily achieved his pilgrimage, Nompar showed much more interest in all the secular points along the way. He paid his respects to the king of Cyprus for two or three days, although he found the country very hot and not very healthy. He stayed some five weeks at Rhodes, as much the contented tourist as many who have followed him. Departing for Sicily on 20 September his ship was caught in a desperate storm and was nearly wrecked. When the exhausted company came to land at a small harbour on Sicily's southernmost point Nompar conferred with his squires and they all decided that it was unwise to attempt any further sea voyage in

25. The Earl of Warwick making an offering at the Holy Sepulchre in the hall where arms were hung

winter. They acquired horses and rode on to Palermo and both in the city and on the way Nompar described castles with great interest, casting a professional eye over their site and fortifications. While sightseeing in Palermo he met a knight from Bearn, and the two knights from neighbouring parts of Gascony talked of their native country. They became friends and the knight, who had received a strong castle from the king of Sicily for his service, invited Nompar to stay with him. The castle was in mountainous country, strong and well-built, with beautiful views and good hunting and his host tried to amuse his guest with such sport. Nevertheless the lonely Nompar kept remembering his wife and was delighted at a message from Palermo to the effect that a ship was in harbour bound for Barcelona. The early southern spring was on the way and Caumont returned to Palermo, bought provisions and embarked in mid-February.[21] A month later he had arrived in Barcelona and could turn his steps towards home. He stopped at Pau to see the castle built by Gaston Fébus, the famous fourteenth-century count of Foix, which impressed him as the most beautiful and best built he had ever seen. Caumont particularly enjoyed a porch at the entry to the hall which boasted frescoes of all the beasts, both male and female. Fébus, who had been a passionate huntsman and author of the *Livre de Chasse*, obviously enjoyed being surrounded by reminders of his favourite pastime. Nompar finally arrived home on 13 April 1420 and at the end of his account provides a fascinating list of the souvenirs he had brought home to give his wife and the lords and ladies of his county – relics and quasi-relics, Eastern cloths, purses and rings.[22]

The Gascon lord was one of the most devout of the high-born nobles who made the long journey to the Holy Land and his account, pedestrian though it is, gives some sense of this. He had little to say about people, and nothing at all about the squires and others who accompanied him, but he demonstrated a reasonable, rather professional, interest in castles and fortifications. It is somewhat surprising to note that he was well versed in standard classical lore, citing Menelaus, Helen and Paris off the island of Cytherea; Minos, the famous labyrinth and the Minotaur off the shores of Crete; and Jason and the Golden Fleece off Colchis in Turkey, though not realising in this case he had the wrong place. His Christian concern was obvious in his praise for the knights at Rhodes who continued their campaigns against the Turks unlike, he adds tartly, other Christians who preferred to fight among themselves.[23] Nompar obviously enjoyed his pilgrimage and it is sad to realise that only eight years later he was killed in an ambush during the continuing struggle between the French and English in Aquitaine while he was still under forty.

SANTIAGO DE COMPOSTELA

The pilgrimage to Santiago de Compostela in north-west Spain, which was often described as 'St James in Galicia', was probably the most popular of the three great pilgrimages during the Middle Ages, for it was difficult enough to provide a sense of penitential accomplishment but also accessible to those who could not afford the long voyage to the Holy Land. There is even amusing testimony to its popularity in a moral tale provided by the thirteenth-century preacher, Jacques de Vitry. He tells the story of the talkative servant of a rich man who was warned by his master that he did not want to hear any bad news when he returned from Compostela for he would be eager to celebrate with his friends and neighbours. On his return he was met by a silent servant leading a lame dog. His curiosity aroused, the master questioned the man on what had happened to his dog. Reluctantly the servant unravelled a whole string of woes. The dog had run past the mule who had kicked it so vigorously that the mule's halter broke. Thereupon the mule ran through the house, scattering the hearth fire with its feet so that the house was burnt down and the pilgrim's wife perished in the fire. Compostela was a universally recognised peg on which to hang such a tale in the thirteenth century. In various guises the tale continued to be popular for centuries appearing suitably brought up to date as a dialogue used in American schools in 1856, and as a popular French song in the 1930s.[24]

Pilgrims going to Palestine were seeking the holy places, both real and fantastic, connected with the life of Jesus and events in the Bible. At Compostela the cult had grown up around a late and legendary account which claimed that the Apostle James had preached in Spain and that his body had been brought back to Galicia for burial by two of his disciples after his martyrdom at Jerusalem in 44 AD. Nothing was heard of this tomb until it was miraculously discovered at Compostela in 838 while at almost the same time St James was believed to have come to the aid of the faltering Spanish army at the battle of Clavijo and been responsible for the death of thousands of Moors. The first church built at Compostela was sacked by the Moors at the end of the ninth century and its bells taken away to Cordoba but the town was soon reconquered by the Spanish Christians and rapidly became a growing centre of pilgrimage, recognising St James as a powerful patron in the continuing fight against the Moors. Whatever the historical accuracy of the story concerning St James' burial or the discovery of his tomb (believed by many Spaniards but not by others), the force of the medieval belief cannot be questioned.

From the eleventh century on it was strong enough to impel large numbers of pilgrims from all over Europe to take the long, dangerous and exhausting journey through France, over the Pyrenees and across northern Spain to a small town in remote Galicia. The over 500 miles of the pilgrims' road from Roncesvalles to Compostela traverses extraordinarily varied terrain, descending from the Pyrenean pass inextricably linked with Roland and Charlemagne to the flat sunbaked plains of Castile and Leon, then rising again over the precipitous slopes of the Cantabrian range to arrive at the damp green hills of Galicia.

Such a journey, menaced by wild beasts in the forest and unfriendly inhabitants in the towns who quite naturally mistrusted the hordes of hungry, thirsty and often quarrelsome and incomprehensible wayfarers, was difficult for even genuine pilgrims. The pilgrim roads were also crowded with numbers of unwilling pilgrims of doubtful reputation since a pilgrimage was often assigned as an ecclesiastical penance or a court-enforced punishment. It is no wonder that the pious injunction to feed and lodge any pilgrim of St James was often disregarded by cynical residents along the way. The popular twelfth-century *Guide du Pèlerin* had several moral stories to encourage proper charity by giving horrid examples of what might happen to those who refused a pilgrim's honest needs. There was the weaver of Nantua who denied a pilgrim's request and at once the cloth on which he was working fell to the ground, mysteriously torn in half. Even more drastic was the story of the pilgrim who sought lodging in Poitiers near the church of St-Porchaire but was refused entry to all the houses in the street except the last. During the night a fire burnt down the houses of all those who had turned him away, only the one which had sheltered him was spared.[25]

The pious task of providing food and shelter for the flocking pilgrims was first undertaken by individual hermits aided by gifts from the charitable. It was then taken up in a more organised fashion by the Benedictine abbeys, mostly owing obedience to Cluny which were founded along the pilgrimage routes as the traffic grew. In time a whole network of hospices and hospitals developed along the route to Compostela to help the poor and the

26. *Statue of St James
holding a pilgrim's staff*

ill. These were generally run by the Augustinians and headed by
the famous hospice at the Pyrenean pass of Roncesvalles. These
institutions soon gained a wide reputation for in 1321, for example,
Edward II provided safe-conducts for messengers sent to England
to collect alms for the hospital of St Mary Roncesvalles 'in con-
sideration of the benefits constantly given in that hospital to poor
pilgrims visiting the shrine of Santiago'. Bernard-Ezi II, the same
fourteenth-century lord of Albret who requested so many pilgrimages in his will of 1341, showed a more practical concern for
such pilgrims by leaving 50s *bordelais* to every hospice on the route
of St James between Bordeaux and Pamplona. In the thirteenth and
fourteenth century secular confraternities dedicated to St James
also developed. Originally founded to favour pilgrims en route to
St James and to give them lodging, they gradually began to assist
all pilgrims. The confraternity at Paris, centred at St-Jacques-aux-
Pèlerins, has already been mentioned and its hospice must have

been a particularly busy one for it recorded that in 360 days in 1368 they had lodged and fed in their hospice 16,690 pilgrims who came and went to Mont St-Michel and elsewhere. They were still lodging thirty-six to forty every night and were in dire need of more beds, coverlets and sheets.[26] Such assistance and the general information on routes, dangerous rivers and sights along the way which was to be found in the *Guide du Pèlerin* would be most useful for all those pilgrims who travelled to Compostela by the land routes. Obviously some of the hospitals at least expected to serve the whole gamut of pilgrims. In the fifteenth century, for example, Leo of Rozmital, when returning from Compostela through Spain, was forced to leave three members of his retinue in the hospital at Guadalupe because of illness. Social rank was recognised there, for the voluble Tetzel who wrote the German account of their travels, commented that everyone received service according to his station but all got the necessary care.

> Each one, rich or poor, as his sickness requires is waited on daily by the physician, the apothecary and the kitchen staff who serve him during his sickness, so that, as I think, he could not be waited on so well in his own home.

The hospital returned to those who regained their health everything they had brought in with them and if they lacked provision gave them assistance without charge. In order to maintain its resources, however, the hospital took over all the belongings of those who died there.[27] Many pilgrims must have found such services a welcome refuge when ill in a strange land.

However, by the second half of the fourteenth and throughout the fifteenth century most English pilgrims went by ship rather than risk the long and dangerous trip through war-torn France. The sea voyage was sufficiently daunting, for a fifteenth-century poet remarked pessimistically that 'Men may leve all gamys / That saylen to seynt James', and then went on to describe vividly all its discomforts and dangers. Pirates or enemy sailors were yet another hazard. Sir James Audley was captured at sea early in the fourteenth century while on his way to Compostela and a century later the duke of Brittany interceded with Henry V for the release of some pilgrims from his duchy whose vessel had been taken by English sailors.[28] Nevertheless the patent rolls of the time record a profitable trade in licences issued to ship-owners to take pilgrims there and back. For example, from February to July 1395 Richard II licensed the departure of 1,630 pilgrims, as well as two other ships from Bristol whose number of passengers was not specified. The king also insisted that the master was responsible for collecting 6d from each pilgrim for the king's use – a useful supplement to the royal income.[29] When William Wey sailed from Plymouth to Compostela in 1456 he wrote of seeing more than eighty ships in the harbour of which thirty-two were English. The priest from Eton was a curious observer as well as a collector of pious tales for he includes the music and the verse of 'the song of the little boys of Spain tumbling before the pilgrims' for the coins tossed to them.[30] In fact the relationship of England with Compostela remained close during the fifteenth century and even the king might send an offering. In 1445 Robert Puryton, sub-prior of Winchester, was authorised by his prior to go on pilgrimage to Compostela and to take the royal alms from Henry VI which were equal to fifteen gold nobles. In response to this generous gift the cathedral chapter of Compostela had a solemn mass of the apostle said at the high altar, in the presence of Robert and 'a multitude of pilgrims some of whom were English subjects' and admitted the royal family into their confraternity.[31]

Many of the more important people who made their pilgrimages to Santiago did so in the intervals of other occupations in Spain. Baudoin de Lannoy, brother of Ghillebert, served as an envoy to the king of Portugal for the duke of Burgundy in 1428–9. Philip the Good was debating a marriage with the king's daughter Isabel, later to be his third wife, but wanting to be quite sure of the lady's attractions before the wedding had sent along Jan van Eyck to paint her picture. The portrait then had to be sent back for the duke's approval before the diplomatic mission could proceed. In the enforced interval Baudoin and his fellow negotiators fitted in a pilgrimage to Compostela, a sightseeing trip to Moorish Granada and were shown the historic glories of Portugal by the king himself.[32] Pilgrimage was even more incidental to the activities of

John of Gaunt in his great expeditionary force to Spain in 1386. Froissart describes how several French knights having made their pilgrimage most devoutly to 'baron monseigneur saint Jacques' heard of the imminent arrival of the English fleet and immediately set off for La Coruña to strengthen the garrison there and hold the town against the English. They were in good time and prevented English seizure of the town but could not delay their landing or their encampment on the shore near the city. The English needed to disembark their horses who had already been fifteen days at sea and, even with the best of care and fresh water, were still suffering from the movement of the sea. Gaunt paid off his ships to prove his intention to remain in Spain but, after a month of stalemate, near La Coruña, decided to move on to Compostela and mustered his large force, an army which also included his wife and daughters as well as a number of other noble ladies. Compostela was a small and not very defensible town so its leaders wisely came to an accommodation with Gaunt's forces, agreeing to allow them in the town and treat them well unless the king of Castile came to fight them. In such a case Gaunt's troops promised to withdraw so that the town should not suffer. This settled, a ceremonial procession of the clerics of the town came out to welcome the duke and duchess and to present them with the keys of the city. When Gaunt, his wife and daughters arrived in town they went at once on foot to pay their respects to St James's relics and then settled themselves into their lodgings. Froissart talks of the plentiful supplies available for them but remarks disapprovingly that the archers especially drank so much that most of the time they went to bed drunk and the next day their bad headaches rendered them incapable.[33]

This not very edifying spectacle was paralleled by what Leo of Rozmital found at Compostela in 1466. He and his retinue arrived to find the archbishop a prisoner with his mother taking command of the cathedral which was being besieged by a local lord supported by the people of Compostela. The count and his retinue had considerable problems trying to see the church and still remain on the right side of both parties. They finally succeeded in entering due, the writer suggests, to the baron's importance and the clergy's expectation of a rich gift. They paid their respects at the altar and the shrine and, seeing the large number of coats of arms of lords and travellers hanging in the chapel, Rozmital left his there too. The church and its sculpture were admirable, they felt, but its current condition was that of 'a wilderness' with horses and cows stabled in it and its defenders cooking and sleeping there.[34] The devout Nompar de Caumont briefly recorded his pilgrimage to Santiago in 1417 but primarily as a table of the distances from Caumont to Compostela and back, showing that he travelled an average of nearly twenty miles a day during the fifty-eight days it took him. Nompar did elaborate on the battle field at Najera where the Black Prince had won a major victory over Henry of Trastamare in 1368 while commanding an army of Gascons and English. Like other less devout tourists he was fascinated by the church at Santo Domingo de la Calzada which harbours a white rooster and hen and gives a long account of the miracle which it celebrated.[35] Otherwise, silence.

ROME

The pilgrimage to Rome occasioned less comment, partly because it was such a familiar destination since so many ecclesiastics had frequent business in Rome with the papal curia. Pilgrims visited the main churches and some of the places connected with the early days of the church but, to clerical regret, they were often more impressed by the city's pagan history. The story was even told of St Gregory the Great urging the destruction of all the antiquities, because the believers who had come to Rome for the salvation of their souls were so taken by the marvellous ancient marvels that they spent their time admiring them instead of meditating piously on the real nature of their journey.[36] Boniface VIII proclaimed a jubilee year in 1300 hoping to increase the flow of pilgrims and another jubilee in 1350 attracted enormous crowds and prompted the building of a Via dell Peregrino leading to the Pont Sant' Angelo. It also encouraged many Romans, especially those who lived near St Peter's, to turn themselves into temporary but rapacious inn-keepers. They were accused of forcing pilgrims off the street and into their houses and then overcharging them mightily. Such jubilees were not necessarily popular with contemporary monarchs. When the pope requested Edward III to allow English pilgrims to depart for Rome and to encourage a truce in Gascony to make their journey easier, he was quickly rebuffed by the English king who wanted all Englishmen and their money at home for his own military needs.

In the second half of the fourteenth century national hospices began to flourish in Rome with the specific intention of providing safe and congenial lodging for foreign visitors. The English hospice was founded in 1362 when a house owned by an English seller of beads living in Rome was sold to the confraternity of the English at Rome for the use of poor, infirm, needy and wretched persons from England. Despite rather mixed beginnings – the first house had a prostitute next door and St Bridget of Sweden as a near neighbour – the hospice prospered and extended its holdings. By the end of the fourteenth century funds were collected for it in England and people in England became members of the confraternity. Among the more useful bequests was that of a woman who in 1390 left the hospice her three best beds which were to be furnished with her best pillows, sheets and coverlets. By the beginning of the fifteenth century the hospice controlled sufficient lodgings to be able to rent out some of its houses to English representatives at the curia who were both well-to-do and long-staying. Obviously the hospice had begun to give shelter to more than the poor and wretched since the inventory of 1445 mentions twelve quilts in the nobles' chamber, twenty in the paupers' chamber, and five in the women's chamber out of a total of sixty-nine. There were sixty-three beds altogether, so they could sleep about a hundred people. The hospice was probably only full in jubilee years while at other times there might be some 200 pilgrims a year.[37] The general opinion of Rome in the mid-fifteenth century was of a poor city where even St Peter's was dirty and in bad condition. It was sparsely populated for its size with many gaping ruins and woods within the walls where wild animals bred. The citizens, according to one disgusted observer, knew nothing about the antiquities around them but only about the taverns and places of ill-fame.[38]

Kings were not above using all pilgrim traffic for their own ends.

In 1433 Henry VI appointed a collector to receive the 2d due on each noble exchanged by pilgrims and others going to the Roman court, the Holy Land or other holy places – a kind of early foreign exchange tax. Henry was equally concerned that no ship should sail for Compostela with pilgrims without paying for the king's licence and even the powerful Cardinal Beaufort had to petition the king's council in 1426 for a licence to go overseas on a pilgrimage he had already vowed. It is also questionable whether some of the pilgrims' motives were predominantly spiritual. In 1417 John Hall, vicar of Hart, was licensed by his bishop to be absent from his benefices for a year so that he could fulfil his vow of pilgrimage to Rome, but in 1390 seven different chaplains had been licensed by Richard II to 'go on pilgrimage' to the Roman court and obtain a benefice there. Rome does not seem to have been a major goal of pilgrimage for the great, although it might serve as an incidental exercise if the opportunity offered. Thus the earl of Warwick filled in the gap between his arrival in Italy and the joust to which he had been invited at Verona by going on pilgrimage to Rome. Even such an indefatigable pilgrim as Ghillebert de Lannoy only came to Rome once, for the jubilee year of 1450 when he was already in his sixties.[39]

LOCAL PILGRIMAGES

In England Canterbury and Walsingham were the most favoured places of pilgrimage for the upper classes, though many other pilgrims flocked there as well. Even those with only a minimal acquaintance with Chaucer have some idea of the motley, cheerful, rather ribald company that gathered at Harry Bailey's inn at Southwark to make their leisurely pilgrimage to Canterbury through the spring landscape of an English April. We are all the richer for our acquaintance with those varied pilgrims but their party included only a few who had any pretensions to noble birth – and Chaucer seems to imply that even for them it was more pretension than reality. The travel-stained knight, his son the gallant squire, and the refined prioress were merely pale reflections of the great and the mighty who thronged the cathedral during the popular days of the pilgrimage to 'the hooly blisful martir'. In 1220 the young Henry III presided at the translation of the relics of the murdered Thomas Becket to their new resting place, specially built in the chapel behind the high altar. There they were lodged in a great iron chest, plated with gold, standing on a marble base and covered with a painted wooden lid which could be raised for the edification of the pilgrims.

27. Pilgrimage badge of Thomas Becket, a typical pilgrim souvenir

The fact that Canterbury was on the main road from Dover to London undoubtedly had some influence on the number of important pilgrims, foreign as well as English. Many of the great, though travelling on other business, would pause at Canterbury, pay their respects to the saint and make some offering at his shrine. King John of France, leaving England in 1360, visited the cathedral and made generous offerings of jewels as well as coin at the shrine. He had already given alms to many of the hospitals along the way as well as a special royal gift of twenty nobles (£6 13s 4d) at Sittingbourne to Sir Richard Lexden, 'an English knight who is a

Hermit'.[40] The Emperor Sigismund, when he came to visit Henry V in 1416, also paid a visit to Becket's shrine, as did Baron Leo of Rozmital and his retinue fifty years later. They, however, left a detailed account of the shrine with its many jewels and richly decorated gold coffin, 'large enough for a middle-sized person to lie in'. They saw all the relics, St Thomas's spring and the wonder-working picture of Our Lady and were particularly pleased when the choir sang a beautiful hymn in the count's honour.[41]

Canterbury was a frequent stopping-place for English kings in their travels around their realm but one of the more unusual royal visitors to the shrine was Mary, the sixth daughter of Edward I. Mary was one of the few royal princesses of England to become a nun. There is no hint why she was so chosen, although it has been suggested that it was due to her grandmother's 'inconsiderate piety', for Queen Eleanor of Provence had settled at the convent of Amesbury and wanted her granddaughter near her.[42] The child was professed as a nun in 1285 at the age of seven and given an annual revenue of £100, which was later increased to £200 and an annual allowance of forty oaks to provide fires in her chamber. Mary appears to have found the convent rather a boring place and she must have been a sore trial to any abbess trying to enforce the episcopal regulations against nuns gadding around outside their convents. She was often at court – sometimes for such legitimate social occasions as the marriage of her sister Elizabeth or to assist the young Queen Margaret, Edward's second wife, before the birth of her second child. When she went to court she often stayed a long time and took a large retinue for a simple nun. Not only did she have a train of twenty-four horses with a groom for each and did much of her journeying in a litter with accompanying ladies and damsels, but her cavalcade was occasionally swelled by pages, messengers and minstrels. Many of these trips to court also included trips to various shrines, Walsingham and Bury St Edmunds as well as Canterbury. When she and Queen Margaret heard of Edward's serious illness in the summer of 1307 they immediately set off on pilgrimage to Canterbury to pray for a cure. It was a futile journey, although they did not hear of the king's death until they returned to court. A few years later, Mary again went to Canterbury, accom-

panied by her cousin Isabella, granddaughter of Edmund of Lancaster, who had also been made a nun at Amesbury under Mary's
keeping. Since in the course of their rather meandering travels
Mary lost so heavily at dice that she had to borrow from one of her
servants there is a strong implication that she held a rather relaxed
view of the obligations of pilgrimage.[43] Her visits to Walsingham,
near the northern coast of Norfolk, were in the current fashion of
aristocratic piety. The shrine was famous for its vision-inspired
replica of the house at Nazareth where Mary was greeted by the
Angel Gabriel and for its ancient well-known statue of Mary with
the child Jesus, which was burned at Smithfield at the time of the
Dissolution. Henry III's devotion to Walsingham set a fashion
which was followed by royalty and nobility until the early sixteenth
century. So pervasive was this upper-class atmosphere that one of
its recent historians particularly emphasises the continuing flavour
of snobbery and of 'only the very best families'.[44] Such an attitude
is further exemplified by the desire of Bartholomew Burghersh the
younger, one of Edward III's leading military men and diplomats
and a founding member of the Order of the Garter, to be buried
within Walsingham Chapel, a difficult privilege to obtain. Whether
the king's daughter made her pilgrimages to Canterbury, Walsingham or Bury St Edmunds the impression made is not one
of extreme devotion. Rather these seem to have been essentially
junkets, a socially acceptable way for a bored nun with luxurious
tastes and a good income to get away from the convent where she
had been installed through no wish of her own.

In France pilgrimages were equally important and popular with
a wide choice of regional shrines as well as those known throughout
the nation and abroad. Chartres was the great centre of devotion
to Mary, where her ancient statue and tunic, presented by Charles
the Fat in the ninth century, had made it a place of pilgrimage for
centuries. The glorious cathedral eloquently proclaims the vitality
and force of that devotion among all ranks. Kings and queens often
came. Louis IX made several pilgrimages and once he brought
Henry III too. Philip the Fair and Philip VI both visited the cathedral to give thanks after their victories over the Flemings and
offered rich gifts. Edward III and the Black Prince, at least according

to Froissart, were persuaded to make peace in 1360 when an unprecedented storm which burst over their army while they were near Chartres was taken as a sign from Our Lady. Edward vowed at the cathedral that he would make peace, and did so.[45] Rocamadour – literally the rock of St Amadour, supposed to have been a companion of St Martial and Veronica – was a centre of pilgrimage for the south. It clung to the rocky cliff in the *causse* country of south central France in the valley of the Alzou and was particularly popular with pilgrims from Spain, Portugal and Italy as well as the French. In 1305 Edward I's trusted secretary, John Bensted, went to Rocamadour, probably more on business than on pilgrimage. He had been commissioned by the king to consult with Sir Othon de Grandson, then pursuing the cause of English diplomacy with the pope in Avignon, and had sent off a messenger from Paris. Bensted waited for the return of the messenger at Rocamadour, quite possibly because such a busy pilgrimage spot would be incurious about visitors from far away.[46]

The famous French shrine of the north was Mont Saint-Michel, St Michael in Peril of the Sea, which drew its pilgrims especially from Normandy but also from Germany and Flanders and which acquired a military and patriotic lustre during the Hundred Years War by its determined and successful resistance to the English conquest of Normandy. Even under present tourist conditions and with the causeway which no longer leaves pilgrims or tourists at the mercy of the treacherous sands and the galloping tides, it is easy to feel some of the elation with which the tired pilgrim arrived at last at the entrance to the abbey on the tip of its lonely rock. Thousands came and many died. The obituary of 1318 records eighteen drowned in the bay, twelve caught and buried in the quicksands and thirteen who were suffocated by the dense crowds in the sanctuary.[47] It could be a fearsome thing to be enjoined to do penance by making a pilgrimage to the Mont as the stern archbishop Eudes Rigaud had required. The great came as well, and no doubt under rather easier conditions. Louis IX was there in 1256 and Philip III came to give thanks for his return from Tunis when his father and so many other nobles had perished in that ill-advised crusade. The pilgrimage of Charles V in the fourteenth century was described by one of the monks with considerable rhetorical flourish. The king was described as:

> so ravished by the marvels that he saw in such an august place, so dear to blessed spirits, especially the Archangel Michael, that he dissolved in tears from the compunction of his heart and the fervour of his great devotion.[48]

Such highborn, and no doubt generous, visitors allowed the monks to report themselves in 1250 as 'with God's grace ... opulent'. By the fifteenth century a proper ritual of greeting distinguished guests had been punctiliously elaborated. The king and queen of France, the dauphin and the duke of Normandy were to be met with full honours at the steps of the rock. Other less important royal relatives and papal legates were to be met in the upper part of the town with somewhat diminished solemnity, while archbishops, bishops and counts would only be met at the guard house with fewer formalities and no ringing of bells. Protocol did permit a prelate to preach if he wished, as Rigaud did when he visited the monastery in 1263.[49]

There is little doubt that the pilgrimage to Mont Saint-Michel was seen as particularly efficacious because of the dangers along the way. This was also true of one of the most unusual spots of medieval pilgrimage, that of St Patrick's Purgatory in remote and wild Donegal. St Patrick's Purgatory was the name given to a cave on Station Island in Lough Derg, a stern and lonely place. It was believed that any man who dared to enter there, penitent and with true faith, and spent twenty-four hours 'in the face of unknown and unspeakable horrors', would be purged of his sins and at death would go straight to heaven.[50] It would appear that many of those who frequented it – mostly French, English and Hungarian – were curious to see if they could find out the fate of their friends or relatives through visions of purgatory and its inhabitants. Only the squire of the distinguished Sire de Beaujeu declared extravagantly that he and his master had been favoured with lively visions of all the torments of hell and then of the earthly paradise and had seen *moult de merveilles*. St Patrick's Purgatory perhaps gained its European reputation as being the end of the known world, for medieval Ireland was considered extremely remote and wild. It was generally enough known in the fourteenth century that Froissart, when he met Sir William de Lisle at Ospringe and found that he had been in Ireland with Richard II, at once asked him about the 'hole of St Patrick' and the truth of the tales about it. De Lisle described his trip there from Dublin and how he and an English knight had had themselves enclosed for the night. He had suffered from wild dreams but did not feel they were visions. Rozmital too had heard of the shrine but felt no compulsion to make that distant detour.[51]

The pilgrimage of Raymond, viscount of Perelhos, a Catalonian noble from Roussillon, who went to St Patrick's Purgatory in 1397, is characteristic. Raymond had been brought up at the court of Charles V of France and later served King John of Aragon and two popes. He mentioned that he had listened to many visiting strangers at the court of Charles V talking of the strange and remarkable things in several parts of the world and was desperately anxious to see some of them for himself. When he heard of the death of his old master, the king of Aragon, he was much concerned about his soul and, remembering what he had heard about St Patrick's Purgatory, decided to visit it. Gathering a retinue and armed with the vital licences and safe-conducts he finally got to Ireland and was ferried with 'many others from several nations' to the monastery on the island. After the proper ceremonies he was locked into the cave, but not before he had knighted his two sons as well as an Englishman and a Spaniard. Such a pilgrimage spot was considered to have a special value as a place for dubbing knights, underlining the spiritual foundation of chivalry. During the viscount's enclosure he had the visions he desired, seeing the king of Aragon in purgatory and also catching sight of a kinswoman he did not know had died. She was expiating her weakness in spending too much time painting her face but fortunately both she and the king were on their way to heaven. So many of the accounts of the pilgrims to the spot – including that of a noble Hungarian who told his story to an Irish notary in Dublin on his return – emphasise their fear and their visions that our more pragmatic age is led to wonder if the urge to fall asleep in the cave, and the horrid dreams which resulted, were not due to a lack of fresh air. In addition most of the pilgrims were exhausted after the prolonged fast and the long-drawn-out religious ceremonies. The much travelled and strictly matter-of-fact Ghille-bert de Lannoy was there in 1431 and gives an admirably detailed account of the nature of the place and the door 'like a Flemish window' which closed off the grotto. Lannoy had himself shut in for a couple of hours meditation and, having been told that at the bottom of the hole was a mouth of hell which St Patrick had stopped with a stone, he verified the continued presence of St Patrick's stone. The Burgundian was one of the last important visitors for in 1497 the pope ordered its destruction, although the exact reason for the order was not given.[52]

The desire for pilgrimage was obviously strong among the great as among the simple and continued with quite astonishing force until the end of the Middle Ages and beyond. Pilgrimage in some shape or form has been a constant human passion. By the end of the Middle Ages it seems to have had a strong admixture of wander-lust and curiosity as well.

CHAPTER SIX

KNIGHT CRUSADERS

The crusading knight has always provided one of the more glamorous visions of the Middle Ages and historical novelists have frequently found in his adventures a rich vein of profitable romanticism. The reality is both more complex and more interesting since crusaders were impelled by so many motives. Genuine idealism and religious fervour were inextricably interwoven with more secular dreams of adventure, of escaping the monotony of everyday, of satisfying combat, sanctified by its religious purpose but with hopes of rich booty and glory. The continued papal encouragement of the crusade as an instrument of policy not only provided a useful method of diverting warfare and violence from within Europe to the Moslem ruled territories of the Holy Land, but also gave religious sanction to the idea that violence against non-Christians or heretics was a praiseworthy activity. Such a concept could be, and was, diverted into many odd channels. This was clearly demonstrated by the tragic Fourth Crusade of 1204 which overthrew the Christian Byzantine Emperor at Constantinople and set a Latin emperor in his place. As well, there was the growing papal tendency to apply the term 'crusade' to a number of outbreaks of local political warfare. Nor were kings blameless, for they acquired the habit of conveniently vowing a crusade in order to raise the tax known as the crusading tenth on the ecclesiastics within their kingdom, and then to apply the money raised to some secular emergency. Certain individual crusaders of these centuries emerge clearly from the ranks of their anonymous fellows to embody the range of motives which drove them and to illustrate how ideals changed with the course of years and the pressure of events.

During the thirteenth century while the Latin kingdom of the crusaders still maintained its continually threatened foothold along the coast of Syria and Palestine, periodic expeditions were sent from Europe to lend much needed help to the Holy Land. Armies, like pilgrims, no longer found it possible or practical to take the long overland route through the Balkans to Constantinople, across Asia Minor and down through Syria. The growing naval strength of Venice and Genoa meant that sea transport was quicker and less

28. *Departure of St Louis and his company on his first crusade in 1248*

expensive. The crusade led by Louis IX of France in 1248 proposed to arrive at the Holy Land by way of Egypt. It captured Damietta but then suffered disastrous losses when it attempted to go up-river to Cairo. The subsequent retreat of the French army, hindered by the illness of many of its members, ended in the capture of the king himself as well as many of his nobles while the common soldiers, who promised no opportunity for rich ransoms, were generally butchered by the sultan's forces. Once the king's large ransom had been paid and Louis released, he went on to Acre, the great Latin crusader port, where he spent the next three and a half years attempting to improve the fortifications, the morale and the future of the Latin kingdom. Jean, sire de Joinville, a noble of Champagne who accompanied the king and became his friend as well as his admirer, has written of their expedition in one of the most personal of all surviving medieval accounts.[1] It is in many ways naïve and ingenuous but it gives a vivid picture of the thoughts and reactions of a representative thirteenth-century noble to this extraordinary journey.

Joinville does not explain why he decided to go on the crusade, although his list of the noble friends and relations who took the crusader's vow suggests that there was a kind of group agreement. He was in his early twenties and undoubtedly a religiously sanctioned adventure must have had a particular attraction. We know that the king as well as the pope encouraged a propaganda effort by the clergy to boost recruiting. Many vigorous sermons were preached in the atmosphere of a revivalist meeting, urging men of all ranks to come forward and take the cross, the sign of their adherence to the crusade. Joinville does tell us that he regarded his crusade as a military pilgrimage and that he had the Cistercian abbot of Cheminon invest him with the staff and scrip of the pilgrim. Financing such a major expedition presented problems for him, as for many others, and Joinville went off to Metz to pledge the greater part of his estate in order to provide himself with enough cash. As he took his penitential departure from Joinville, barefoot and in his shirt, he tells us that he would not look back 'for fear that my heart should weaken at the thought of the lovely castle I was leaving and of my two children'.[2]

It seems odd to us that there is no mention of sadness in leaving his wife though the crusade preachers often complained that family affection was one of the strong dissuasions for possible crusaders and that some particularly determined wives locked up their husbands to prevent them from taking the cross. The wives had a legitimate complaint. Crusading husbands were always away for at least a couple of years – Joinville did not return home for six – and the wife was left with the responsibility of running the castle and the estate with whatever officials had been left behind and of maintaining income and privileges in a period when powerful neighbours often used force to make good their claims. The legal immunity given to crusaders was frequently not respected. In Joinville's case, his wife was also left with two small boys, the younger of whom had been born in the middle of the farewell festivities. It is a curious anomaly that Joinville frequently faults King Louis for his cold and even uncourteous behaviour to Queen Marguerite but writes no word about his own wife, except to describe her family connections.

Before leaving, Joinville and his cousin had sent their baggage ahead to meet them at Auxonne where they took ship down the Saône and Rhone rivers to Lyon and Arles, while their great war-horses were led on the tow path alongside the boats. The young knight's account shows his quick eye for the things that interested him – the hills of sprouted wheat and barley stockpiled in Cyprus by the king's officials and the barrels of wine piled so high they looked like barns. He describes the fine sight provided by the landing of the count of Jaffa's galley at Damietta. It was driven by 300 oarsmen, each with a shield of the count's arms and a pennon

29. St Louis, the best-known crusader of the thirteenth century

with the arms embroidered in gold; 'The galley seemed to fly; and what with the beating of the pennons in the wind and the ship's trumpets and drums and Saracen horns, the noise was like lightning crashing from the heavens.'[3] The focus of Joinville's interest helps to provide sharply personal glimpses of many individuals in that miscellaneous army: the king, whom Joinville admired and loved and whom he portrayed as a human being; Queen Marguerite, brave through all her perils, indomitably rallying from childbed the Italian merchants of Damietta to finance the king's cause; the count of Poitiers, Louis' brother Alphonse, so openhanded when playing dice that he would give handfuls of money whenever he won to any of the lords and ladies loitering near the door of the hall; the count of Eu, a young and boisterous practical joker, who took advantage of his tent's proximity to Joinville's own dining tent to set up a little catapult which the count would fire down the table when Joinville and his knights sat down to eat, breaking jugs and glasses.[4] These were glimpses of the great but Joinville's brief vignettes of a wide range of individuals are equally vivid. There was the Saracen who had befriended Joinville during his captivity and whose last word as they parted was a warning always to hold tightly to the hand of young Barthemy he had with him, a bastard son of the Lord of Montfaucon, so that the Saracens would not sell him as a slave. Even more poignant is his account of the eighty-year-old knight who, after the king's capture, slept by the bed of Queen Marguerite, whose child was almost due, and held her hand in reassurance against her recurring nightmares of fierce Moslems and captivity.[5]

Joinville was not primarily a sightseer. The places he saw were merely a backdrop against which the crusade took place and his descriptions of far-off places and their local inhabitants have none of the vividness or acuity to be found in his portrayal of life among the Franks. He went on pilgrimage to the shrine of Our Lady of Tortosa (Tartus), the most important Christian shrine in Syria where there had been a shrine of the Virgin since before the year 387, but tells us nothing about the place or the way there. The episode is highlighted in his mind by the purchase of camelhair cloth for the Queen and the laughable confusion that arose when it was presented to her, for she received it kneeling, thinking it was a gift of relics.[6] Since Joinville was not by nature a traveller, and had the common medieval terror of sea voyages, one crusade was enough for him. When Louis decided on a second crusade in 1270 Joinville openly deplored the expedition and insisted that, so far as he was concerned, his earlier crusade had allowed the royal officials and those of the count of Champagne to ruin and impoverish his people so that a second absence would be at the expense of the well-being of his own people. His disenchanted attitude became more and more general as the thirteenth century wore on and the situation of the Latin kingdom became more precarious although there remained a core of truly devoted crusaders.

Edward of England had a less emotional and pious devotion to the crusade than his uncle, King Louis, but an equal determination to try and save the Holy Land from total reconquest by the Mameluke rulers of Egypt. Edward went personally on crusade in 1270 but arrived in North Africa only after Louis' death. The prince did not feel that this dispensed him from his crusading obligation so after spending the winter in Sicily he set sail for Acre with his wife Eleanor and a devoted group of young nobles and knights. Among them were two Savoyards, Othon de Grandson and Jean de Grilly, who had come to England more than ten years earlier in the suite of Count Peter of Savoy, the uncle of Edward's mother. They had soon become household knights of the young prince and served him in administrative and diplomatic capacities for many years, with a special connection with Gascony and its problems. There was obviously a tie of friendship between the two Savoyards, born of long companionship.

Edward's expedition of 1270–2 had few practical effects but he continued to consider seriously how help could be sent to the beleaguered Christians of the Holy Land. During the 1280s there was a baseless hope in the west that an alliance could be reached with the victorious Mongols, whose empire now extended from Armenia to China, to bring aid to the Christians against the Moslem rulers of Egypt. The Mongols at this time had many Greek and Nestorian Christians within their lands and seemed to encourage the dream of conversion and alliance but no concrete result developed. The sultan of Egypt only had to wait for a favourable moment to wipe out the few remaining Christian settlements in the Holy Land. Grilly, dismissed by Edward in 1287 for abuse of his power as seneschal of Gascony, fulfilled his personal vow to return to Syria and was put in charge of the French troops there. He led them when the Moslems attacked Tripoli in force but managed to escape safely from that disaster and general massacre. After the collapse of Tripoli the city of Acre finally understood the danger it was in. Grilly was sent to the papal court to seek help from the west. Little was made available and the Italian soldiers recruited were turbulent and undisciplined. Grilly returned to Acre where he was once more joined by Othon de Grandson, leading the English fighting men sent by Edward I. Their long friendship must have been at least partially responsible for Grandson's vigorous efforts to rescue Grilly, again fighting at the head of the French contingent, when he was wounded in the final Moslem assault of May 1291. Grandson succeeded in commandeering Venetian ships, placing Grilly and the other wounded soldiers aboard, while he himself only joined them when the final fall of the city was imminent. Crusading was over for Grilly, who returned to Savoy where he died soon after the turn of the century,[7] but Grandson, despite his losses, stayed on for a while in Cyprus and then went to Armenian Cilicia, in the company of several Cypriot barons and leaders of the military orders, to answer an appeal from its hard-pressed king. By 1293 he returned to Savoy and then to England where he continued to be one of Edward's most trusted friends and officials.[8]

Nevertheless, his passion for the crusade, perhaps heightened by his despair over the loss of Acre, was not extinguished. It has been persuasively argued that it was Othon de Grandson who was responsible for putting together another project for a possible crusade in the first years of the fourteenth century. The *Memoria*, as it was called, dealt with a whole range of problems touching the reconquest of the kingdom of Jerusalem: the best season to leave Europe, the best port in the Near East for the debarkation of an army sent from the west and its preferred line of march to Jerusalem. It went on to discuss the matters that would arise when Palestine had been reconquered: the route by which to invade

30. Individual combat between a Christian knight and a saracen

Egypt, the ways to gather the needed money and how to reorganise the kingdom.[9] The plans came to nothing but Grandson was still not deterred. In 1312 he himself again took the cross and proposed to go to the Holy Land. It was an extraordinary decision for a man who was well into his sixties and only comes to our attention because he was attacked as he made his way down the Rhone to get the papal licence and blessing from Clement V, his good friend from Gascon days. Grandson was robbed of 20,500 gold florins and other goods and he and his household were held captive by a band of marauding Savoyards and Dauphinois. The pope was appalled at this act of sacrilege against a knight of such devotion, noted for so many works of piety, and wrote to the archbishop of Lyon and two of his suffragans that Aymon de la Palud, the band's leader, must repay the total sum, restore the goods within fifteen days and provide satisfaction to Grandson for his injuries or suffer personal excommunication and interdict on his lands.[10] Even if restitution was actually made this rude interruption was sufficient to deter the aging Grandson from his final crusading attempt. In 1319 he paid 10,000 gold florins to be absolved from his crusading vow on the grounds of old age and bad health.[11]

The dream of the crusade remained in European minds but it

attracted greater lip-service than genuine enthusiasm. The kings of France and England, who had stood in the forefront of the crusading movement during the thirteenth century now found themselves enmeshed in their private quarrels and would not allow either their money or their fighting men to dribble overseas on a fruitless mission. Their continued hostilities precluded any real attempt to bury their animosities sufficiently to encourage a major joint expedition. John Bromyard, the lively fourteenth-century Dominican preacher, regretted the decline in crusaders willing to go to the Holy Land, suggesting they were deterred by their fear of captivity among the infidels, the great expense, or devotion to their family or estates. Those who went, Bromyard declared, were driven by curiosity or amusement and expected on their return to boast of all they had seen and heard, mingling fiction with fact. The stay-at-homes bragged around their own fires of the great deeds they were capable of against the infidel, so long as no one called their bluff.[12] The crusade for the Holy Land was over in all but name and for the rest of the Middle Ages westerners generally came to Palestine as pilgrims. Nevertheless a new Moslem enemy was ultimately to menace Europe itself and force the resumption of the crusade in self-protection. The rise of the Ottoman Turks from a minor tribe with a foothold in Anatolia to a conquering force which displaced the Byzantine empire in Asia Minor and moved into the Balkans threatened not only Latin lands in southern Greece but Hungary itself by the end of the fourteenth century.

However, during the greater part of the fourteenth century the immediate goal of the crusading enthusiasts tended to be the wild north-east frontier of Europe – Prussia and Lithuania – where the Order of Teutonic Knights sought the assistance of fighting men from all over Europe. The Teutonic Knights, as the Teutonic Order of St Mary's Hospital in Jerusalem was more conveniently known, had been founded in Palestine at the end of the twelfth century and had originally been regarded as a minor relation of the Templars and Hospitallers. Its primary focus, like that of the other orders, was service in Palestine. This was transformed by the slowing down of crusading activity in the Near East and the papal decision to encourage resident missions in the wilds of the East Baltic by the provision of a permanent force of military professionals to fight the heathen there. The Teutonic Knights seemed well suited to such a function but they cautiously refused to commit themselves until they were assured of a free hand and practical sovereignty in Prussia. By the end of the thirteenth century their *raison d'être* in Palestine had been totally swept away with the fall of Acre and the Mameluke successes in Armenia but they had conquered most of Prussia and Livonia. From the beginning the northern crusades were wars of conversion by military force, accompanied by much killing, ravaging and plundering in the poor settlements. Christianity was not preached, it was forcibly imposed with raw overtones of the divinely established racial superiority of the German nobles over the Balts and the Slavs. At this crucial moment when their enemies hoped to attack them, as the Templars were being attacked in France, with accusations of sodomy and witchcraft, the Grand Master moved the Knights' headquarters to their castle at Marienburg where they were independent lords. The Knights then focused their crusade on a continuing battle with the pagan Lithuanians of the Baltic and with the Russian leaders whose strongholds of Pskov and Novgorod tempted them with their riches.

The great attractiveness in the fourteenth century of the 'crusade

31. The Castle of Marienburg, the headquarters of the Order of Teutonic Knights

to Prussia', as it is usually referred to in contemporary accounts, was the outlet it provided for a nomadic fighting population which could no longer wage war in Palestine. The voyage to Prussia became a recognised stage in the careers of many nobles, French and English as well as the Germans who had provided the major share of the forces in the previous century. It had several special charms for young knights, apart from offering a religiously approved solution to the boredom brought on by an unexpected truce or peace. It was less distant, less difficult and less expensive than the voyage to Palestine and an expedition to Prussia could easily be achieved in one season. The Knights were good hosts, providing many feasts and glittering social occasions at Marienburg and their other castles. The actual campaigns were often short, for the really serious fighting had already been done. This allowed plenty of time to enjoy the hunting in the great forests of Prussia, a fact which a French chronicler suggests was the main reason for the western nobility's enthusiasm for such an expedition.[13] Winrich von Kniprode, who became Grand Master in 1351 and ruled the order for over thirty years, was particularly active and influential in recruiting crusaders from the west to aid in putting constant pressure on Lithuania, by this time the main battleground for the Knights. The Grand Master's investment in more impressive and elegant castles for the Order and in lavish entertaining was repaid with the arrival of more and more foreign knights.

From the time of Henry III the Teutonic Knights had always been favourably regarded by the English kings, who had granted them an annual rent as early as 1235. The tradition was continued by subsequent kings up to the time of Henry IV.[14] Though it was not a large sum it demonstrated English interest and English knights were among the crusaders as early as 1327. Henry of Lancaster, that fourteenth-century paragon of chivalry, went off to Prussia in 1351, after a series of brilliant campaigns in Gascony. It was an unfortunate trip for him; on the way he was assaulted and robbed of all his money, while on arriving in Prussia he discovered that no campaign was planned for that year. There was no choice but to return home unsatisfied. Earlier in the fourteenth century King John of Bohemia had made three separate expeditions to Prussia –

partly to enhance his claims on Poland with which the Order had a continued struggle – and on one occasion took with him the French poet Guillaume Machaut. Both men proved of great propaganda value to the Order when they returned to western Europe. King John proclaimed in the preamble to one of his charters the value of the Order as an impregnable wall to defend the faith against the Lithuanians while Guillaume included in his popular poetry reference to the conquest and conversion of the Lithuanian 'miscreans'.[15]

One of the distinguished crusaders enlisted by von Kniprode was Gaston Fébus, the famous count of Foix, who took advantage of the truce in 1357 between France and England to voyage to the east.[16] Fébus certainly did not have a particularly religious motivation for his crusade. His journey was a useful way for the young man of twenty-six to get out of an awkward political situation at home. It also provided him with the justification for announcing a special crusading levy on the inhabitants of his lands to pay back the 24,000 écus that he borrowed from the Flemish merchants to finance his trip. The description of his voyage suggests what a pleasant form of travel the fourteenth-century nobility considered such an expedition. In 1357 Fébus sailed from Bruges (not yet isolated from the sea), accompanied by a considerable force of men. He and his retinue went to Konigsberg (Kaliningrad), making a detour along the way to Norway and Sweden to give Gaston, a keen huntsman, a chance to try his skills against the reindeer. He emphasised their insatiable search for pasture in summer and commented on the great herds to be found moving in the forests and on the tundra, noting that in winter the reindeer fed on the bark of birch trees and on the lichens which could be dug out from under the snow.[17]

Fébus had arrived in Konigsberg with his companions by February 1358, in good time to share in the spring reyse, or raid. By this time all the warfare in the north was in the form of such expeditions, very rarely longer than a few weeks at a time because of treacherous weather conditions. The Knights and their associates struck out into the wild country of wood and slough, not against a sharply defined enemy to be met in battle but against the wild and desperate inhabitants of forests and small settlements who employed guerilla tactics against their enemies. The fighting was brutal and repressive, fire and sword being used indiscriminately to capture men, women and children. Nevertheless, for the knights of the time for whom their own serfs barely had human form and heathens certainly did not, it had a glamorous veneer. On the conclusion of the *reyse* a magnificent feast was held in one of the Order's great castles. By the second half of the fourteenth century a remarkably clever form of propaganda had been devised and publicised in western Europe to feed the knights' relentless hunger for reputation and prestige. The Table of Honour, as it was called, consisted of ten or twelve knights considered to be outstanding. The choice was made by the attendant heralds who chose from the assembly those most renowned for their travels and their bravery and ranked them in order of preeminence. The leading knight was given the honour of 'beginning the board', a distinction proudly boasted about, as Chaucer reminds us when he describes the qualifications of his knight.[18] Fébus was certainly one of the chosen number but we do not know whether he 'began the board'. In any case he did not remain long in Prussia after the fighting and the feasting were finished but travelled back to southern France by way of Germany. He was back in his own lands in October 1358, just a year after he had sailed from Bruges. It had been a successful, interesting and not too long foray, adding to his glory and reputation at little expense to himself.

Later in the century Henry of Derby as a young man in his mid-twenties followed the path of his grandfather, Henry of Lancaster, and went twice to Prussia in 1390 and 1392. The second expedition was diverted into a pilgrimage to Jerusalem but on the first Henry spent some eight months in the north, dividing the winter months between Konigsberg (Kaliningrad) and Danzig (Gdansk) on the Baltic Sea. Henry sailed from England in July 1390 and arrived in Danzig on 13 August. There he learned that the summer campaign had already begun and that he must travel quickly to catch up with the main force. His company rode eastward, guided by two German knights appointed by the Grand Master and by the 21st had entered the great forest of Lithuania where they caught up with the main army, crossing the Memel river by the 24th. Their raid had a number

32. Gaston Fébus happily at home in his palace at Orthez

of successes, including the capture of the outworks of the Lithu-anian capital of Vilnius (Vilna), a feat which was credited to the attacks of Henry and his men. A siege of the other outlying forts was unproductive and after five weeks' illness among the troops and with supplies dwindling, they were forced to withdraw. This was one of the longer campaigns but even so Henry and his con-tingent were back in Konigsberg by 20 October where they settled down to enjoy themselves. It was a very expensive stay, primarily financed by John of Gaunt. Henry's large retinue indicated the state and elegance which befitted his position. He maintained eleven English knights, eighteen squires, three heralds, six minstrels, household officials and yeomen as well as uncounted and undiffer-entiated servants. His cost for wages alone was £564 and a further £400 was spent on gifts. The maintenance of his household with the necessary supplies and lodging and the cost of travel brought his expenses to £4360 in all.[19] The very detailed accounts suggest the luxury and amusements that a group such as Derby's could enjoy. There were gifts of wild animals such as young bears and a wild bull as well as the more usual courtesy presents of horses and hawks. Henry's love of music was satisfied not only by his own band of minstrels but by the arrival of many other musicians who arrived to entertain the household and whose fees are duly recorded.[20] Henry obviously enjoyed this long stay in Prussia since he was anxious to return in 1392, but this time his welcome was not as warm. Having left England on 24 July he arrived in Danzig on 10 August. His trip to Konigsberg was much less hurried than on the previous occasion and when he finally arrived on 2 September it was to find that there was to be no campaign in which he could engage. The Order was willing to give him £400 towards his expenses and he left after a couple of days, arriving back in Danzig by 7 September. From there his mind turned to pilgrimage, not crusade.

Henry of Derby's wanderings were extensive but bear no comparison to those of his contemporary, Jean Boucicaut, knight and ultimately marshal of France, whose life was written while he was still alive and provides a most flattering picture of him. It illustrates most clearly what its editor has called the 'vagabond and adventurous humour of our ancient valiant knights'.[21] Since the young Boucicaut was eager to go wherever fighting was to be found it is not surprising that he went three times to Prussia. The description of his very practical reason for so doing is illuminating. He wanted 'as good men who wish to travel commonly do, to increase their value'. The first time he stayed a season and returned to France. Since there was no major fighting going on in France, and thus no outlet for his energies, he went back to Prussia 'where it was said that this season they should have a pretty war'. His third voyage to Prussia in 1391 was more to his liking since the election of a new Grand Master who had mustered a large army to invade the kingdom of the Letts, north of the Dvina river, meant 'the greatest and most honourable war there in a long time'.[22] But all these expeditions to Prussia had not extinguished Boucicaut's unflagging interest in fighting. He had also, with his good friend Regnault de Roye, travelled to the Turks' lands in Greece and agreed to fight with the sultan if he attacked other Saracens. Once again disappointed that there was no war, the aggressive knight returned to Europe and then went on pilgrimage to Jerusalem. His eye for adventure and the main chance remained sharp. Hearing that the count of Eu, who had also come to the Holy Land on pilgrimage, had been seized at Damascus by the men of the sultan of Egypt, Boucicaut, who only knew the count as a relative of the French king, immediately went to Damascus, joined Eu and remained with him when he was taken to Cairo. The sultan imprisoned the count and all his retinue, including Boucicaut, for four months. Once they had been freed they were off to visit the hermitage of St Paul of the Desert and the monastery of St Catherine at Mt Sinai before returning to Jerusalem. After they had done the expected pilgrimage circuit they went to Beirut to seek passage on a ship sailing westward but were again seized by the Moslems – obviously they offered rich pickings to any captor. It was another month before they were freed and could get off to Cyprus and Rhodes on their way back to France. They were greeted at court with great enthusiasm and Boucicaut's reputation was enhanced by the praise heaped upon him by the count of Eu.[23]

In 1391 Boucicaut was recalled from his last voyage to Prussia to be named marshal of France, a singular honour for a young man of twenty-five. With the vehement encouragement of the count of Eu, he joined the great force mustered to fight the Turks under the command of John Count of Nevers, son and heir of Duke Philip the Bold of Burgundy. It was the last great international crusading army, brought into being by the alarm of King Sigismund of Hungary who had sought western assistance against the constant westward movement of the Ottoman Turks, already in control of the Balkans. Although the church was divided by the Great Schism, both popes issued bulls recommending a crusade and the European kings paid some attention to their plea and that of their fellow monarch. The French were willing, the duke of Burgundy enthusiastic in support. The French and Burgundian forces of some 10,000 men were joined by 6,000 German troops and a contingent of 1,000 English fighting men under the command of the half-brother of Richard II, John Holland the earl of Huntingdon. The force set off in the spring of 1396 and was joined at Buda by King Sigismund's army of some 60,000 men. In addition there were troops from Wallachia and perhaps 13,000 adventurers from Poland, Bohemia,

Italy and Spain. It was the largest army ever gathered together to fight the infidel and had the advantage over the earlier crusades of shorter lines of supply and reinforcement and a less exhausting march. But, as had been the case so many times before, Sigismund, whose actual territories were in danger, wanted a defensive campaign while his allies wanted a great offensive whose success would allow them to penetrate Anatolia and drive triumphantly on to Jerusalem itself. Sigismund was forced to agree. In early August the army set forth down the Danube which it crossed at the Iron Gate, the gorge where the river breaks between the mountain ranges of the Carpathians on the borders of what are now Roumania and what was formerly Yugoslavia. It took eight days to ferry the army across the river into the sultan's dominions, and then it marched south. At the well-protected Turkish fortress of Rahova, Boucicaut and the count of Eu launched a precipitous attack and had to be rescued by Sigismund's Hungarian forces. The town was successfully stormed and the population, predominantly Bulgarian Christians, put to the sword, although a few of the wealthy were spared for ransom. From there the huge army moved on to Nicopolis, the major Turkish stronghold on the Danube, most strategically located in a natural position of great strength which had been newly fortified. The Christian army was not equipped for siege warfare but had to hope that they might be able to starve the enemy into submission. Two weeks of inactivity before Nicopolis brought out all the weaknesses inherent in such a large force and encouraged rashness and foolish over-confidence typified by the attitude of Boucicaut and his good friend the count of Eu. When the sultan with his own army approached any hopes of sensible joint action were ruined by the unquenchable passion for individual glory which such men as Boucicaut saw as the only way to conduct an engagement. The battle on 25 September 1396 showed the superiority of both the tactics and discipline of the sultan's troops. The French vanguard was sucked into attacking an apparently weak line of light cavalry only to find their way was then barred by stakes. When they dismounted to pull them up they were then fallen on by the great body of Turkish troops held in reserve. In the end, it was not a battle but a massacre and, despite great feats of individual bravery, the French army was almost wiped out. Sigismund's dispirited Wallachian contingents retired without ever fighting and Sigismund's own army was scattered despite a brave attempt to reconquer the battlefield. Sigismund himself was forced to flee on one of the Venetian boats which had been blockading the river and his followers struggled home in whatever way they could. The Turks spared only a few captives from the French army because of the wealth to be gained from their ransoms – the counts of Nevers, Eu and La Marche, Enguerrand of Coucy and Guy of La Tremouille. The remaining survivors were beheaded at the sultan's command before the eyes of the horrified French captives. Nevers recognised Boucicaut in the line of doomed men, not considered important enough to ransom, and saved his life by signing to the sultan that he was worth as rich a ransom as himself. Nicopolis was a disaster for European armies and its unfortunate result made obvious how anachronistic and dangerous the rash zeal for personal glory of 'chivalrous' lords such as Boucicaut had become. The enormous ransoms asked for the prisoners were gathered, chiefly at the expense of the duke of Burgundy and King Sigismund, and the noble captives finally returned to Europe in 1397.[24]

This setback did not deter Boucicaut from continuing his warlike journeys, for in 1399 he led a contingent of 1,200 knights to the east to aid the hard-pressed Byzantine emperor, Manuel II, but no one seemed to have the money to pay them so they soon returned. During the period when France was closely involved in the affairs of Genoa Boucicaut served as its governor from 1401–9. This led him into constant struggles with Genoa's old enemy Venice and also to a further expedition to the east to reinforce the Genoese hold on Pera, the great port just opposite Constantinople then being besieged by the Turks. He was back in France in time to fight at Agincourt in that jealously sought position of honour, the vanguard, where he was again captured, this time with no opportunity for ransom. Boucicaut died in captivity in Yorkshire in May 1421, a man of fifty-five whose life had been a model of late fourteenth-century chivalry. He had gained personal renown and riches but had also caused major disasters for the French through his rash tactics and stupid underestimation of his opponents. His crusades – both against the Turks and in the north – seem to have been motivated by a desire for military activity and personal glory with only a bare veneer of conventional piety. As a knight on the social round Boucicaut was a great success, as a crusader he was a disaster.

The Moors in the Iberian peninsula and the neighbouring North African coast provided still another focal point for crusading activity throughout the Middle Ages. By the end of the thirteenth century much of the Iberian peninsula had been reclaimed for Christianity by the kings of Aragon and Castile but the continued existence of the Moslem kingdom of Granada and the danger of Moorish invasion over the straits of Gibraltar meant that fighting continued. Sporadic campaigns were waged against specific Moorish strongholds in the kingdom of Granada and around the Straits and expeditions were launched against Moslem North Africa, whose Moorish pirates had made the Barbary coast a terrifying obstacle for Christian sailors. Such efforts were usually launched by the Spanish or Portuguese kings and primarily attracted their own nobles. Wandering European knights would also join the forces, if the opportunity offered. Sir William Douglas, for example, the admired Scottish nobleman who was planning to go to Jerusalem in 1330, went first to Spain to help the king of Castile fight the Moors. As the battle arrays of the opposing kings were moving into position Douglas was convinced the Spanish were beginning the attack. He was determined to be in the vanguard and immediately spurred his horse towards the enemy, closely followed by his own knights. Although Douglas had expected the rest of the army to advance they remained in place. The precipitate forward party was surrounded and cut to bits by the Moors, killing Douglas and all his followers. Their vainglorious bravery had proved fatal.[25]

Ghillebert de Lannoy is the last of this group of knight crusaders, a man whose zest for travel included crusades as well. When only a young squire he made two trips to Spain to fight with the king of Castile's forces against the Moors but, even at this early age, he displayed a passionate curiosity about all the regions through which he passed. When he fought at the sieges of Antequera and Ronda in 1410, for example, he immediately applied for a safe-conduct from the Infante of Castile as soon as a truce had been proclaimed and went to spend the next ten days in the Moorish capital of Granada, admiring its palaces and gardens like any modern tourist.[26] Three years later he was to be found on an expedition to Prussia. The situation had changed in the north since the decisive defeat of the Teutonic Knights by the combined forces of the Lithuanians and the Poles at Tannenberg in May 1410. Although the Knights continued to exist, their attraction as a crusading centre evaporated as the myth of the legitimacy of the northern crusade against Lithuania and Poland, which had been officially Catholic for over a generation, was finally destroyed and papal support for the Knights withdrawn. Lannoy was a member of the last group of European knights to come to the Order's castle for a *reyse* against the Poles. With a company of Burgundians he left Sluis in the early spring of 1413 and sailed to Danzig from where he went on to the Teutonic Knights' great stronghold at Marienburg. It was an extremely powerful castle and Lannoy observed that it was adequately provisioned for 10,000 men for one year or 1,000 men for ten years. Since the proposed expedition was not yet ready Lannoy took advantage of the delay to sail to Denmark and buy himself some new horses at a Danish horse-fair. He returned in time for a *reyse* against Pomerania, a not very glorious affair lasting only sixteen days in which towns were burned and beasts seized. Lannoy was wounded in the fighting and was knighted by one of the knights in the company, an accolade that gave the twenty-seven-year-old squire both pleasure and improved social standing.[27]

After the completion of this brief expedition Lannoy went on to the Order's province of Livonia in the hope of joining a winter raid. He met the provincial Master at Riga but was informed there was to be no fighting. The inquisitive young man took advantage of the Master's courtesy to arrange a visit to Novgorod, the capital of the great trading empire of north Russia. The trip through the northern forest in midwinter was strange and fascinating to a man from Flanders, for all the travelling had to be done on sleds and the winter conditions there contrasted with the temperate climate to which he was accustomed. Lannoy was a sharp, succinct observer. He commented on the effects of the cold – the cracking of the forest trees, the rabbits in their white winter coats, the way his beard and eyelashes froze at night, the piles of frozen meat displayed in the market. He spent nine days in Novgorod and found its churches impressive but its walls weak, while the slave market where women were bought and sold horrified him. His status was recognised by the local bishop who sent him large supplies of food and drink during his stay – a mark of prestige that gave him real pleasure. He then went on to Pskov, disguised as a merchant, and travelled back to Livonia by sled across the frozen rivers and lakes.[28] After this excursion Lannoy slowly returned to Marienburg and made his farewells to the Grand Master, having decided to return home by the long land route through Poland, Bohemia and Austria. The kings of Poland and Bohemia treated him with warm hospitality, at least partly because they were anxious to make a favourable impression on the duke of Burgundy whom Lannoy already served. The trip to Prussia with all the extra excursions included took about a year.[29]

By Lannoy's time, despite flurries of activity, the feasibility of a crusade against the oncoming Turks was much discussed but no real movement was launched. In 1421 Henry V and the duke of Burgundy sent Lannoy on an avowedly diplomatic mission in the east, but with the further mandate to reconnoitre a possible route for a crusade and to observe the nature of the defences in the Holy Land. Ten years later Duke Philip sent another of his officials, Bertrandon de la Broquière, on a similar journey which produced another report. There is little question that Duke Philip had a genuine interest in a possible crusade. Beyond the information and reports provided for him he was responsible for staging the flamboyant Feast of the Pheasant at Lille in February 1454. This entertainment was marked by an extravagant profusion of complex contrivances and pageants whose scale is suggested by the fact that the music was provided by singers and organs within a stage-set church and by twenty-eight musicians concealed in a large pie. At the end of the spectacle Philip took a solemn vow to go personally on crusade and even, as a vainglorious gesture, to fight in single combat with the Grand Turk.[30] In obedience to ducal pressure, many lords also made crusading vows, though often carefully

33. Duke Philip the Good of Burgundy

hedged, but despite all the glamour and expense the initiative evaporated into insubstantial rhetoric. The occasional naval skirmish had been mounted against the Turks in the intervening years but even the final Turkish capture of Constantinople, the once great capital of the mighty Byzantine empire, only roused the west to further elaborate but futile gestures. Crusading at the end of the Middle Ages had degenerated into a merely fashionable activity, mounted in easily reached districts against insubstantial opposition and primarily designed to enhance the curriculum vitae of an ambitious or impecunious knight. Such expeditions could improve the individual crusader's status in society but European rulers had no power, nor any real desire, to challenge the political reality of the Turkish advance into the Christian lands of eastern Europe.

CHAPTER SEVEN

DIPLOMATS ON THE ROAD

A frequent, colourful sight along the roads of medieval Europe was the retinue of an ambassador bound for the papal curia or a royal court on a mission for his king. The size of his accompanying party was determined by the importance both of the ambassador himself and the mission on which he had been despatched. Many medieval lords and barons spent considerable time acting as diplomats and they were normally accompanied by ecclesiastics of carefully calculated rank. The greater the importance and prestige of the ambassador the greater the compliment to the ruler to whom he was sent and the more obvious the importance of the ruler who had commissioned him. The theory and vocabulary describing the ranks of diplomats and their corresponding functions developed rapidly during the Middle Ages and by 1436 a handbook of diplomatic practice, the first applying to secular as well as papal diplomacy, had been written by Bernard du Rosier. This Frenchman exemplified one avenue of promotion for able clerics for, having served as a lecturer on civil and canon law, he was later despatched on various diplomatic missions and became first provost and ultimately archbishop of Toulouse. His *Short Treatise about Ambassadors* was designed as a practical handbook which du Rosier completed while on an embassy to the court of Castile.[1] His work was considerably more high-minded and theoretical than its bluntly pragmatic sixteenth-century counterparts. Rosier recognised the many kinds of business on which ambassadors might be employed but divided their activities into two main categories, the embassies of ceremony and those of negotiation. An ambassador might be sent to one court for a single occasion or issue or he might be required to make a circular tour of several courts. In either case Rosier insisted that no ambassador should set out unless he was sure of being adequately repaid, although he should be ready to leave promptly once this all-important matter had been settled.

Equally important was the vital matter of the necessary credentials and instructions. There was usually a final audience with the king where credentials and instructions were handed over. The envoy might have several sets of instructions – generalised ones which could be made public and perhaps secret ones as well, which were not to be disclosed to the other party and were often given by word of mouth. By the fifteenth century there was also the possibility of written secret instructions, as in the case of Henry V's letter to Sir John Tiptoft, written in English by the king himself and under his signet. Sir John had been assigned to accompany the Emperor Sigismund when he left England in 1416 and Henry wanted Tiptoft to be aware of the state of the negotiations regarding the French prisoners in England and to see that Sigismund, and he alone, was given this information.[2] The proper formal credentials were essential as Ghillebert de Lannoy had known when he was commissioned by Henry V and the duke of Burgundy to undertake a voyage to the east, calling on monarchs along the way. Lannoy had been issued his credentials in Paris but on his way home his baggage carts were attacked by freebooters and the documents, as well as money and goods, were stolen. Ghillebert had to make another special trip to King Henry to have his official letters replaced before he could leave on his voyage.[3]

Once everything was in order Rosier suggested that an ambassador should make a solemn and public departure, using such publicity as a way to increase his own prestige, to spread the news of his mission and thus to encourage the powers to whom he had been sent to be more willing to receive him. The embassy should move at a reasonable but not excessive speed, and in a style which reflected adequately the dignity of its principal figure. This need to make status visible was a medieval commonplace. Froissart put it in more individual and colourful terms when he described the retinue of Lord William Douglas of Scotland who arrived at the port of Ecluse in Flanders (the modern Sluis on the Belgian-Dutch frontier and now fifteen miles inland) in 1330. Douglas entertained on his ship for twelve days, surrounded by his two knights banneret, seven other famous Scottish knights and twenty-five young and highly born squires, with trumpeters and nakerers (nakers were the medieval version of kettledrums) to proclaim their presence. Their company was served generously with wine and spices from gold and silver vessels, a proper display for such a lord 'who represented the person of the king of Scotland'.[4]

The time spent in travelling could be usefully employed, for the tedious hours on the road were to be put to use by the senior members of the delegation in instructing their juniors in their duties while the younger men were also to take over all the disagreeable tasks involved. On their arrival the court to which they had been sent must go out to meet them at some distance from their final destination – the distance and the formality of the greeting to be determined by the social standing of the ambassador, the import- ance of the sender and the gravity of the mission, for any mission was enhanced by choosing a person of high social rank as its chief. Once the arriving embassy had been suitably greeted a ceremonial public procession accompanied them to the presence of the ruler to whom they had been despatched. Such cavalcades could be very elegant, depending on the impression which the receiving ruler wished to give. In western Europe they were usually rather cheerful affairs. The ambassadorial procession, dressed in its finest clothes and announced by its own trumpeters, passed through streets dec- orated with banners and garlands and was greeted with pealing bells and perhaps even cannon. This was followed by a first formal audience at which the ambassador presented his credentials and either he, or more commonly the ranking ecclesiastic, made a formal and elaborate speech explaining the reason for the mission, an intimidating endeavour which has been described as 'an exacting exercise in Latin eloquence'.[5] This was followed by a ceremonial banquet and in a fifteenth-century book of etiquette the marshal of the hall, responsible for the placing of the guests, was reminded that a messenger from a king, or even a noble, should always be placed one rank higher than his normal place in order to do the necessary honour to his master.[6]

Since embassies might be sent merely to attend a special occasion such as a coronation or wedding or the final formal ratification of a treaty, they could be encouraged to take their leave with fitting formality as soon as the specific ceremony was over. Embassies charged with negotiation were another matter. They took time and the ambassadors had to be alert, firm but conciliatory, while keeping in mind the desired end and the possible concessions that could be made. Rosier emphasises that an ambassador must be unfailingly polite and should not lose his temper – a counsel of perfection particularly difficult for the high-spirited medieval baron. During negotiations the ambassador might have to send home for supplementary instructions, an unfortunate and time-consuming operation but preferable to the total breakdown of negotiations. When the ambassador had finished his business he should leave as soon as possible, making a formal, public and polite goodbye. If a truce or a treaty had been negotiated, formal ratification by the principals usually followed at a later ceremonial occasion. The returned ambassador was to submit his report as soon as he got home, sometimes a matter of urgency. Gontier Col, the secretary of King Charles VI, who served as secretary for the French embassy sent to Henry V in the early summer of 1415 when the charade of peace negotiations and arrangements for a marriage to Charles's daughter Catherine were still being played out, hastily wrote a long report for the archbishop of Bourges, the head of the mission, even before he got back to Paris. Col summarised all that had occurred up to the date of departure and promised to bring the formal speeches of Archbishop Chichele and the French reply to them to Paris with him. The distraught secretary apologised for his delay but explained that his horses had been seasick on the Channel crossing and he had been forced to hire others, an act which required him to borrow money as unfortunately he was short of funds.[7] The way of the diplomat was not always easy even then.

Technically an ambassador had the benefit of a considerable number of legal safeguards and by the fourteenth century the legists

34. The marriage of Philip of Artois, count of Eu to the daughter of the duke of Berry, a diplomatic marriage described by Froissart

had begun to define their privileges. They were supposed to be immune for the period of their embassy, both in their persons and in their property, with freedom to enter, cross or leave territories without being hindered or violently attacked. They were to be exempt from taxes and local tolls and were entitled to be supported by the public treasury. The concept was lofty; its practical application was often weak or non-existent, for acting as an ambassador often involved considerable activity or real physical peril. Aeneas Silvius, for example, when sent to negotiate peace terms with Alfonso of Aragon, had to pursue the reluctant king even when he went hunting. Honoré de Bonet, the fourteenth-century French prior who wrote *The Tree of Battles*, a highly popular text on military law and the problems that might arise during periods of warfare, discussed the kind of almost insoluble difficulty that might bedevil an ambassador. Bonet puts forward the hypothetical case of the ambassadors sent from the king of Scotland to his ally, the king of

France. They travelled by ship and landed at a port in English Gascony. Before they could make their way to Paris they had to hire horses and carts for their belongings. While travelling north they were met by a French soldier who recognised the equipment as English, therefore legitimate bounty in wartime, and promptly seized it. The envoys complained bitterly to the French king when they finally arrived at Paris but the soldier continued to argue that since the horses and carts were the property of his English enemies he had taken them in lawful war. Bonet resolved the case in a legalistic fashion which was bound to encourage further difficulties. He argued that if the ambassadors had real need of what they had hired then everything should be immune to capture but if they had brought things they did not really need or 'any man for their entertainment which they could well do without' then the soldier's seizure was perfectly reasonable.[8] No wonder there was confusion and that clerics were favoured on embassies since they could rely on the protection of the church and their special status to discourage brigandage and capture.

Not even clerical status preserved diplomats from the inherent difficulties of the road. Walter Mauclerc, bishop of Carlisle, who was sent to Cologne in January 1225 regarding a possible marriage for the young Henry III, wrote about the hardships of his midwinter mission. When the bishop with his retinue and equipment had embarked at Dover they were forced back to the harbour 'afflicted beyond telling by the fury of the sea and the storms'. Walter was unable to disembark either his belongings or his horses but, recognising the need for haste, he and one servant managed to take passage on a boat carrying pilgrims. Once safely disembarked at Gravelines and furnished with two horses by the kindness of a merchant they had met on the boat, the bishop and his servant set off for Cologne over two hundred miles away. They made good time for they reached the city within a week but Walter wrote feelingly to the king about the horrors of his trip:

But hardly any pen would be adequate to record how many adversities we have sustained on that journey, at one time on account of the harshness of the ways, at another on account of the intemperate winds, at another through continued fear and weakness.

After describing his various efforts, none of which met with great success, the bishop again underlined his difficulties, reminding the king that 'we have laboured under continuous infirmity and have lost many horses on the journey, and we have spent nearly all the money which you have delivered to us'. His final request for more money to be sent to him if he was to continue his mission strikes a timeless note.[9] Even unsuccessful diplomacy seems to be an expensive business.

Marriages, an integral part of medieval diplomacy, were also very costly affairs as the ceremonies surrounding the betrothal of Henry III's sister Isabella to the Emperor Frederick II reveal. Frederick was an extraordinary medieval monarch and fascinated his contemporaries. When his messengers arrived at Westminster in February 1235 seeking the hand of Isabella as his third wife it did not take the king and his council long to deal with the final formalities arising from the earlier negotiations working toward such a marriage. On 27 February they gave their agreement to the German ambassadors who insisted that they had to see the princess in person. She was brought to court, a young woman of twenty-one, and – according to the chronicler Matthew Paris who revelled in all the details – displayed her beauty and her suitable ornaments to the Germans. The inspection satisfactorily completed, the ambassadors confirmed the emperor's matrimonial intention and put the engagement ring on her finger. Since the messengers insisted that Isabella should be ready to depart soon after Easter (8 April) there was an enormous flurry to put together a trousseau worthy of a royal bride. She was provided with a crown of pure gold studded with precious stones, gold and jewelled rings, necklaces and other ornaments as well as large supplies of gold and silver, for the table platters and pitchers were of gold while even the kitchen equipment glittered with silver. All this was paid for by a heavy aid of 30,000 marks (£20,250). Isabella and her valuable trousseau were put in the special care of the bishop of Exeter and Ralph FitzNicholas, who served as the royal ambassadors for this ceremonial voyage.

Her company, the archbishop of Cologne and the German ambassadors were all guests at a great feast at Westminster on 6 May. The following day they started for the coast, accompanied by the king himself and a large party of men on horseback. Having stopped at Canterbury to pay their respects to the shrine of St Thomas they proceeded to take ship at Sandwich where the king, by ordering all the abbots of nearby monasteries to provide a suitably magnificent retinue for his sister, was credited with gathering three thousand men on horseback. Isabella bid a sad farewell to her brother, whom she was never to see again, and then sailed from Sandwich on 11 May with her retinue. The voyage to Antwerp, which was in territory under imperial jurisdiction, took four days. On arrival the princess was greeted by the customary procession of clerics with lighted candles, singing songs of joy to the accompaniment of pealing bells, but also by a strong guard since there was fear of a French attack. During the five day trip to Cologne she was constantly entertained by master musicians playing on all varieties of instruments. Her arrival at the city was a festive one for the citizens streamed out to meet her. They had decorated the city with flowers and ornaments and provided in her honour a mock battle in which staves were broken. The medieval love for devices was already apparent in the thirteenth century for the citizens of Cologne had also created a boat which appeared to be rowed on dry land but was actually pulled by horses under silk cloths while clerks, accompanied on hidden organs, made music. Isabella was conducted through the main square of the city in a royal procession but the Cologne matrons were not satisfied with a mere glimpse of a veiled figure so she obligingly threw back her cape and hood so that all could see her beauty. After this she went to her lodgings in the palace of the archbishop where a chorus of young girls with musical instruments played and sang all night – perhaps not the ideal welcome for a tired traveller. The emperor himself was not present for he was busy warring against his son Henry and it was six weeks before the princess moved on to Worms where the marriage finally took place on 20 July. It appears to have been a splendid occasion for Matthew Paris reported the presence at the feast of four kings, eleven dukes, thirty counts and marquises as well as the prelates.

It is to be hoped that Isabella enjoyed her trip and its splendours for they were her last public acts. In fact, her brother the king later complained bitterly to the emperor that she had never worn in public the magnificent crown provided at such expense. The emperor had consulted his astrologers as to the suitable hour and waited until the morning after the wedding to consummate the marriage. Immediately announcing that Isabella was pregnant with a son he handed her over to the care of Moorish eunuchs and similar elderly servants. Nearly all of her own retinue were sent back to England though the returning ambassadors at least were given three leopards by Frederick for Henry III's menagerie in the Tower of London.[10] Isabella bore Frederick a daughter and a son before her own death in childbirth in 1241. Earlier that year she had the unusual pleasure of seeing her brother, Richard of Cornwall, who passed through the emperor's domains on his way home from a crusade in the Holy Land. He was received with great magnificence and spectacular entertainments as well as concern for his health. Matthew Paris has a remarkably detailed account of this visit too which he undoubtedly got first-hand from Richard when he stopped at St Albans after his return home. Both Earl Richard and the monk seem to have been particularly impressed by the two Saracen dancing girls who balanced on balls while juggling other balls and singing. Unfortunately Isabella was not part of court life, since Frederick had adopted the Moorish practice of totally segregating his wife from the court, and Richard even had difficulty seeing his sister. It took several days before he got the emperor's permission to have what seems to have been a single meeting.[11] Such total isolation from family ties was often a harsh reality for the young princesses used as counters in the making of diplomatic alliances. This fact may account for Edward I's rather callous reaction to the death in 1305 of Blanche, duchess of Austria and the sister of Edward's young second wife. When ordering the queen's confessor to break the news to her, the king urged him to keep her from grieving unduly. After all, he said, if the queen wanted to mourn she should have done so when her sister first married and went to Austria for from that time one could regard her as 'dead and lost'.[12] In contrast, the frequent marriages between the English and French

35. A fifteenth-century cavalcade

royal families tended to encourage the maintenance of family ties and even numerous visits.

Edward I had a number of trusted nobles of the second rank whom he constantly employed as diplomats and negotiators among whom Othon de Grandson was one of the most trusted. He typified the negotiating diplomat often used to support a head of mission who enjoyed higher status but was less informed about the business in hand. Othon worked hand in glove with the clerks and officials who elaborated policy and devised the arguments by which they hoped to win their points. Because he was so continuously used on missions to the papal curia, both on general matters and on the specific problems of Gascony when the popes were trying to encourage peace between England and France, Grandson became a highly informed, influential and trusted mouthpiece for Edward's policies. When he was sent from Gascony to the curia in May 1289 he led a mission including most notably William Hothum, a learned Dominican much employed by Edward I, as well as other knights and servants. The retinue was a moderate one, mounted on forty-seven to sixty horses, but the business took Grandson some ten months for he did not return to England until March 1290. His tasks were many. He was to deal with the pope over the proposed crusade, for the Christian presence in the Holy Land was under continuing attack and this was a matter of constant concern to both the king and the pope, as well as to Grandson himself. The marriage proposed by Edward between his son and Margaret, the heiress of Scotland, had to be discussed. In addition, Grandson was entrusted with money to pay the annual pensions given to certain cardinals to encourage them to further English interests, to pay off outstanding English obligations to the pope and to provide the salaries of certain papal notaries who acted as the English king's proctors at the curia.

Although there is little colourful detail in the accounts of the ten months it is clear that the travelling was difficult. Grandson and his companions had a hard passage over the Alps for the horses had to be led and both man and beast suffered from illness. The knight himself, as well as several of his servants, were tended by physicians and needed drugs. Four members of the party died and their funeral rites had to be properly celebrated. In submitting his accounts Grandson quite correctly included the cost of foreign exchange but it is startling to realise just how circumscribed was the circulation of the varieties of coins for in travelling from Gascony to Italy and back to England the party had to exchange and use twelve different local moneys.[13] The exchequer officials agreed to this expense but were not always so obliging. It is amusing to note that when Grandson was again in Rome on diplomatic business for the king in 1300 he took advantage of the occasion, since it was jubilee year, to visit the pilgrimage shrines there. The eagle-eyed exchequer clerk thereupon withheld his salary for the forty days he spent doing this and not paying attention to royal business.[14] Grandson was a respected voice for English affairs at the curia over many years and gained personal rewards for it. He was named a papal knight, furthered the clerical careers of his nephew John, who ultimately became bishop of Exeter, as well as of other family members and dependents in Lausanne. Grandson never married and never lost his concern for his family lands in the *pays de Vaud* and it was to Neuchâtel that he retired after the death of Edward I. Edward II used, or attempted to use, the elderly expert in negotiations at the papal court for his last unsuccessful request to him was in 1316 when Grandson must have been over seventy. The old knight, whose ties of friendship with Edward I as prince and king had lasted some fifty years and brought him honour and riches, was happy to remain at home, freed from the burden of travelling the roads of Europe on weighty royal business.

As early as the thirteenth century ambassadors might find themselves on far more exciting and far-flung travels than the familiar routes between the English and French court or the papal curia. The travels of Sir Geoffrey Langele from Genoa to Tabriz in 1292 carrying two gerfalcons to the Mongol ruler of Persia provide a lively example. In 1287, while King Edward was in Gascony, his court had been visited by Rabban Cauma, a Nestorian monk serving as an ambassador for Argon, the Il-Khan of Persia, and a correspondence was begun between the two rulers. In those last desperate years of western struggles against Mameluke strength in the Holy Land, European Christians continued to hope that the Mongols, who had some sympathy with the Nestorian Christians, might aid them in their fight. It proved an impossible dream but this embassy to take the Il-Khan the falcons he coveted was a minor consequence of the diplomatic courtship of the Mongol rulers. The journey was long, arduous and expensive, as the accounts which detail their expenses from Genoa to Tabriz and back bear witness. The return journey alone is estimated to have cost £3,363 2s 8d.[15]

Langele headed a group of twenty people including a chaplain, a clerk, a barber who also acted as a physician, four men-at-arms and seven servants. A squire, Nicholas of Chartres, was responsible for the funds and on the outward journey was also charged with providing the falcons' daily ration of beef and carrying them. The length of their journey and the difficulties of the country through which they had to pass encouraged a wide range of purchases – furs, cloths (some adorned with Langele's arms), tents of cotton, pavilions of ox-skin, sacks for bread and skins for wine, pots and crockery as well as some crossbows for protection. The ambassador and his retinue went from Genoa to Brindisi, then sailed to Constantinople and reached Trebizond, the great port on the south shore of the Black Sea, in the late spring of 1292. From there it was about 300 miles to Tabriz across the high mountainous terrain of Central Armenia. When they arrived at Tabriz they had difficulty completing their mission as the khan was absent. At last the falcons were handed over and the embassy was given a leopard to take home to Edward in return. The retinue left Tabriz in late September and after three weeks of travelling arrived back at Trebizond. There they had to arrange for shipping for themselves and the leopard, pay off the porters who had transported their baggage and acquire provisions for their voyage. By 13 October they had found a ship sailing for Constantinople, though the trip took another three weeks. A week at anchor in the Byzantine capital allowed a luxurious change of diet for the accounts mention oysters, ducks, chestnuts, pears and apples while even the leopard was provided with mutton instead of chicken. Twelve more days at sea finally brought them to Otranto on the eastern heel of the Italian peninsula. Having acquired the essential horses they rode overland, spending Christmas in Rome and finally arriving in Genoa 11 January 1293. The accounts end there, casting no light on the difficulties of travelling with a leopard over the Alps in midwinter.[16] Here, as so often, one regrets that there were so few medieval diarists.

Such exotic places were not the usual territory of medieval ambassadors during the thirteenth or fourteenth centuries. Great nobles used as ambassadors were far more likely to find themselves shuttling interminably between the English and the French courts and the papal curia because of the unsolved and almost insoluble problems between the two kingdoms. Many of the years of the Hundred Years War were spent not in warfare but in confrontation between diplomats, with the pope attempting to bring both sides to a peace or at least a truce. Henry of Lancaster, cousin, companion and counsellor of Edward III was at the centre of the influential group around the king. Admired and respected all over Europe for his prowess, his warlike skills and his good manners, Henry also managed during the activities of his busy life to write a charming treatise on the spiritual life, *Le Livre de Seyntz Medicines*. This multi-talented man was often Edward's choice to head a prestigious mission. In fact Henry served the king so well, in diplomacy as in war, that in 1351 Edward as a mark of personal favour, raised his title from earl to duke of Lancaster – the first duke named outside the immediate royal family. In 1354–5 Duke Henry was particularly busy along the diplomatic front since great efforts were being made to conclude a peace with France. The pope was attempting to mediate between the two monarchs and had sent Cardinal Guy of Boulogne to Guines near Calais where a treaty was worked out between the English and French representatives. It was then arranged that both kingdoms should send solemn ambassadors to Avignon to ratify the agreement. Both missions were recruited from the very highest ranks. The French sent the duke of Bourbon, the archbishop of Reims, the count of Armagnac and the much esteemed knight, Geoffrey de Charny, while the English were represented by the duke of Lancaster, the earl of Arundel, the bishop of Norwich and many other magnates. The bishop had been engaged in the negotiations at Calais so King Edward's secret instructions on departure were given to Lancaster and Arundel specifying exactly what the king was willing to compromise on in his demands. These, which were meant to be kept secret were expanded by another secret credential which they could show if required. The duke was well provided with money – his expense account survives – and he and his company made an impressive entrance into Avignon on Christmas Eve with thirty-two of their 200 horses magnificently equipped with trappings. The chronicler Knighton, who gives us some idea of the colour of the occasion, explains that when Lancaster approached the city so many bishops, dignitaries and even citizens – a cavalcade of more than 2,000 – came two miles out of the city to meet him and conduct him to the pope in dignified procession that the great bridge over the Rhone was jammed from early morning to mid-afternoon. Finally Lancaster arrived at the papal palace, made his formal reverence to the pope and then went to the residence arranged for him. The embassy remained in Avignon six weeks, with Lancaster providing lavish and expensive hospitality – Knighton explains that, in preparation for the required entertainment during his stay, 100 barrels of wine had been placed in the cellars before his arrival. Such openhandedness amazed all the curia. Nevertheless, despite the enthusiastic welcome and the generous provision of diplomatic dinners the embassy achieved nothing. The French refused to ratify the agreement made at Guines and the English refused to give up their claim to the throne of France and, more seriously, their right to hold the duchy of Aquitaine without homage to the French king.[17] The expenditure of time, money and the presence of the greatest in both realms had led, as so often before, to another impasse between the two kingdoms.

Another conference in 1392 between the French and English at Amiens, when the same problems were still being discussed, suggests the efforts that often had to be made for the discussions to remain peaceful. Froissart explains the various measures taken by the French king. All the English expenses during the conference were to be defrayed by the French and King Charles had given strict orders that no quarrelling or riot was to take place with the English during their stay in Amiens. The detail of the instructions suggests how difficult it was to contain such an explosive situation and how easily tempers flared. French knights and squires were not to suggest any jousts with the English, no pages or varlets of any French lord were to cause riots or quarrels in the inns, under pain of losing their heads. Four corps of guards of 1,000 men each were to be stationed at the four main squares of Amiens and were not to move from their posts even if there was a fire in the night, a terrifying catastrophe in an overcrowded medieval town. French knights and squires were forbidden to be out at night without a torch, though the English could be. Innkeepers could not demand payment for food or drink nor steal or hide any of the English bows or arrows, though they could accept them if they were given as presents of courtesy. The conference arrived at no conclusions, since their demands differed so greatly, but Froissart records that at least the two sides parted in good humour.[18] The draconian regulations had served their purpose.

Only some ten years later King Henry III of Castile, whose wife was the daughter of John Gaunt, sent an embassy on perhaps the most exotic mission of the whole Middle Ages. Henry was particularly anxious to extend his diplomatic relations and increase his prestige and had sent two of his knights to the east to report on the forces and intentions of the rulers there after the disastrous Christian defeat at Nicopolis by the Turks in 1296. The Spanish knights were present at the battle of Ankara in 1402 when the forces of the almost legendary conqueror Timur (also known as Tamerlane the Great) defeated and captured the Turkish ruler Bayazid. Timur treated the Spaniards with distinction and sent back an envoy of his own to the king of Castile with a complimentary letter and rich presents. On the strength of all this activity Henry III decided to send another embassy to Timur. The king's choice for this mission fell upon Ruy Gonzalez de Clavijo, a knight of good family and experienced at court. He was accompanied by another knight and a friar who was a master of theology, as well as a small retinue. They left Puerta Santa Maria, near Cadiz, in June 1403 and did not return to Spain until March 1406. During that time they had travelled all the way to Samarkand and back and Clavijo had written a remarkably detailed and informative account of all the places he had seen. He was a good observer who described what he *saw*, not what someone else might have said about it, and he strikes a remarkably detached and unawed note whenever riches and glories were displayed to him. In fact he is so dispassionate that it is a pleasure to find him getting truly excited over his first view of a giraffe, which was being conducted to Timur as a present from the sultan of Egypt. He gives a very clear, accurate description of the extraordinary animal but then bursts out 'to a man who had never seen such an animal before, it was a wonderful sight', a sentiment many later observers have shared.[19]

Although the tone of Clavijo's work is so restrained he obviously took full advantage of his opportunities to look around him at all the new and strange things he was seeing and to record them as best he could. As always in a medieval description of a long sea voyage there were the inevitable becalmings and storms, the various islands with their different crops and histories, the startling view of the volcano of Stromboli. But much of his emphasis was on visiting everything possible so as to see for himself and he was unwilling to put much trust in the many rumours and secondhand tales that circulated in such a crossroads as Rhodes where pilgrims, men of the fleet and travellers and merchants from the Near East all met and exchanged news. Finally the Spanish embassy's ship arrived at Pera, across the Golden Horn from Constantinople, on 24 October. Four days later they were received by the emperor who appointed a guide to show them the churches and relics of the imperial city. The emperor obviously had personal control over some of the more important shrines and their relics as Clavijo remarked that they had to return a second time to the monastery of St John the Baptist, which had the most important relics of Christ, because the first day they had been there the emperor had gone hunting taking the key with him, having forgotten to give it to the empress. The Spanish knight seems to have been a conscientious but occasionally exhausted sightseer, as after a detailed description of the Hippodrome and the famous high column 'at least six lances in height' which could be seen from the sea, he records that it was in memory of some great event and had an inscription on it, 'but as the writing was in Greek, and it was getting late, the ambassadors could not wait to have it read to them'.[20]

Clavijo and his colleagues had ample time to visit Constantinople and to sort out their impressions for their voyage to Trebizond was rendered impossible by gales. Their ship foundered, although they managed to get safely ashore with all the presents they were carry-ing to Timur, and they had to return to Pera and spend the winter there. They finally sailed on 20 March 1404 and got to Trebizond three weeks later. After two weeks in that city they set out for Timur's capital, travelling through Armenia and Persian Azerbaijan and arriving at Tabriz on 11 June. Clavijo was much impressed by the size and riches of the city, the wide range of merchandise, the number of mosques and 'the finest baths that, I believe, can be seen in the world'.[21] The free flow of merchandise at Tabriz, Sultanieh – not so large but with even greater trade – and Teheran was impressive, but the difficulties of the road and the speed of their travel took their toll. Seven of the party were seriously ill and had to be left at Teheran to await their return. Clavijo felt that they were well taken care of but even so two died.

The Spaniard was especially interested in the speed of travel. He commented on the general provision of post horses at frequent relay stops to facilitate communication with the ruler and to speed the transmittal of news. He was told that the trip from Tabriz to Babylon (the medieval capital of Egypt near Cairo) could be achieved in ten days – a remarkable achievement for a distance of around 1,000 miles. The discreet ambassador does not dwell too heavily on the almost breakneck speed with which Timur's men urged them on to the capital, but he records Timur's preference for a messenger who does fifty leagues (around 150 miles) in a day and a night and kills two horses in the process. It appears to have been a general practice to kill horses by hard riding and many carcases were seen along the roads.

After travelling over the burning plains of Khorasan – frequently at night because of the great heat – they arrived at the banks of the Oxus on 21 August. The river was fed by the snow waters from the mountains and was flooded from May to October, but a system of

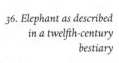
36. Elephant as described in a twelfth-century bestiary

large flat boats, made of logs clamped together with iron and with gunwales about five feet high, could provide passage for as many as 150 at a time. Since all Timur's troops had to cross the Oxus on their expeditions to the west such a fleet was an absolute necessity. Finally on 8 September the Spanish ambassador and his party were taken to a palace and garden about a league outside Samarkand to have an audience with Timur. The occasion was an overpowering one. The Spaniards surrendered the presents they had brought for Timur and were met just within the castle gate by six elephants with castles on their backs, decorated with banners and filled with men. Timur himself sat in front of the entrance to the palace on silk embroidered carpets made comfortable with round pillows. The great ruler was dressed in a silk robe with a high white hat topped by a spinel ruby surrounded by pearls and other precious stones. After they had made the required bows the ambassadors were brought close to the aged, almost blind ruler so that he could see them. He spoke highly of the king of Castile and received the letter they had brought graciously. They remained for a month in Samarkand, seeing Timur at various palaces and being invited to several feasts which Clavijo describes in all their curious detail. Finally they were taken out to the plain where Timur's Mongol horde was encamped (some 20,000 by Clavijo's reckoning) in a veritable tent city of great elegance and richness, though the effect was somewhat spoiled by the excessive dust that coated faces and clothes. Every convenience was there, including tents for the sale of provisions and even tents for hot baths where the bath-men had great boilers to heat the water. Timur's own pavilion was so large and so tall it looked like a castle. Divided into separate chambers and filled with crimson carpets embroidered in gold, it was sur-rounded by a canvas wall made of brightly coloured cloths. Since it was a time of celebration and weddings all kinds of entertainment was provided but Clavijo was most impressed by the elephants who were painted green and red, often had swords bound to their tusks, and were urged on with drums so that 'when they all ran together, it seemed as if the earth trembled'.[22] The glories of Samarkand itself, with its shopping street covered with a vaulted roof and punctuated by fountains, its gardens and vineyards with noble houses, the fertility of the land which was rich in meat and birds and fruit – Clavijo was especially fond of the marvellous melons – made a profound impression on the Spanish party. The city, they felt, was about the size of Seville and Timur had crammed it with all kinds of craftsmen, making goods for both peace and war. The previous June a train of 800 camels had come from Cathay laden with the finest of Chinese merchandise while spices were shipped north from India. The Spaniards saw the end of a legend. Timur's last illness had already begun when they departed in November 1404 with no formal leavetaking nor any letter for the king of Castile.

37. Camels and donkeys. Illustrations in a mid-thirteenth-century Bible from France

The return journey exposed them to winter conditions even harsher than the summer heat they had experienced on their way. The crossing of the Oxus was easy but the trip across the plain of Khorasan was made through the heavy snows of mid-winter. On one occasion it was so deep that thirty men with long poles were sent ahead of them to open the road. It was the end of February 1405 before they got to Tabriz where civil war, sparked by Timur's death, enforced their stay till almost the end of August. Once allowed to proceed, the road to Trebizond was not difficult and, with relatively short delays, they returned from there to Pera where they found a great ship sailing for Genoa at the beginning of November. The Italian port was reached at the beginning of January and the travellers paused for a month before they could get a ship to Spain, arriving in San Lucar, not far from Cadiz, on 1 March 1406. It was a most extraordinary trip for any medieval man and far beyond the usual pattern of diplomatic travel. The Spanish knight had seen all the fabled wonders of Samarkand at the peak of its power and had covered much of central Asia. His long diplomatic journey had no lasting effect but Clavijo's stories at court and in retirement in Madrid during the six years before his death must have helped to keep alive a curiosity about the riches of the far corners of the world so dramatically illustrated by Spanish explorations before the end of the fifteenth century.

Perhaps the most indefatigable traveller of all these medieval ambassadors was Ghillebert de Lannoy and his activities suggest the wide-ranging expertise expected from such a man. Born into a distinguished Flemish family, both he and his two brothers, Hue and Baudoin, were trusted councillors and servants of the duke of Burgundy. Ghillebert's close contact with Duke Philip the Good began early and he rose rapidly in the duke's service after the battle of Agincourt, where he had been wounded and taken prisoner by the English. His career brought him lucrative appointments, respect at court, a founding membership in the prestigious Burgundian Order of the Golden Fleece, and a series of assignments which took him across much of the known world. Given Ghillebert's wide-ranging travels on pilgrimages, crusades and for his own pleasure as well as on diplomatic missions it is easy to understand his advice to the duke of Burgundy that no man should be chosen as a member of his grand council before he was at least thirty-six. He declared that a man is a vagabond until he is twenty-six, and then it takes ten years to see how he will turn out.[23] Our understanding of such a traveller is made easier by the fact that Lannoy not only composed the formal diplomatic reports on his various missions, but also kept a journal of all his various voyages whatever their purpose. He was an excellent observer, precise and curious about everything that met his eye but laconic and unemotional. The clear prose of the serious official and man of affairs soon replaced the love ballads he wrote in early youth when he served as squire to Jean de Werchin, seneschal of Hainault, who was himself a recognised poet. Lannoy's *Voyages et Ambassades* is a straight-forward account of his various military expeditions, diplomatic missions, official appointments and frequent pilgrimages from his first raid on the Isle of Wight at the age of thirteen to his final trip to Rome for the holy year of 1450 when he was almost sixty-five. The core of this work is his detailed report on a two year journey of diplomacy and reconnaissance undertaken for Henry V of England and Duke Philip of Burgundy in 1421.[24] Both rulers had a real desire to lead another crusade and sent Lannoy, a trusted familiar of the duke with experience of the east, to explore the political climate and report on the military aspects of the terrain which might affect a possible crusade. This was an unusual mission in its mix of activities and the reconnaissance in the Holy Land was kept secret from much of the party, being effected under the cover of a devout pilgrimage in which Lannoy was only accompanied by a herald, the acknowledged medieval military expert. On his return home Ghillebert filed a separate account of the detailed military information he had acquired on such matters as the nature of harbours and their anchorage, the availability of good water and possible provision for horses with Duke Philip and the English council, since Henry V had died during his voyage. Lannoy's true diplomatic activities had involved formal visits to the rulers who controlled the land route by which soldiers could march overland to Syria and Palestine. The support, or at least acquiescence of these powers, would be essential for the passage of an army.

It was an adventurous journey. Lannoy left his castle at Ecluse (Sluis) in May 1421 with a party of eight but he sent his people, the luggage and the jewels on by ship while he himself took the overland route through Brabant, Westphalia, Bremen, Hamburg, Lubeck, Stettin to Danzig (Gdansk). There he rejoined his party and presented his letters of credence and the assigned gifts to the Grand Master of the Teutonic Knights. Lannoy reported with considerable satisfaction that the Master had done him great honour, giving several dinners for him and presenting him with two horses while Artois king-at-arms, the accompanying herald, received two sables. The choice of the proper diplomatic presents was always a thorny one though precious jewels, fine cloth from the ambassador's own country or some notable piece of craftsmanship were always acceptable. Included in Lannoy's baggage was one of the most unusual diplomatic presents of the century, a gold clock destined for the sultan of Turkey. A gold clock small enough to be carried on such an expedition so early in the fifteenth century is in itself a surprise but, because the sultan of Turkey for whom it was destined had died before Lannoy arrived and civil war was raging in Turkey, the clock could not be delivered. The conscientious ambassador carried it with him on his two year journey and on his return gave it back to the council of Henry VI. From that point the gold clock retreats obstinately into the mists of history and our questions remain unanswered – what kind of clock was it? did it still run after all its vicissitudes? and who finally got it?

Leaving the Teutonic Knights Lannoy and his party went south through Poland and found the Polish king in a small town near Lemburg (Lvow) where he was enjoying hunting. The king's hospitality was generous for he had a lodge of green leaves and branches made for the ambassador and took him with him to trap live bears. He also gave him two very rich dinners during which Lannoy sat at the king's own table. The Polish king was allied to the ruler of Turkey against the Hungarians but the king warned him of the sultan's death and the subsequent upheaval which made it unsafe for land travel. Before leaving the ambassador was loaded with rich presents – horses, silk cloths and a hundred marten and sable skins – and proceeded to take a route through the Ukraine, then under the control of the duke of Lithuania. His ceremonial meetings with the duke were particularly interesting since Lithuania was almost a borderland between east and west. At the duke's table he met an embassy from Novgorod and one from Pskow, both in northern Russia. There was also an unforgettable Tartar with a beard that hung below his knees and was covered by a kerchief. The duke kindly armed him with letters, written in Tartar, Russian and Latin, to help him pass through Turkey and more practically gave him

38. *A diplomatic dinner in which King John I of Portugal entertains John of Gaunt*

two Tartar guides and six Russians and Wallachians. The duke repeated the Polish warnings about the war in Turkey and assured him that it was impossible because of this to travel down the Danube. Once again Lannoy and his party were loaded with presents before they set off while Ghillebert also took advantage of this stop to send his clerk back to the English king, no doubt with a report of their travels so far. As Lannoy continued southward he met the lord of Wallachia and Moldavia and gained from him more exact information regarding the seriousness of the war raging in Turkish territory, both towards Greece and in Asia. The diplomat's original plans had to be abandoned so he decided to head for the great Genoese port of Caffa (Kaffa) on the Black Sea.

Embassies in such wild country were not all ceremonies and gift-giving. In making his way to Akerman on the mouth of the Dniester river, Lannoy had gone on ahead to find lodgings but when he attempted to enter the town at nightfall he was beaten, robbed and tied to a tree on the banks of the river clad only in his shirt.

Fortunately he managed to escape the next morning and was assisted by the lord of Wallachia and Moldavia who caught the robbers and turned them over to Lannoy to put to death if he wished. The return of his money made him merciful so he let them go free 'for the honour of God'. From Akerman some of his party and the baggage went to Caffa by ship but Lannoy himself and the rest of his companions went overland for eighteen days through what he calls a great Tartar desert where travel was hazardous. One night while the party was sleeping in a wild and lonely place hungry wolves scattered their horses, leaving the twenty-two people in their group wandering for a whole day and night while the wolves followed them for a considerable distance. Finally one of the Tartars managed to round up the horses and, 'thanks to God and many pilgrimages vowed' as Lannoy remarks with fervent piety, they all got safely back together.[25] It appears likely that Lannoy had been given specific instructions by King Henry and Duke Philip to plot

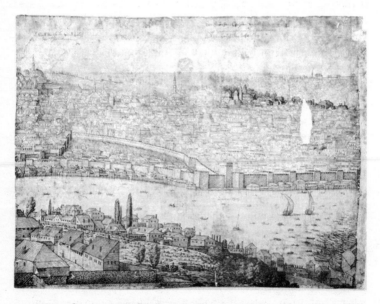

39. Part of a panorama of Constantinople in the mid-sixteenth-century, still close to its appearance before its fall to the Turks. Phanar quarter with the city wall at the harbour

the possible land route of an army because, even after all his hair-raising adventures, he persisted in attempting to find a guide who would enable them to circle the Black Sea and thus go by land to Jerusalem. The region was so unsettled and his information so discouraging about the distances, the many races, languages and beliefs of the inhabitants that Lannoy finally conceded the necessity of going to Constantinople by ship.

The Byzantine capital was the last official diplomatic point on Lannoy's journey. The ambassador presented his letters, King Henry's gifts and the letters of the peace arrived at between the kings of England and France (the Treaty of Troyes 1420). In the depressed atmosphere of Constantinople, beset on all sides by the advancing Turks and in desperate need of western help, Lannoy talked of the peace achieved and the desire of the two kings to advance the union between the Latin and Greek churches – a union that had been broken in 1054 and which for the Byzantine was a matter of fundamental patriotism as well as of religion. Papal ambassadors were in the city to discuss the religious problems with the old Emperor Manuel and his son John and Lannoy spent many days listening to the arguments. John took the ambassador hunting and picnicking while Manuel presented him with velvet cloth and a gold cross, enclosing several relics and adorned with a fine pearl. The cross was carefully taken home and after being set in a silver angel was presented to the Lannoys' chapel of St Pierre at Lille. After leaving Constantinople Lannoy left the rest of his party and his baggage at Rhodes while he and the herald visited the Holy Land, both as pilgrims and to reconnoitre the terrain.

This long and difficult mission was not the last which Lannoy carried out for the duke of Burgundy. His geographical knowledge and diplomatic experience resulted in his being sent to the Emperor Sigismund concerning the Burgundian desire to help put down the Hussites, the vigorous heretical sect in Bohemia. He was dispatched to King James in Scotland in 1431, that remarkable journey in which he not only managed to make the long detour to St Patrick's Purgatory but also went to call on Henry V's widow living in retirement at Pleshy. He was one of the Burgundian representatives at the church council in Basel and also at the Congress of Arras in 1435 when his master the duke of Burgundy finally threw over the English alliance and again joined forces with the French king. Even such a listing of the high points of his career clearly illustrates what a valued and utilised diplomat he was. His own writings show him to have been an intelligent, rather conservative, experienced man who was well rewarded by Duke Philip for his services. However, the most lasting impression of Ghillebert de Lannoy, as well as of other less fluent medieval ambassadors, is that they were men of hardihood and ingenuity, of culture and formal good manners, of genuine if conventional religious faith, but above all of curiosity, of an unshakeable interest in all the sights and marvels to be found in the diverse parts of the world they reached.

CHAPTER EIGHT

PERIPATETIC ECCLESIASTICS

The large and impressive retinues to be met on the roads of medieval Europe were not necessarily those of kings or nobles. The splendour of Becket's equipage, for example, forcefully reminds us of the ostentation with which highly placed clerics might travel. The size and magnificence of their retinues depended as effectively as those of their secular counterparts on the rank, riches and reason for travelling of each one. There was one major difference, however, for non-noble birth was not the barrier to rank and riches for a cleric that it was for his secular companion. In the thirteenth century above all, the rise of the universities and of the orders of friars made the church a career particularly open to talent and could provide great temporal rewards. Such outstanding bishops as Robert Grosseteste, the universally admired bishop of Lincoln, and Eudes Rigaud, the Franciscan archbishop of Rouen, were not only notable ecclesiastics but forceful figures in their kings' councils. Although Rigaud's family was of the minor nobility of the Ile-de-France, Grosseteste's origins were certainly non-noble and both bishops won their promotions primarily through their impressive intellectual reputations. By the late thirteenth and early fourteenth century many bishops were named from the body of king's clerks, civil servants promoted to high office in the church as a reward for their administrative service. The aristocratic bishop, who owed his advancement primarily to the importance of his family and the king's desire to clinch that family's support, comes into particular prominence by the late fourteenth and early fifteenth century and then often gained the richest and most influential sees. These categories were not at any time mutually exclusive nor represented the whole gamut of the episcopate so it is not surprising that within the same official rank there might be enormous disparities in wealth and its display. Since all bishops were also important magnates with territorial as well as ecclesiastical responsibilities they were often even more mobile than their secular counterparts.

The young clerk starting at the bottom of the ladder of advancement would often be a subordinate official in a large household, perhaps that of a bishop or noble or, more importantly, of the king or queen. He would then naturally share in the travels of that household. As he became more skilled and experienced he was gradually used on more difficult matters, perhaps even on diplomatic missions or journeys to the curia, first as a subordinate and then as a leader. He would be rewarded by appointment to benefices (clerical offices which paid annual revenues) controlled by his patron. Since the pope had the richest rewards at his disposal, trips to the papal curia were often ardently sought after, for to catch the pope's eye and impress him as being particularly able was the quickest road to preferment in the church. An English clerk at the papal curia in the early fourteenth century wrote to John Lutterel, then chancellor of Oxford university, advising him to get himself named as an envoy to the curia, serving the king or a bishop or earl, for about three months. Such a period of time would allow Lutterel to have some previously well-planned disputations with the theologians in the papal court and this could show him in a particularly favourable light. His adviser was convinced that such tactics would gain Lutterel great profit and honour. The advice was taken and Lutterel made a good impression, being rewarded with minor ecclesiastical dignities and prebends, but he died before he could attain a bishopric.[1]

The successful clerk who was promoted to the episcopate was an important figure in his own right and necessarily travelled frequently. The pressure of important business with the papal curia might require the bishop's personal attention at Rome or Avignon or at one of the church councils which flourished in the first half of the fifteenth century. At home it was his duty to pursue the ecclesiastical visitation of his diocese, investigating the behaviour

40. Matthew Paris's
drawing of a church
council at London

of his clerics and their carrying out of their duties as well as the
maintenance of church property and revenues. In addition, as one
of the magnates of the realm, he was frequently summoned to
appear at parliament in England or *parlement* in France as well as
at church assemblies, and to attend such other great events as
coronations, royal weddings or special feasts. Many bishops, whose
skills had originally been honed as subordinate clerks on diplomatic
missions, later found themselves playing a more important role in
such negotiations. In following some of these ecclesiastics on their
various rounds we can gain a more realistic idea of their extraordinary mobility.

Eudes Rigaud, the Franciscan archbishop of Rouen from 1248 to
1276, left behind a record covering twenty-one and a half years of
his episcopate which is almost a daily journal of his activities and
travels. The distances covered by the hardworking archbishop in
the pursuit of his various tasks have been worked out and come to
the startling total of 54,131 miles. Almost every year he was on the
road at least half the time and averaged some 2,500 miles.[2] Obviously
neither weather, the seasons of the year, the state of the roads,
nor even his own rheumatism were allowed to circumscribe his
voyaging. The immediate question that springs to mind is where
was he going and what was he doing on all these trips? Primarily
he was engaged on the visitation of his own diocese and those of his

six suffragan bishops of Normandy, for Rigaud was an exceptionally conscientious archbishop and pursued this duty with vigour and continuing zeal. He did not restrict himself to his limited round. When he felt his archiepiscopal powers were threatened by an appeal from his suffragans to the pope Rigaud hurried to Rome to deal with their arguments in the pope's own presence and did not allow himself to be deterred by the difficulties of crossing the Alps in mid-winter. He was well acquainted with the best known pilgrimage spots in France and visited them himself when possible. In the spring of 1260 he went on pilgrimage to Notre-Dame-du-Puy and St-Gilles-du-Gard, while in the summer of 1261 he made a pilgrimage on foot from Paris to Chartres. It is a distance of some fifty-five miles and took the archbishop, then probably in his fifties, a week. He occasionally imposed pilgrimages as a penance when disciplining both clerics and seculars brought before his court. On one occasion an erring priest was sent to Mont-St-Michel and another to the southern shrines of St-Gilles and Rocamadour. The three laymen sent to the distant shrine of St James at Compostela had been guilty of murdering a lay-brother and that strenuous pilgrimage was only the culmination of their public and mortifying punishments.[3]

Not all Rigaud's concerns were ecclesiastical ones. He worked closely with King Louis IX, who was particularly concerned with strengthening royal power in Normandy which had only returned from English rule in 1204. Rigaud was used and consulted by the French king and even the laconic entries in the journal suggest that there was an important tie of friendship between the two men. When Louis was seriously ill in April 1259, and afraid he was about to die, he sent for Rigaud who immediately set out for Fontainebleau. The archbishop's own health was so poor – he was suffering both from fever and rheumatism – that he had to be carried in a wagon. The king regained his strength rapidly but the exhausted archbishop, returning to Normandy after the crisis had passed, was forced by his illness to remain in bed at St-Cloud for six weeks. Apart from frequent trips to Paris for meetings of *parlement* or merely to give advice to the king, Rigaud also had the secular duty of sitting as Master at the twice yearly sessions of the royal exchequer at Rouen. He shared in the final negotiations of the treaty of Paris in 1259, meeting with Simon de Montfort in that summer for discussions over dinner, soon after several days spent with the king. When the treaty was finally achieved Rigaud was given the privilege of proclaiming it publicly before the kings of both England and France in December 1259.[4] The archbishop was always perceived as a useful envoy on English matters and was sent on a second trip to England in the summer of 1260 when Simon de Montfort was under attack at the court of Henry III and Louis was attempting to make peace between the two. Rigaud was in his late sixties when he accompanied the French king on his final crusade to Tunis in 1270 (an unrecorded distance which should be added to his administrative journeys) and travelled back to France in the sad cortège carrying the king's bones. Even this rather restrained listing of the indefatigable archbishop's activities is sufficient to exhaust most modern travellers, but it is also illuminating to explore the conditions under which this peripatetic life was lived.

Like all important medieval travellers Eudes Rigaud was always accompanied by a retinue. The size of ecclesiastical retinues, especially when the prelate was engaged on an official visitation, was a matter about which popes frequently legislated, since those visited were usually legally required to provide hospitality and could be beggared by too extensive a company. Jacques de Vitry tells the cautionary tale of a bishop on visitation whose cook demanded so many special dishes for his master that the hard-pressed host was driven to sacrilege. Exclaiming bitterly, 'I have nothing more to give except the flanks of the Crucifix', he had the figure roasted and put on the bishop's table.[5] In the thirteenth century an archbishop was supposed to have no more than forty to fifty mounted attendants, a bishop twenty to thirty and an archdeacon from five to seven. Rigaud seems to have travelled with a core of clerics, diocesan officials and fellow Franciscans. These had received special papal permission to ride horses, a mode of travel not normally allowed to mendicant friars. This central group amounted to about twelve people and must have been supported by enough servants, grooms and valets to assure adequate food and lodging on the road. We have one personal glimpse of the archbishop and his household from the chatty chronicle of Salimbene, the Italian Franciscan. He records that when Rigaud passed through northern Italy on his way to Rome in February 1254 he was welcomed at Mantua by the papal legate who wished to send his seneschal as a harbinger and to pay Rigaud's expenses as far as Bologna. The self-sufficient archbishop refused his generosity, saying that he and his household could live with suitable splendour on half the revenues of his see. Salimbene saw for himself the archbishop's behaviour in Ferrara where he reported that Rigaud was attended by eighty mounted attendants and 'a proper household'. This was a very large party, perhaps swollen by individuals joining him for mutual support over the Alps or by the need for extra officials to assist him on the long journey or at the papal court. According to the chronicler the archbishop always arranged, even in foreign parts, to have two large silver bowls placed on the table in front of him to hold food for the poor and to have himself served with two platters of every kind of food. One he ate from, the other was poured into the bowls to be distributed as alms. No doubt Salimbene got particular pleasure in singing the praises of a holy and learned archbishop who was such a prominent member of his own order, but he was sufficiently realistic to remark that Rigaud was also rather ugly.[6]

Almost all the archbishop's travels were made on horseback, usually at a rate of some fifteen miles a day. His trip to Rome pushed him to greater speeds, occasionally as much as thirty-seven miles a day, for he left Rouen on 29 December 1253, crossed France, traversed the Alps and arrived in Rome by 11 March – a relatively fast trip for such a good-sized company. The range of his travels indicates that the roads cannot have been as bad as has sometimes been suggested and that there must have been a wide network of passable roads to allow him to travel to all parts of Normandy. Only once does the archbishop have himself transported – when he rushed to the bedside of King Louis – and only once does he mention taking a boat down the Seine from Mantes to Meulan with his friend the bishop of Evreux.[7] The problem of finding lodgings seems to have caused few difficulties. As archbishop of Rouen Rigaud was lord of a good number of manors and he often used these places as centres when he was on visitation. His favourite appears to have been

Deville, a comfortable place only a couple of miles outside Rouen's walls and apparently preferred to the archbishop's older house within the city. The use made of Deville when the archbishop was attending daily exchequer sessions in Rouen suggests that he was an early example of a commuter. The archbishop also had a house in Paris, much needed as the king required his attendance there more frequently. Between 1258 and 1264 (the period when relations between England and France were of particular concern to Louis) Rigaud spent two to three months a year in the capital. When he was absent on more distant trips he was naturally a welcome guest at various Franciscan houses – and must have particularly enjoyed the four days he spent in Assisi on his way to Rome – or could frequently call on the hospitality of his fellow bishops or important abbeys. On visitations the abbeys and religious houses usually owed him procurations, that is, hospitality or a substitute payment. Sometimes this included beds and other utensils, while the archbishop provided the food to be cooked; on other occasions he seems to have found it necessary to have all the essentials with him.

Rigaud's journal, or register of visitations, is a very matter of fact and laconic record of the peripatetic life of an outstanding churchman of his time. The details it provides of what the archbishop found in the course of his visitations and the remedies he sought to apply to keep both clergy and laity law-abiding Christians emphasise the enormous effort that a good bishop could put into maintaining a proper level of religious life in his diocese against the pressures of human weakness, back sliding and perversity. The portrait of Rigaud which emerges from these entries is that of a very conscientious man, full of energy and vigorous common sense. When the amount of his travelling under the slow, uncertain and uncomfortable conditions of the Middle Ages is added to the quantity of work he achieved the result compels modern admiration and astonishment.

Rigaud was unquestionably an exceptional man. Bishop Richard Swinfield of Hereford, who was a generation younger, is more typical. The fortunate survival of the account roll of his household for ten months of 1289–90 throws considerable light on the travels, retinue and expenses of an average bishop.[8] Swinfield was trained in theology and well thought of as a preacher but he undoubtedly gained his bishopric by his years of devoted service to his predecessor in the see, Thomas Cantilupe. Cantilupe was a member of a prominent baronial family (his uncle had been bishop of Worcester and his father steward for King Henry III). He had studied at Paris, been made a papal chaplain by Innocent IV, supported Simon de Montfort at the time of the Barons' War and was made bishop of Hereford in 1275. He chose young Swinfield as his chaplain, secretary and friend and Richard in return spent much of his episcopate (1282–1317) pursuing the canonisation of his old master. The cause was ultimately successful after Swinfield's death though there is a large element of irony in the naming as a saint one who had died under sentence of excommunication by John Pecham, the impulsive archbishop of Canterbury. From the evidence of the household roll and the bishop's register Swinfield would appear to have been conscientious in his duty of episcopal visitation and he would go to London when necessary for parliament. The household account shows him making a mid-winter trip to the post-Christmas parliament of 1289–90 and making a present to the king and the queen but he only stayed six days in London and then started on his homeward trip. Occasionally he fell back on the excuse of ill-health for not attending parliaments or meetings of the bishops. In 1297, for example, he wrote to the archbishop of Canterbury begging to be excused from such a meeting since he did not dare to undertake the labour of the long journey while suffering such weakness.[9]

Unlike Rigaud, Swinfield was not constantly on the road. In the period covered by his household roll two thirds of his time was spent at his favourite episcopal manors, a month in going to and from London and the remainder on the visitation of two different parts of his diocese. However, like other secular lords he travelled frequently between these various manors. Most popular were Sugwas, a few miles west of Hereford; Prestbury, near what is now Cheltenham, where the bishop had a large house and deer park; and the three manors clustered near the eastern boundary of Herefordshire – Bosbury, Ledbury and Colwall. Colwall at the foot of the Malvern Hills was also good hunting country and the bishop had several huntsmen whose duty it was to supply the episcopal table with venison. The bishop also benefited from the salmon and eels caught in his weir on the river Wye at Sugwas. Such supplies, and many others, were very necessary for the bishop was required to offer considerable hospitality. For example, when he celebrated Easter at Colwall on 2 April 1290 his clerk records some seventy horses in the stable over the week-end, although the average number was around thirty-five to forty. His accounts also remind us that the Easter egg has a long history, for an incredible 1,400 were bought for 3s 8d. Easter dinner also included beef, pork, young deer and a large number of pigeons, some of them coming from his dove-cote at Bosbury.[10] It was at these times that the bishop might entertain his powerful and prickly neighbours such as Humphrey de Bohun, earl of Hereford or the magnificent Clare earls of Gloucester. Almost all the information garnered from the accounts is consonant with the pattern of life of an ecclesiastic who was also a magnate and who was expected to maintain an important household. The bishop gave adequate alms and supported a couple of poor scholars at Oxford and he also enjoyed music. When in London two of the king's harpers were given generous presents of 20s each though the harpers of the abbot of Reading and Lord Edmund Mortimer only received 12d each.[11] The mention of other minstrels and jugglers suggest that it was an accepted convention to tip the entertainers on any occasion. Semi-annual wages were paid to the various members of the household and cloth was bought for their robes. Horses for the bishop and his household, as well as for the carts, were purchased and exchanged while the saddles and other equipment were periodically replaced or repaired. Swinfield's household roll suggests the well organised, stable existence of a bishop who, though not particularly distinguished, made his ecclesiastical and manorial rounds in the accepted pattern of his time.

Some bishops appear to have done almost all their travelling before their promotion. John Grandisson, the bishop of Exeter 1327–69, is a good example of a scholarly prelate who settled happily into his niche and resisted as far as he could any efforts to dislodge him. Grandisson undoubtedly gained from his family connections – his uncle was Sir Othon de Grandson and his father William also served the king and reaped the rewards of that service. John was started on a career in the church at a very early age for he appears to have received his first benefice when he was about fourteen. He studied theology at Paris under Jacques Fournier, later Pope Benedict XII, but currently better remembered as that bishop of Pamiers whose register had so much to say about the inhabitants of Montaillou. The young cleric moved on from Paris to become a papal chaplain, was named archdeacon of Nottingham in 1322 and, four years later, was sent off by Pope John XXII on a very delicate diplomatic mission.[12]

The pope was anxious to bring peace between the English and French and sent the archbishop of Vienne, the bishop of Orléans and the young archdeacon on this mission. They were armed for their task with daily wages of fourteen gold florins for the archbishop, ten for the bishop and four for the archdeacon in addition to useful letters ordering all archbishops, bishops, prelates and religious orders in the districts which they passed to provide them with all their necessities. When they set off in September 1326 the political situation in England was already coming to a head with Queen Isabella leading the revolt against her husband Edward II and the Despensers while the struggle with France over Gascony was pushed to the side.

The ambassadors had no trouble making their way northward from Avignon, through Burgundy and Champagne, to find King Charles IV of France at Château-Thierry, but crossing to England and obtaining the necessary safe-conducts was another matter. They finally crossed at the beginning of December and then spent almost a month in Canterbury awaiting the royal will. London had been in a state of turmoil since mid-October and on 7 January 1327 a parliament summoned by the queen and her supporters in the name of Prince Edward met and eight days later declared Edward II deposed. John and the French prelates appear to have been in London during this exciting period, since they arrived in London on 4 January and only sailed back to France on 26 January. Discreetly their written report gives no hint of what was going on but merely states that they did their business with the queen and the leading people of London. They were ordered by the pope to return to

Avignon in May if they could not help in reconciling Edward and Isabella. This was an impossible task but John seems to have continued his diplomatic activity searching for a way to conclude peace in Gascony in the company of the archbishop of Vienne. The notification of his choice as bishop of Exeter reached him at St-Macaire, a Gascon outpost on the Garonne, in August 1327. Grandisson returned to Avignon where he was consecrated in the Dominican church by the cardinal of Praeneste in a ceremony attended by cardinals, prelates and many nobles. It took some time for the new bishop to get permission to leave the curia but he finally received the necessary papal licence, made his farewell calls and reported with considerable satisfaction that 'it was said many were doleful at his departure'.[13] On 23 December he set out for England though mid-winter was a bad time for travelling. John had proposed to cross France with the greatest speed but he was delayed by frost, snow and intemperate winds so that it was only at the beginning of February 1328 that he crossed from Wissant to Dover. Any newly consecrated bishop had to comply with certain formalities. First, he had to take the oath of obedience to the archbishop of Canterbury, so Grandisson hurried to Canterbury and, since the see was vacant, took the required oath to the prior and chapter as the administrators. From Canterbury he had to go to the king, present the papal bulls naming him, do fealty to the king for the see's temporal holdings and was then invested with them. He found the young Edward III in York at the beginning of March, was well received and fulfilled the necessary business with dispatch. Religious and secular requirements both completed, Grandisson headed for Gloucestershire and his father's home at Oxenhall, where he and his household stayed for nearly a month. His elderly father was no doubt glad to see one son so well settled in a position of importance; his mother was perhaps even better pleased to have a bishop for a son, for she was a great-niece of St Thomas Cantalupe who had recently been canonised.[14] After his family visit the bishop returned to Northampton for the April parliament, having taken lodgings at Hayford nearby. Only after all these various duties had been completed did he set out for his own diocese, arriving at Honiton 9 June and being formally greeted at the episcopal manor

of Clyst near Exeter by a solemn procession of the dean, the treasurer, the sub-dean and many canons of the church who then all
stayed to dine with him.

Such an active eighteen months seems to have left the new bishop
with a strong desire to remain at home and not travel the roads of
England. In January and February 1330 he excused himself from
appearing in London, either for the meeting of parliament or the
coronation of Queen Phillipa, claiming that it took the messenger
so long to get to him that it was impossible to arrive in time, that
the distance was so great, the season so bad and the roads in such
poor shape that he should be forgiven for his non-appearance.[15]
Some years later Grandisson had a letter from the Black Prince who
was on his way to Plymouth to embark for France and had issued
a number of requests to clergy and religious in the West Country
to provide him with horses and carts. The bishop reiterated his
complaints about the Devonshire roads, especially in March, since
they could hardly be travelled by oxen let alone horses. He also laid
great emphasis on his inadequacy as a horseman, claiming proudly
that there was no other bishop in England or France who was so
bad on horseback as himself. In fact, the sedentary bishop boasted
that for three years he had not ridden sixty miles around Exeter nor
even mounted a horse since Michaelmas[16] – how the conscientious
Rigaud would have disapproved! Nevertheless Grandisson was in
many ways a good bishop, active in raising scholarship and the
level of learning among his diocesan clergy. His passions were the
completion and beautification of his cathedral, and his own library,
part of which he left to his cathedral on his death. Grandisson was
a rich man, connected to many of the noble families of the realm –
his sister had married William Montague, the earl of Salisbury –
but having settled into his comfortable see he seems to have been
anxious to put aside his early years of travelling.

One of his contemporaries, Amanieu de Lamothe, archbishop
of Bordeaux from 1351 to 1360, provides a striking French example
of what birth and patronage could achieve without much merit.
The greatest weakness of Pope Clement V, the first Avignon pope
who had previously been archbishop of Bordeaux, was his unbridled
passion for promoting his own relatives. He named two of his

cousins to the see of Bordeaux in quick succession and surrounded himself with Gascon cardinals. One of these, Gaillard de Lamothe, a cardinal for forty years, carried on the tradition of preference for those related to Clement V. Amanieu de Lamothe had been rewarded early in his clerical career, being made a canon of St-Caprais, Agen, when he was only fifteen and named bishop when he was thirty. His family, the lords of Roquetaillade, belonged to the heartland of Gascony, south of the Garonne and not far from Bazas, where they had built a new and elegant castle. The arch-bishop obviously found the papal court at Avignon more attractive than his diocese and probably less politically embarrassing, for he remained at the curia during 1355–6 when the Black Prince made his first stay in the duchy of Aquitaine and used the archbishop's palace in Bordeaux as his own residence. When the archbishop decided to return to Gascony in the summer of 1357, the Black Prince had already sailed for England, accompanied by his royal prisoner, King John II.

The accounts of the archbishop's treasurer, Pierre de Fita, mark with precision the various stops made by the company as they took the main road from Avignon through Nîmes, Montpellier, Toulouse, and then north and west to Bazas and Roquetaillade.[17] It was a journey of about 320 miles, which they accomplished in two weeks, spending two restful days in Montpellier and another two in Toulouse. Obviously the archbishop and his retinue made very good speed despite the August heat. The accounts are sufficiently detailed to note when they stopped for drinks for man and beast and they frequently mention the purchase of water laced with salt, no doubt a necessary safeguard on that dry hot plain in midsummer. Generally the company appears to have put up at inns, sometimes sending a harbinger ahead to procure the necessary lodgings, but the last two nights, as the archbishop moved into his own diocese, he was put up at the expense of the bishop of Condom and the bishop of Bazas. The make-up of the retinue is not detailed, although reference is made to the twenty-seven horses included. A great many entries deal with those horses – their needs, their equipment and even medicine for them. Since the treasurer was merely keeping a running account of expenses for a short period he does not itemise, except incidentally, the members of the company or their functions. A rather surprising group to be mentioned are the trumpeters to whom a gift was made at the archbishop's command after the retinue had arrived at Roquetaillade. They may have been part of the company or come out specially from Bordeaux to celebrate the return of the archbishop. Once Lamothe had ensconced himself at his family's estate he remained there for over a month. In September he went to Lormont, the country castle of the archbishops some five miles north of Bordeaux on the right bank of the Garonne. There he could enjoy his gardens and fields as well as the vintage wine. Like Grandisson, Lamothe did not believe in travelling any more than the absolute exigencies of his position required, and preferably made sure of pleasurable interludes.

Richard Courtenay began his clerical career with several definite advantages. At the end of the fourteenth century to belong to the most important family in Devon and to have an uncle who was archbishop of Canterbury were unusual assets. Archbishop William Courtenay was particularly devoted to his nephew and encouraged his clerical career, for in his will he called him 'his dearest child and foster son', generously bequeathed him 100 marks, several books – including a dictionary in three volumes – and his best mitre 'in case he becomes a bishop'.[18] The archbishop's foresight, or, perhaps more realistically, his practical recognition of the ways of clerical promotion, was quite justified as Richard became bishop of Norwich in 1413 when he was only thirty-two. Unlike so many other of the travelling ecclesiastics described, Courtenay's activity was primarily intellectual and diplomatic. He had taken his first degree at Oxford in law in 1399 and was ordained priest in December 1400. The young priest's reputation at Oxford was high, for he served as chancellor of the university in 1406–8, and again in 1411 when the university and Archbishop Arundel collided over the position of the Lollards at Oxford and the vexed question of university privileges. Courtenay was forced to resign the chancellorship in September by King Henry IV but was re-elected in November by a defiant university. The squabble was finally settled with some help from Prince Henry with whom Courtenay was already on good terms, as he had accompanied the prince on one of his expeditions into Wales. Courtenay had begun to make himself useful as a diplomat as well, having conducted Henry's sister, the young Princess Philippa, to Copenhagen to marry King Eric of Denmark.

There seems little doubt that Henry V enjoyed the company of the aristocratic, intelligent, and good-looking young cleric only a few years older than himself who seemed capable of dealing with a wide range of royal business. Soon after his accession he had him made bishop of Norwich but kept him at court to serve on a number of diplomatic assignments. Richard Courtenay was a leading figure in the series of glittering, expensive and totally inconclusive embassies that masked Henry's decision to reopen the war with France. With due regard for elaborate protocol the ambassadors moved backwards and forwards between France and England with their magnificent retinues – as many as 500 horses and *'bien pompeusement habillés'*, one chronicler says.[19] They were greeted sumptuously and feasted in the grand manner, while during the spring embassy of 1415 they were also entertained by great jousts in Paris. These took place up and down the Grande Rue St-Antoine near the French king's palace of St-Pol, while the leading French nobles vied with each other in the magnificence of their array. Courtenay was the spokesman for the king's demands, which were always extreme, as Henry exploited to his own advantage the fatal split in France between the factions which struggled to gain control of the weak and mad Charles VI.

Courtenay was not only a diplomatic mouthpiece but also pursued his own intellectual interests. When in Paris on an embassy in 1414 Courtenay had met Master John Fusoris, a Paris medical doctor who was also highly esteemed for his knowledge of mathematics and astronomy as well as an ability to make clocks. The bishop and Fusoris had a long discussion on astrology – always closely allied to astronomy in the Middle Ages – and Courtenay bought seven astronomical instruments from him for 400 crowns. Since the bishop needed to have the rules by which they operated he arranged to dine with Fusoris at an inn at St-Denis on their way home from Paris and persuaded him to ride with him and the earl of Salisbury as far as Pontoise. Courtenay had also bought books from Fusoris – such secular works as romances and an Ovid as well as a small bible and a biblical commentary. In fact, like so many others, the bishop had found Paris goods so exciting and had also bought so much jewellery, mirrors and goldsmith's work that he could not pay Fusoris all he owed him and had to borrow to get home.[20] The acquaintance was pursued when Courtenay was again in Paris in February 1415 while Fusoris managed to have himself attached to the French embassy to Winchester that summer. Courtenay had invited him to bring along a treatise on the astrolabe and one on the sphere as well as geometrical puzzles for King Henry. Fusoris was introduced to the king and presented his treatises, receiving the royal thanks and forty nobles as well as the money still owed to him by the bishop. Such intimate relations with the English court at a moment when hostilities were recommencing were bound to arouse suspicion. Fusoris was arrested and charged with treasonable conversation though after a few months imprisonment he was allowed to live quietly in Reims. At Winchester the Paris doctor had warned Courtenay, always a man of delicate health who was becoming very stout and complaining of dizziness, that he should consult the best English medical men and not join any English expedition, as he would be easy prey for any illness. The medical advice was excellent but disregarded. Bishop Courtenay, as keeper of the king's jewels, was with Henry's army at the siege of Harfleur. He died in mid-September 1415 at the early age of thirty-four, a victim of the dysentery which killed so many of the soldiers.[21]

A monastic contemporary of Courtenay's was John Whethamstede, abbot of St Albans for thirty-three years. St Albans was one of the greatest Benedictine houses in England and its position just a day's journey from London meant that it was host to the important and the famous. Abbot John was not pleased when he was notified by the archbishop of Canterbury of his appointment as a member of the English delegation to the Council of Pavia in 1423. Church councils were frequent and often long-drawn out affairs during the early years of the fifteenth century and the abbot was an unwilling but very voluble traveller. His account of his journey to Italy and back forms a fascinating contrast to the continuous travels and brief entries of Archbishop Rigaud.[22] Whethamstede's

41. Abbot John
Whethamstede of St
Albans, the reluctant
traveller

Latin prose was full-blown and pompous, for the abbot was proud
of his extensive, if ill-digested, classical knowledge and loved to pen
elaborate letters home from many of his stopping-places. As a
reluctant traveller whose flesh trembled at the prospect of 'drinking
the chalice of an overseas journey' and with the added horrors of
an Alpine crossing, his rather uncomfortable passage of the Channel
in March 1423 inspired a letter to his brethren on the perils of the
waves with assorted references to Neptune, Thetis the sea-nymph,
Circe, Apollo and Aeolus the god of the winds. Once on dry land
his spirits recovered somewhat and he set off on horseback from
Calais through Picardy, Flanders and Brabant to Mainz on the
Rhine. There he was pleased to be invited to dinner by the cardinal
legate but immediately after fell ill with a fifteen day fever. On
recovering his strength he wrote again to the monks, describing his
illness and praising his doctor, and then resumed his journey
through southern Germany to Austria where he crossed the Alps.
The abbot was a very self-centred man. He lists, but does not
describe, the towns through which he passed on the way to Pavia
and gives no hint of the nature or number of the retinue he must
have had with him. On arrival at Pavia he discovered that because
of an epidemic in the town the council had transferred itself to
Siena.

The change of locale meant further travelling but before proceeding the abbot sent four of his retinue back to England bearing further letters, also replete with classical references. On a more practical level, he also sent off to the duke of Milan for a safe-conduct through his territories. Whethamstede resumed his journey after its arrival but with little enthusiasm and many delays. The summer heat had already begun, the abbot felt the need of a good doctor and was delighted when a Venetian gentleman he had met on the road gave him a letter of introduction to a physician in Florence. The abbot spent some time in that city where he discovered that the kind stranger was in fact a most learned man and castigated himself for having failed to note and take advantage of his knowledge. Finally arriving in Siena, Abbot Whethamstede enquired how the council was progressing and was informed that nothing notable had happened. As a monk the abbot might have been upset to hear that the bishop of Lincoln had been orating intemperately against the exempt religious of his jurisdiction, which of course included the Benedictines, though even the bishop's own delegation had greeted with relief the fact that the prelate had been put out of action by an attack of fever. No particular activity was going on at the council, nor any expected in the near future, so Whethamstede decided to take advantage of the lull to go to Rome and visit the pope, who was avoiding the council. Before departing he wrote to the presidents of the Benedictine order in England informing them of the dangerous proposals of the bishop of Lincoln, and also sent a reproachful letter to his brethren on their failure to write to him. The traveller's disappointment when there is no news from home is a perennial complaint.

The journey to Rome was difficult and the abbot remarks in one of his few geographical asides on 'the place of horror and vast solitude' which one had to cross to reach the papal city.[23] An audience with the pope was arranged within a few days of his arrival and John had the opportunity to put forward his request for a number of privileges for the abbey. On his return to his lodgings he was struck down by a serious attack of dysentery but was cheered by the pope's dispatch of a plenary indulgence by the hands of Thomas Polton, then bishop of Chichester, who was resident at the papal court as English proctor. The ailing abbot was convinced that he was going to die, but revived after being vouchsafed a vision of St Bernard in a dream. The saint assured him he would recover if he would read his books and study them with diligence – obviously heavenly approval for his own preferences. When his health returned the abbot had two further audiences with the pope, gained the privileges requested and then took his leave to return to Siena. While he was catching up on the proceedings of the council during his absence a messenger arrived from England with a welcome bundle of letters which also brought bad news for dissension had broken out in his abbey and its holdings. Whethamstede immediately paid the messenger suitably but sent him back carrying a vigorous letter of reproof as well as the news of his recovery and of the continued absence of the pope from the council.

By this time the homesick abbot felt it was time to return. He went to the bishop of Carlisle, the president of the English delegation, and made his excuses on the grounds of ill-health. Since Whethamstede had made no contribution whatsoever to the conciliar proceedings the bishop was quite happy to release him in order 'to safeguard his health'. On his way back to England the abbot spent seven weeks in Cologne during all the Christmas festivities in order to 'rest from his labours'. He dispatched his companion, the learned doctor of law, back to England while John himself with one monk and seven servants remained in Cologne. The little company arrived in England on 9 February 1424 and spent ten days in London so that the abbot could greet politely the lords of the realm gathered for a meeting of parliament. According to his own report, his return to St Albans on 25 February was a triumphal procession. He announced smugly that the inhabitants of Barnet and St Albans came out to meet him with cries of 'Hosanna, blessed is he who comes in the name of the Lord'.[24] Surrounded by a crowd of horsemen he arrived at the abbey church where a Te Deum was sung and the abbot gave thanks that none of his people had been lost during his absence. The service was followed by a suitable feast for all those who had come to welcome him and after a little conversation about his journey the outsiders were dismissed. Abbot John was at last home and at rest among his brother monks.

Whethamstede was something of an intellectual and wrote pro-
lifically but he had little influence outside his own monastery. His
flowery account of his one great trip is interesting for its exceedingly
self-centred approach and its lack of interest in the places or people
he encountered. His style of reporting irresistibly recalls the school-
boy howler which described Dante as an author who stood with
one foot in the Middle Ages and with the other he saluted the
dawn of the Renaissance. Abbot John adopted that same precarious
posture and his prose suffers from the weaknesses of both periods.

It would not seem right to end a series of sketches of peripatetic
ecclesiastics without a bow to that indefatigable traveller, Aeneas
Silvius Piccolomini, who after years of employment as secretary
and diplomat for cardinals and the emperor rose to ecclesiastical
heights and was elected Pope Pius II. Aeneas was a humanist, full
of curiosity and good humour, and his descriptions of his travels
are quite different from the brief entries of Eudes Rigaud or the
pedantic pomposity of Abbot Whethamstede. His *Commentaries* are
still delightful reading just because they tell so much about the
character and ideas of Aeneas Silvius himself as well as the many
places he saw and the people he met. After his attendance at the
Congress of Arras in 1435 as secretary to Cardinal Albergati, the
papal legate, Aeneas was sent to Scotland by the cardinal on a
mission to King James I.[25] Although Aeneas is very garrulous about
his trip he tells us nothing of his diplomatic objectives, though it
seems likely that the purpose was to mobilise Scotland against
England and, by stirring up trouble in the north, to distract English
attention from the consequences of the Burgundian change of allies.
Aeneas had difficulty getting from Calais to England as the English
were suspicious of the reason for his journey but he finally managed
to cross with assistance from Cardinal Beaufort. Once he got to
England he was still unable to get a safe-conduct to go to Scotland
and had to return to the continent. During this delay he put in
some time sightseeing and spoke approvingly of London with the
famous church of St Paul, the wonderful tombs of the kings in
Westminster Abbey and 'the bridge like a city'. He was particularly
impressed by the golden shrine of St Thomas at Canterbury, covered
with diamonds and other precious stones and reported that it was

considered sacrilegious to offer there any gift less precious than silver. As a proper, and possibly gullible, tourist Aeneas had been told of the fame of Strood in Kent 'where men are said to be born with tails' but had seen no examples.[26] Having recrossed the Channel to Sluis he found a ship for Scotland but the crossing took twelve days as the ship was battered by two gales which drove the unfortunate vessel all the way to Norway.

In the best medieval tradition of how to survive a storm at sea Aeneas had made a vow of pilgrimage and on landing in Scotland walked barefoot ten miles to Our Lady of Whitekirk, a well-known local place of pilgrimage. Piccolomini wrote a clear description of Scotland as he saw it, though it was not a very complimentary view for he found it generally poor and rude, with no wine, very cold weather and not many crops. Unlike Bartholomew the Englishman two centuries before, however, he had no comments at all about the native dress. As a good observer Aeneas noted that at the time of the winter solstice when he was there, the day was not more than four hours long. Certain prejudices have long histories for the Italian noted that there is 'nothing the Scotch like better to hear than abuse of the English'.[27] His sea voyage over had been enough to make him decide to return by land, so he disguised himself as a merchant, crossed the Tweed and sought hospitality in the nearest town of the rough border country. The experienced traveller had taken the precaution of providing himself with some loaves of bread and a jug of wine, both scarce commodities in the north, which ensured him a cordial welcome. In the evening the men of the locality went off to take refuge in a neighbouring peel-tower, fearing a Scottish raid. They left the women behind with their startled visitor explaining that the Scots would only rape the women, not kill them. Aeneas virtuously refused the offer of two of the girls to sleep with him in the barn to which he was taken, but his night was still a restless one for the heifers and goats who surrounded him nibbled happily on the straw they continually pulled out of his pallet. At least his sleep was not disturbed by Scottish raiders. Happily leaving the desolate border country behind him he travelled south through Durham and York where he particularly admired the size, design and brilliant glass of the cathedral. The rest of his voyage was uneventful and though he was unable to get official permission to leave England he found no difficulty in bribing his way onto a boat at Dover. Aeneas Silvius has been described as 'a freelance journalist, and one of the best who ever set pen to paper'.[28] He wrote of his travels with a lively pen and is distinguished from so many of his earlier predecessors, and even his contemporaries by his unquenchable curiosity about people and places. To read his *Commentaries* is to learn something of the man himself and to know very clearly what he thought of the persons and places he saw. The circumstances were still medieval, the tone suggests the coming changes.

CHAPTER NINE

THE SOCIAL ROUND

The vivid crowded pictures from medieval manuscripts which tend, almost unconsciously, to provide our mental image of the Middle Ages focus most unforgettably on the patterns of life of the noble and wealthy and illustrate the activities that most interested them. Naturally, in such a situation there was much emphasis on war in all its forms – siege, attack and battle – for this was the *raison d'être* of the knightly class. Following close behind, however, come the innumerable depictions of those much loved and popular social occasions, feasts and tournaments. The familiar January illustration from the *Très Riches Heures* shows the wealthy and cultured duke of Berry presiding at the New Year's day feast, an occasion for great display and exchange of presents. Such feasts, usually in far more modest form and including more ladies were part and parcel of medieval life. They were, as they have always been, a necessary grace note to the more serious business of diplomacy, negotiation and reconciliation as well as the required and enjoyable flourish which celebrated such occasions as coronations, weddings and the great holydays of the ecclesiastical year. They brought together not only the immediate members of the court or household but also distinguished visitors and travellers from afar. Christine de Pisan, the French court poet at the end of the fourteenth century, empha- sised in one of her ballades the qualities of the proper knight. Among the more unexpected were his duty to haunt the courts of kings and princes, to accompany noble strangers and above all to be a great traveller in pursuit of honour, proud and enterprising in feats of arms.[1] Her emphasis on the importance of a far-flung search for occasions to display prowess and demonstrate prestige in the most exalted places was generally shared by the nobles themselves. To improve one's status at court, at feasts and other gatherings, one had to have gained prestige and, if possible, riches at the tournament, thus providing a dominant motive for social travel by the upper-class knight.

The tournament has come to be regarded almost as a shorthand symbol for the chivalry of the Middle Ages, a conception much encouraged by the enthusiasm of chroniclers and authors of romances as well as their illustrators, for the loving depiction of such spectacles, especially in their later, more theatrical form. Nevertheless the tournament is a somewhat ambiguous symbol for the nature of these meetings changed enormously between the twelfth and fifteenth century. The tournament of twelfth century France, where the practice originated, consisted of a great mêlée of companies of opposing knights who fought a running battle over the chosen countryside with standard weapons. Such bloody contests did not lend themselves to ornament or female attendance, for they covered much territory and often led to death or serious injury. Their supporters praised them as a valuable way to train young knights in the armed skills needed for serious warfare, and young and impecunious knights sought them out as an approved way to gain riches, and perhaps social position as well, through their prowess.

The case of William Marshal is an example of the rewards to which success in the tournaments could lead. The poet who wrote

42. Early fourteenth-century tournament

his life got much of his material from William's faithful squire and described the knight's tourneying days in loving detail.[2] William Marshal, born around the middle of the twelfth century, belonged to the minor Anglo-Norman nobility. His father had served King Stephen as marshal in his household and later supported the Empress Matilda, but William was the second son of a second marriage, so that his worldly prospects were gloomy. His father sent him as soon as he reached adolescence to a relative, the chamberlain of Tancarville, in Normandy, to be trained in that household in military skills and gentle behaviour. The boy spent some pleasant years there, though his behaviour gave no hint of his future ability. He was finally knighted by his kinsman and began the life of knight errantry which was to occupy much of his young manhood. The pattern was a familiar one at this time for the twelfth century saw a large number of young men of the noble and knightly class, who had taken up arms and had been dubbed knights but were still referred to as 'youths', a stage in their careers which continued until they married and founded a family. The problem was to find the resources which made marrying and settling down possible, for they were often younger sons with minimal expectations of an estate and few resources with which to command a profitable marriage. Not surprisingly, these 'youths' had a passion for the roving life and the desire to find adventure and prizes. They frequently travelled in groups and shared a mutual enthusiasm for tournaments where the rewards could be glittering for the successful contestant. William Marshal who was distinguished, according to his biographer, by his strong physique and his handsome hands and feet, used tournaments to put his skill at arms to the test. The first aim was to seize an opponent's horse, then his sword and force him to declare himself your prisoner. The victor kept the horse and its harness, any weapons thus gained and, if the knight declared himself a prisoner, was also paid a ransom. All this could mean considerable riches. In one of his first tournaments, for example, William entered the mêlée and seized the bridle of one knight, dragging him from the fray. He took his oath as his prisoner and then plunged back into the fray to capture two more knights. The author of his life describes this achievement in purely material terms: 'In the morning the Marshal was poor in money and goods, but by evening was well provided with palfreys, rounceys, sumpters and handsome harness.'[3]

Such successes could also bring a young knight to the favourable attention of the great men of his time, increasing his prestige and also his chances of being offered a valuable office. Here again William Marshal exemplified the hopes of such young men. Brought to the attention of Henry II by his warlike abilities, he was made a companion of the king's eldest son and taught his charge useful tactics for the mêlées as well as his own fighting skills. William maintained his passion for participation in tournaments and frequently travelled the circuit of such events, for they were common all over northern France and the Low Countries though most popular in Normandy and Brittany. At a particularly elegant tourney near Epernay the Marshal had been given permission to attend with only one companion. Much of the fashionable chivalric world was there with their rich harness and fine horses from Spain, Lombardy and Sicily, including the duke of Burgundy, the counts of Flanders, Blois, Clermont and a swarm of knights all anxious to win prizes. William won great praise from the company for his strength and skill in the encounter and also for his courteous behaviour. The most highly born lady in attendance presented a magnificent pike to the duke of Burgundy as the ranking lord. In an excess of politeness it was passed on from count to count until the count of Flanders decided that it should be given to the bravest of the knights, who was of course the Marshal. After some search William was finally found at a blacksmith's forge with his head on the anvil so that the smith with his tools could take off the helm which had been beaten down around his neck in the strenuous fighting. (Henry of Lancaster remarked more than a century later that one could always tell a knight who had fought in many tournaments by his battered nose – no doubt the medieval knight's equivalent of the boxer's cauliflower ear.)[4] The search party waited until the smith had removed William's helm and then presented him with the great fish. He received it with appropriate modesty but the story of how he had been found ran through the tents and was greeted with great admiration.[5]

William's reputation was also aided by a quick wit and panache which made him popular among the minstrels and heralds who in their proclamation of the outstanding deeds of noble men were the medieval publicists. Ambitious knights made sure that heralds and minstrels were given generous gifts and other encouragements to speak well of them and their house. On one occasion William and his companions had arrived early for a tourney at Joigny and gained the field before any of their opponents appeared. A number of ladies were in attendance and, to pass the time, the Marshal struck up a song to which the whole company danced with the knights joining in arrayed in full armour. A young minstrel, who had just been made a herald and was no doubt in need of patronage, followed William's song with one of his own having as its refrain, 'Marshal, give me a new horse'. Just at that moment the first of the opposing knights arrived on the field. William left the dance, mounted his horse and took off against his opponents. He unseated the first he met and, taking his horse, gave it to the young herald who immediately boasted to the dancers of the Marshal's generosity. The knights and ladies all agreed that it was the prettiest exploit seen in a tournament.[6] Such feats merely added colour to William Marshal's reputation, for his later career took him far beyond the temporary successes of a knight errant. He was a faithful servant to the sons of Henry II and was rewarded with marriage to the daughter and heiress of Earl Richard of Pembroke. When the nine-year-old Henry III acceded to the throne in 1216 the elderly earl was unanimously chosen by the barons as his suitable guardian and regent. William's ability as a travelling knight had laid the foundations of his career and had brought him enormous rewards and great prestige. No doubt his biography with its inspiring success story was a popular favourite among the young men who attempted this same road to wealth and position and dreamt of equal rewards. Such tales of knightly adventure, and their literary counterparts in the popular romances, were standard fare as part of the entertainment at any feast or tournament.

Popular as the tournament was among the upper classes there were also currents of opposing opinion. During the twelfth and thirteenth centuries official ecclesiastical opposition was general.

Popes fulminated, bishops forbade specific meetings and preachers thundered against the sins tournaments encouraged, but all with little effect. The popes gradually lessened their opposition during the fourteenth century, having reluctantly accepted the nobles' contention that tournaments were necessary to produce skilled knights, for the popes were exceedingly anxious to encourage knightly participation in further expeditions to the Holy Land. The preachers generally remained consistent in their hostility. From Jacques de Vitry and Robert Mannyng of Brunne in the thirteenth century, who carefully apportioned all the seven deadly sins to the various aspects of tournaments and wrote with disgust of 'the impious who travelled that circuit' to the Dominican Bromyard in the fourteenth century who described 'the tournament of the rich as the torment of the poor', they saw the underside of the glamour that surrounded tournaments.[7] The ostentation and extravagance were bought at the expense of further impositions on the lower classes; food and lodging were often paid for with 'wooden money' tallies, which were never redeemed, while largess went to flattering minstrels and heralds instead of the needy poor. Occasionally a preacher would use the familiar background of a tournament to catch his audience's attention with a good story before drawing the inevitable moral. One of the most amusing of such tales comes from *Fasciculus Morum*, a preacher's handbook probably compiled near the end of Edward I's reign. It deals with two knights who had sworn an oath to share their winnings. One was brave and active and went happily to an announced tournament while the other was cowardly and stayed in bed, feigning illness, when he heard of the strength of the opposing party. The first fought bravely and won several horses, news which encouraged his companion to an immediate recovery when the tournament was safely over. The two began their journey home but when they reached the point where their ways separated the timid knight reminded his fellow of their arrangement and asked for his share of the horses from the tournament. The courageous knight was also quick-witted and reminded his companion that he had won two things in the tournament, 'good horses and good blows'. Out of loyalty to his oath he felt his companion should share in both, so he promptly drew his sword and gave him a good beating.[8] As the nature of this popular story shows, vigorous sermons, threats of ecclesiastical censure or the refusal of burial in consecrated ground for those killed in tournaments had little effect. The upper classes of medieval Europe enjoyed the jousts and tournaments and often travelled long distances to take part in them.

Nevertheless time brought changes. In the thirteenth century both England and France were ruled for the greater part of the century by kings who did not enjoy tournaments themselves and often opposed the holding of them. In addition neither Henry III nor Louis IX found it wise to favour these meetings since both were plagued at times during their reigns with rebellious vassals and did not wish to encourage any opportunity for further ill feelings and disorders. There is an interesting suggestion that Louis IX was particularly delighted when Charles of Anjou, his youngest brother, was named king of Sicily because Charles did nothing but make tournaments and jousts in the kingdom of France, much annoying the king.[9] In England too it was the young barons who were most interested in holding the great mass tournaments which were most likely to cause death, serious wounds and bad feeling and often involved the accompanying squires in riotous fighting in imitation of their masters. An English chronicler describes the young men's enthusiasm for such an encounter: 'With the coming of springtime, when kings are accustomed to go to war, when the woods are green, and the birds for joy sing their most cheerful songs, two strenuous young sons of the earl of Leicester, inspired by their fortunate relationship, and not only rich in money but also in the earl's retinue of innumerable soldiers'[10] then published a call throughout England for a tournament at Northampton in the fortnight after Easter. The year was 1265 and Simon de Montfort, earl of Leicester and leader of the rebellious barons, was not anxious to have his sons foment any more quarrels in the already divided kingdom and the meeting was forbidden.

Once England had returned to peace after the Barons' War and Edward, the king's son, had come to full age, tournaments in England came into special prominence. Edward was an enthusiastic advocate of strenuous knightly exercises. He first fought in a tournament at Blyth when he was only seventeen and still wearing light armour, while four years later, in 1260, he went off like William Marshal to enjoy a round of tournaments in France. He did not have William's success but he seems to have thoroughly enjoyed himself. The old-fashioned pattern of the tournament as a mass engagement in which the opposing sides dashed wildly over the countryside changed during the latter part of the thirteenth century. As armour became more elaborate and heavier cavalry was developed the tournament naturally tended to become more fixed in a single place and the gradual softening of manners led to it becoming a more noticeably social occasion. Edward's own passion for the tournament, an enthusiasm which he shared with the younger members of his baronage, his absorption in the Arthurian cult and his concern to set up regulations controlling some of the worst excesses of riotous behaviour at such events worked together to ensure more decorous behaviour. The tournament became a recognised social institution formally attended by the court until the wars in France and Scotland caused the king to prohibit such meetings. Another parallel development in the thirteenth century was the entertainment known as the Round Table. Considerable argument has arisen as to whether this function should properly be called a tournament, for it certainly was not a mass mêlée, or whether it should be considered merely a game in which jousting was one of the activities. Such individual contests between knights using blunted weapons were considerably less dangerous both for the participants and for public order, although fatal accidents did still occur. In any case, the development of tournaments and jousts over the years changed them gradually from rude contests of brute force to highly formalised ceremonials with relatively little danger.

The passion for tournaments, and their frequency at the end of the thirteenth century, is clearly illustrated in the fragmentary accounts of John of Brabant and Thomas and Henry of Lancaster for their expenses between November 1292 and May 1293.[11] John, who had married King Edward's daughter Margaret in 1290, was the oldest, aged twenty-two, while Thomas and Henry, sons of King Edward's younger brother Edmund, were adolescents of fourteen and twelve. The three youths travelled around England spending considerable time with the king's court or with other members of the royal family, and were accompanied by a substantial retinue. When they visited the young Prince Edward's household at Kennington the prince's clerk recorded that John was travelling with thirty horses and twenty-four valets while Thomas and Henry had thirty horses and twenty-one valets. Entertaining on such a scale was costly for their host who absorbed on his account all their expenses for the four day stay. In the five months covered by the accounts John of Brabant, accompanied by Thomas and Henry, was present at no less than six tournaments, all held at various spots in the Midlands. The listed expenses suggest the total preoccupation with sport of all kinds, for they included the transfer of John's heavy chargers to the various tournaments, expenses for saddles, arms and armour bought and repaired, as well as the care and feeding of the falcons and the cost of recovering one that was lost. There were indoor amusements too. John played chess at the Christmas festivities and lost 2s, while payments to minstrels are dotted throughout the accounts. Two unexpected items catch the eye. One of John's servants seems to have overlooked his master's nightshirt

43. *Two fifteenth-century jousting knights, illustrating the arms displayed and tabards and horse trappings*

when packing at Berwick for the trip to Jedburgh and a hackney had to be hired to bring it on – an early case of the forgetful traveller. The nightshirt was no doubt a specially treasured item for most medieval men slept naked, a cold prospect in December in Scotland. In May, while John and the young Lancasters were near London, John was stirred to unpremeditated hospitality. He saw the abbot of Jumièges and his companion passing his lodging on the way to the royal court, drew them into his lodging and entertained them to dinner. One item not mentioned in the accounts is also interesting. Both John and his young wife were in England, for Princess Margaret had not yet left the English court, but there is no mention of her anywhere, although the accounts do accord two occasions in April and May when the young men spent some time with the 'daughters of the king'.

Of all the social occasions of the reign of Edward I, that English king who knew so well how to touch the imagination of his nobles and his people, none was more impressive than the great Whitsun feast of May 1306.[12] It was designed to serve several purposes and used all the impressive and dramatic effects open to the court to further the king's aim of subduing Scotland. With the murder of John Comyn and the assumption of the throne of Scotland by Robert Bruce all hopes of a peaceful settlement there had broken down. The king prepared for war in Scotland soon after Easter with the knowledge that he must reinforce his reserve of knights for the army. There was not a very large group from which to choose, perhaps 1500 all told, and men of small incomes, with lands worth £20 to £40 a year, often attempted to avoid knighthood because of the rising expense of having to provide their own equipment and horses. Edward needed to attract such men since his almost constant campaigns in Wales, Scotland and Gascony had left large gaps in their numbers. On this occasion the king tried a new approach. Prince Edward was now twenty-two and had not yet been knighted and it was customary for a king to dub knights on special occasions throughout the year. Normally these would be his sons or very highly born young men, although their close kin might also be included, for there was a bond of unity between young men who had been knighted at the same time which encouraged a sense of mutual loyalty. Edward used these facts to his own advantage. He had the Whitsun feast proclaimed as the occasion when he would knight his son but he also invited all those who might wish to become knights to join the occasion in London. The king offered all who came a gift of their required equipment – helmet, hauberk, sword, lance and spurs – with the material for ceremonial robes and bed – to be taken from the royal wardrobe at the king's cost. They would then be dubbed by the king's own son on the same day as he himself was knighted. It was a tempting invitation for any adventurous young man with a spark of ambition. It meant a trip to London as the king's guest, the free acquisition of expensive equipment, a seat at the royal banquet after the ceremony and the prestige which would result from being one of the 'class' of knights of the Prince of Wales. In addition there would be the excitement of a stay in the crowded capital.

The invitation seems to have been accepted by some 300 men, mostly young members of the knightly class. As 22 May approached there converged on London not only the aspirants accompanied by their squires and grooms but also the state officials and their re-tinues, the great lords with their womenfolk and households, the ecclesiastics, and the mass of minstrels and hucksters hoping to share in the largess and spending encouraged by such a festive occasion. London must have been crowded to capacity with a sudden ten per cent rise in its population. The result was inevitably pushing crowds, noise, smells and close-packed humanity. The prince and the most highly-born of the aspirants were comfortably lodged in the households of the king or the prince and could make the prayerful vigil expected of a prospective knight the night before the ceremony in the great spaces of Westminster Abbey church. The great majority of the other knights-to-be, officially guests of the king, were put up in tents and pavilions erected hastily in the area around the New Temple and each one had to struggle to find a few feet in the small temple church where he could kneel for the night. After dawn the young men were allowed a little rest from their prayers before they were ceremonially bathed, shaved and dressed in their fine robes for the dubbing itself. The king knighted his son within the palace and then the prince went with his entourage to the abbey to knight the others. The abbey was jammed for the colourful ceremony with crowds who bore little relation to the guests at the well-organised and carefully planned royal spectacles of our own time. Medieval crowds were dense and unruly while the available space was further impeded by the accepted practice of riding horses at special ceremonies, both in the church and in great halls. Suffocation was obviously a constant danger as the Prince of Wales stood on the altar steps to dub the aspirants led up to him through the restless, shifting crowd.

The knighting ceremony was followed by a great feast in the palace of Westminster where the king and his son with the court and the new knights sat down to celebrate the occasion. Such a medieval feast included delicacies as well as normal fare – peacocks, swans and cranes in addition to the more prosaic muttons and bacons, white rolls and wafers instead of heavy dark bread – and, of course, enormous quantities of wine. The chroniclers found nothing out of the way about the food served. Their attention was drawn by the presentation to the king and the prince by a 'multitude of minstrels' of a device, or subtlety, of two swans decked in gold net or pipings, covered by an embroidered green silk. The purpose was to have the new knights vow some deed of arms before this device. Such a vow was a commonplace of the ceremony of knighting, and also figures frequently in literature, but to link it both with the minstrels' device and the actual war in Scotland made it interesting to the chroniclers. They report that King Edward himself vowed to set out for Scotland to revenge the insult offered by Robert Bruce, his son promised not to stay two consecutive nights in one place until he had fulfilled, as far as possible, his father's vow to arrive in Scotland while the other knights vowed to set out for Scotland with the king while he lived and after his death with the prince. In May 1306 Edward was already sixty-seven and ailing as his long stay at Lanercost later in the year demonstrated. The knighting ceremony at the Whitsun feast and the celebrations around it served royal policy by ensuring manpower for the Scottish expedition whose shadow lay heavy over the whole affair. For many of the young men who had travelled up to London to be a part of the glittering occasion it was a highlight in their humdrum lives to be recalled and retold time and time again. They would always remember the splendours of the royal feast and the crowd of musicians, tumblers, acrobats and assorted minstrels who displayed their skills before the elegant company and were royally rewarded for doing so.

Medieval nobles not only went to feasts and tournaments whenever the opportunity offered, they even occasionally wrote books about the chivalrous life. Geoffrey de Charny, a highly respected knight of the mid-fourteenth century who served King John II of France as his standard-bearer and was killed at the battle of Poitiers (1356), wrote *Le Livre de Chevalerie* a few years before his death.[13] In his description of the types of fighting with which a proper knight could occupy himself he still distinguished between jousts and tournaments and considered the latter more honourable because of the expense and effort as well as the danger of wounds and death each time. Charny's whole outlook was a very practical one for he also recognised that such activities could provide the expert with

44. *Aristocratic dance of the type approved by Geoffrey de Charny*

great renown and rich rewards. However, much of his treatise is spent detailing the virtues a knight should have and his required standard of conduct. Much of this is singularly traditional and old-fashioned, both in its piety and its pattern of virtues, but it is also very practical. Charny disapproved of dice when played for greed since it frequently caused the players to suffer great losses, and also of the newly popular *jeu de paume* (an early ancestor of tennis) which, he declared, made men lose their goods and inheritance. It was more suitable for a knight to joust, to talk, to dance and sing decorous songs in the company of ladies.[14] In this same pragmatic vein Charny talks of the right of young maidens and ladies of high estate to wear fine clothes and be adorned with precious jewels, a display he does not consider suitable for men. His reasoning is unexpected. The veteran knight declared that men can go where they like among men and in various countries, they can tourney and joust and join many companies, while women have none of these opportunities. Therefore men can always display their riches in many places and many ways while women, who are kept at home and seldom travel, can only display their goodness, beauty and their estate by their rich clothes and sparkling jewels on social occasions. Such a display can help maidens to marry more suc-cessfully while married women in this fashion please their husbands and show their proper rank.[15]

The value of tournaments and jousts, and the ladies' presence at them, as an outlet for display of status and prestige became more and more important during the course of the fourteenth and the first half of the fifteenth century. The accession of the young Edward III, who shared his grandfather's enthusiasm for jousts and courtly ritual, meant that tournaments were particularly popular during the early years of his long reign, before the turn of the tide of the war in France and the illness of the Black Prince had thrown a pall of gloom over English confidence. In the years before the Black Death King Edward was surrounded by a lively and warlike group of young nobles who rejoiced in chivalric exploits and were remark-able fighters. The early 1340s were enlivened for the English court and the knightly class by a whole series of tournaments in different places in which the king and his retinue might appear in some extraordinary costume. At Smithfield in 1343, for example, the king and his accompanying knights were dressed as the pope and twelve cardinals and challenged all comers. The most spectacular of these occasions was at Windsor in 1344 where the king proclaimed a great tournament for mid-February 'for the recreation and solace of knightly men who delight in the exercise of arms'. Knights were invited from overseas and a general safe-conduct was issued for all who came, embracing themselves, their servants and their goods, both coming and going, and in force for three weeks after the date of the meeting.[16] Nevertheless it was mainly an English affair, attended by the Black Prince and many of the important nobles of the realm. Queen Philippa was present too, with the royal children, the Queen Mother Isabella and many ladies of rank. The proceedings were begun with a great feast. A chronicler assures us that there was abundant food and freely offered drink, while in the evening the lords and ladies joined in various dances and entertainments. Obviously this was one of the occasions when Charny would have approved of the ladies displaying their very finest clothes and jewels. The company enjoyed the three days of jousting and the assorted melodies and diversions provided by the minstrels who flocked to such a profitable showcase to display their talents.

After the jousts were over the king proclaimed that none of the lords or ladies should leave, but should await his solemn pronouncement the following day. In the morning the king and queen in their ceremonial royal robes, followed by the lords and ladies in their best attire, went in procession to hear mass in the great chapel of Windsor. Afterwards the king formally vowed to set up a Round Table in the same state and style as that of King Arthur, while the leading earls, including Henry of Lancaster, vowed to assist in this. The trumpeters and drummers then played the company in to another opulent feast. Plans were even set on foot for the erection of a special building at Windsor to house the Round Table but the project was never carried through.[17] On this occasion King Edward had successfully used pageantry, a superb sporting event before knowledgeable spectators – for in essence this was what a fourteenth-century tournament was – and a generous programme of hospitality and entertainment to reinforce the support and enthusiasm he needed among his fighting class as the war with France rose in intensity. His institution of the Order of the Garter a few years later (probably in 1348) appears to mark the transmutation of the idea of nostalgic devotion to the ideals of the Arthurian Round Table to a more military ideal emphasising an overriding allegiance to the king and the fellow members of the order. The successes of Crécy and Calais may have encouraged such a shift in outlook. In any case, the Order of the Garter which had as its leading member the king's eldest son and gathered the leading warriors of England and Gascony in a prestigious association, served as still another encouragement to the military commanders the king so desperately needed.

The passion for tournaments was just as prevalent in fourteenth-century France as in England, although after the capture of John II French kings were not personally active. Outstanding among the French knights on the tournament circuit in the second half of the fourteenth century was Jean Boucicaut, whose career as a crusader has already been mentioned. Born of a noble family he was brought up at court in the retinue of the dauphin (the future Charles VI) and from his earliest youth showed his passion for arms. His biographer describes with enthusiasm the young man's single-minded pursuit of excellence in knightly skills. The training programme was a rigorous one. Boucicaut would do a somersault fully armed except for his bascinet, jump fully armed to the back of his horse and exercise in full armour to get accustomed to it and to strengthen his arms. He would leap from the ground to the shoulders of a man on horseback, using only one hand to grasp the man's sleeve. Other skills were needed in the attacks on walled towns which formed such a major part of medieval fighting. Boucicaut practised climbing a high ladder against a wall while wearing armour and using only his arms. When he had removed the armour he went up the ladder using only one hand. He practised too the climber's manoeuvre of scaling the narrow space between two walls by using his back and his feet. The physical strength so avidly sought and maintained was further emphasised by a practice which suggests a modern rodeo – the trick of putting one hand on the saddle bow of a great horse and the other between its ears so as to wrestle it to the ground.[18]

These descriptions of Boucicaut's physical feats with their implication that staying in training was as important for a medieval knight as for a modern athlete help to explain why the upper classes, aided by their better diet and better living conditions, were frequently superior physical specimens. Recent archaeological evidence gained from the examination of the skeleton of Bartholomew Burghersh, a leading knight and diplomat during the reign of Edward III, reinforces such a conclusion. Burghersh appears to have been 5 ft 10 in tall, erect and powerful, with what the archaeologists describe as 'an elegant masculine figure', i.e. broad-shouldered and narrow-waisted. His right arm and side were markedly more developed than his left, undoubtedly due to his constant use of weapons. There is evidence of the fracture of a couple of ribs, a twisted ankle and some wear of the right elbow joint – all likely injuries during a strenuous life. He apparently had only slight suggestions of osteoarthritis, a common disease in the Middle Ages for a man in his fifties but, most surprising of all, he had all but one of his teeth at the time of his death. Unlike modern men he did not suffer from periodontal problems but his teeth were worn down almost to the roots, probably caused by the prevalence of a very coarse, tough diet requiring constant chewing[19] – the factor which has brought about the same condition in most elderly Eskimos. This kind of detailed evidence, sadly all too rare, for Burghersh's skeleton could only be identified because of its undisturbed burial inside Walsingham chapel, helps to create a more accurate picture of the physical appearance of these strapping knights.

The most famous joust of the late fourteenth century was that arranged by Boucicaut in 1390 at St-Inglevert between Calais and Boulogne. It was a splendid occasion, vividly illustrated and exhaustively described in Froissart's chronicle.[20] The war between England and France was in another of its periods of prolonged truce and Boucicaut obviously chafed at such boring tranquility. He had the joust cried three months in advance throughout England, Spain, Italy and Germany to all princes, knights and squires so that all would have the time to make the trip if they so desired. The heralds

45. Presentation by a herald of letters proclaiming a tournament

who carried his challenge across Europe explained that Boucicaut and two companions would hold the field for thirty days (20 March–20 April) and would joust with any knight or squire who approached. No combats were allowed on Fridays, Saturdays or Sundays since the longstanding Truce of God forbade fighting on those days. Those who were enemies of the kingdom of France would run a course of five strokes with sharpened lances, friends of the kingdom were restricted to blunted lances. The organisation required on this occasion suggests how elaborately the joust had developed and the large part now played by pageantry. As the date approached Boucicaut and his companions set up their elegant pavilions, shaded by a great elm on which were hung two shields, one denoting peace, the other war. Beside them lay ten prepared lances, five sharp, five blunted. A horn hung from a branch of the tree and each challenger was required to sound the horn and strike the shield appropriate to the contest he wished. Each shield also carried the arms of the three defending knights so that a challenger could choose which champion he wished to engage. Beyond the defenders' tent was yet another handsome pavilion which provided space for the arming and retiring of the knights from a distance as well as being a place where they could refresh themselves. Everything was suitably arrayed and Boucicaut had taken care to lay in a generous supply of good wine and all the necessary provisions at his own expense. Although this was supposedly a non-warlike social occasion there is little doubt that the jousts at St-Inglevert reflected the continuing antagonism between English and French knights which sharpened the excitement and vigour of the combats. Some forty foreign and one hundred and twenty English knights took up Boucicaut's challenge. The English contingent included some of the most important nobles of the realm, John Holland, step-brother of Richard II, Henry of Derby, Percy, Clifford and Philip Courtenay. According to Boucicaut's biographer, Derby's father, John of Gaunt, wrote to the French knight that he had sent his son to learn from him and begged that Boucicaut would joust ten strokes with young Henry. The jousts took place with all the proper formalities but were, perhaps fortunately, rather inconclusive so that everyone could withdraw with their honour satisfied and no deaths or very serious wounds.[21]

During the fifteenth century tournaments proliferated but became more and more occasions of pageantry, social splendour and great expense, a fact which is most vividly illustrated by the treatise on tournaments written in the middle of the century by King René of Anjou. René was a highly cultured man, himself an author and a not very good poet. With rights and claims to a whole string of territories – Sicily, Anjou, Provence, Lorraine – much of his time was spent in unsuccessful battles. In the end he was forced to restrict himself to his French territories of Anjou and Provence where he presided over a cultured and colourful court which was the epitome of late medieval civilisation. His daughter Margaret of Anjou married Henry VI of England and proved exceedingly unpopular in England but Good King René is still remembered with affection in Aix-en-Provence where he spent his final years and, to the lasting profit of his Provençal subjects, introduced the muscadet grape, so generally grown in Anjou. His treatise on tournaments, he carefully explains, was not meant to be an exact description of the current methods of tourneying, but a combination of German, Flemish and French customs, proposed in order to arrive at an ideal form.[22] René of Anjou was far more interested in ceremonial, decor and costumes than the actual combats which were meant to be the reason for tournaments,

46. *René of Anjou*

He also accords a far more important place to the ladies in his arrangements for there were to be feasts and dances every evening at which the ladies could shine. In fact, in this relatively brief treatise there is no real description of the manner of fighting, although it is described as a mêlée, not as individual jousts. On the other hand,

René is informative and detailed about ceremonial matters for the tournament had now become an event at which the defendant and the appellant chose their respective supporters. The expense had become too great for the average impecunious knight and only knights banneret, who supported a retinue of followers, or important lords were welcome guests. Rene also gives full importance to the role of the heralds and pursuivants as what might be called the working referees of the affair. Judges were chosen from a roster of suitable knights and squires by the defendant lord and the heralds then proclaimed the tournament at court and through the kingdom. René carefully delineates the necessary lists and grandstands and then launches into the proper etiquette. There were careful regulations about how the lords should arrive and in what order they should enter the town. They should display their arms on a long stick at the door of their lodging and their banners from an upstairs window, clearly signifying where each lord could be found and adding to the holiday atmosphere of the chosen rendezvous. Since the helms and banners of all the contestants had to

47. The display of helms and banners in a convenient cloister

be displayed before the tournament began, in order to ensure they had a right to take part, René considered it most practical if the judges could be put up in an adjoining monastery, since a good cloister was an ideal place for such a display – it must have been rather disturbing to monastic routine. The average tournament lasted four to five days – the day of arrival, the day of display, the day for all the contestants to take the necessary oath, the day or two days of the tournament itself, followed by the most impressive of all the dinners and the awarding of the prize to the outstanding tourneyer.

In addition to such full-fledged tournaments there also continued to be jousts for the eager knight anxious to engage in his favourite sport. These became more elaborate versions of the type Boucicaut had put on at St-Inglevert, centred on a chosen place marked by a particular device to allow jousting to all comers against the holders of the place. This was now called the *pas d'armes* and René of Anjou was famous for these too. The accounts for the *pas de la Pastourelle*, held at Tarascon in 1449, suggest the emphasis he put on the entertainment aspect of such a spectacle and the expense involved. The players of the cymbals and the tabors only received one florin but Robinet the Frenchman who played that elegant instrument, the dulcimer, before the king and queen for several days during the festivities received six florins. Fifteen florins were also provided in largess for a herald, a pursuivant and a trumpeter – all essential for the proper management of the joust – while Viennois, who was the dauphin's herald, was given a further seventeen florins because he had stayed a full ten days at Tarascon, and no doubt had aided the affair with his expert advice. The centrepiece of this occasion was a beautiful lady dressed as a shepherdess, probably a relative of one of René's most faithful attendant lords, who sat in the middle of her sheep while two knights, representing happiness and discontent in love, fought on her behalf. It was all rather literary and precious and seems to have appealed primarily to a fairly small circle of King René's intimates. Of course, the king had to have new clothes for such an event and was resplendent on the opening day in a doublet of green damask and a mantle of black velvet, while he presented a relative taking part with a horse-covering of black velvet appliqued in green and white with a matching cloak.[23]

This procession of wandering knights seeking fame and fortune at tournaments and jousts suitably comes to a halt with Jacques de Lalaing, a famous knight of Hainault whose real life exploits and fame seem to outshine even such a literary version of the perfect knight as *Petit Jehan de Saintré*. Hainault at the beginning of the fourteenth century had been a small independent principality, more rural than urban and relatively rich. Life was pleasant there for the county had friendly relations with its most important neighbours and no serious internal problems. Count William I was a prudent and skilful ruler who married the sister of Philip VI of France and wedded his daughter Philippa to Edward III of England, while still keeping on good terms with his overlord, the Holy Roman Emperor. The count's court reflected a certain, somewhat old-fashioned, chivalric civilisation where feasts, jousts and tournaments succeeded each other. The merits of Hainault and its chivalrous knights were proclaimed during the fourteenth century by a notable group of writers, including the chroniclers Jean Le Bel and Froissart and also the poet Jean de Werchin, seneschal of Hainault at the end of the century and an early patron of Ghillebert de Lannoy.[24] The fifteenth-century author of the *Livre des Faits* of Jacques de Lalaing continued the Hainault enthusiasm for describing knightly deeds, though the county was now one of the territories under the rule of the duke of Burgundy, for he proudly proclaimed that Hainault produced the flower of chivalry. It was the custom there, he says, that as soon as a nobleman came to an age competent to bear arms he should never cease, no matter what labours or perils beset him, to seek high deeds of arms and to take far-flung voyages so as to spread his renown by his prowess.[25] Lalaing, who was born in 1421 in the family castle near Douai, was a perfect subject for an author of such convictions. His biographer emphasises his all-round skills – sent at seven to learn French and Latin he soon became proficient in both while also acquiring the science of the hunt and of falconry. His career was launched as a result of the patronage extended to him by the young duke of Cleves, the nephew of Duke Philip the Good of Burgundy. Cleves was much taken by the youth when he was on a visit to the castle of Lalaing and urged Jacques to join him at the Burgundian court. The two became close friends who quickly learned to joust and to prove themselves successful in feats of arms. Jacques scored many successes at tournaments, sometimes embarrassing ones as on one occasion at Nancy where two ladies were attracted by the good-looking youth – one gave him a diamond, the other a handsome ruby ring – and each sought him as a cavalier. It would have been discourteous to refuse, but Jacques, on this occasion, beat a hasty retreat from any romantic complications.[26]

His young manhood was spent primarily on the road, for he travelled in Spain, Portugal, France, Italy and England and fought in tournaments and lists some twenty-two times. Everywhere he was met with generous gifts and distinguished hospitality, described with naive satisfaction by his biographer, for the young knight rarely had to pay his own bills. One of the more unusual of his voyages in search of further glory was an expedition to Scotland, first planned in July 1448.[27] Lalaing had decided to challenge Sir James Douglas, the brother of the earl, because of his noble person and great renown. He gained the agreement of the duke of Burgundy who allowed his herald to carry the letters of challenge to 'a little city', Edinburgh, where he found Sir James and the earl. Douglas was delighted and, having received permission from King James of Scotland, returned his consent to such an exercise of arms which were to be carried out according to the customs of Scotland. The whole process was a leisurely one for Jacques' letter of July was only answered by Sir James at the end of September. By the time Jacques had received the response, decided on his companions – his uncle and a highly esteemed Breton squire at the Burgundian court, Hervé de Meriadec – and gathered his equipment it was late in the year. It was December before they were ready to take ship from Sluis with their armour and harness for their meeting with Douglas and for 'any adventures which might happen to them on the way'.[28] They arrived in Scotland without mishap and the final details for the meeting were agreed. The Scottish king was to be the judge and set Stirling as the place for the encounter on 25 February. The two sides would fight on foot, three against three, with lance, sword, axe and dagger, to the finish or until the king stopped the fight. Lalaing's biographer describes how the French challengers entered the lists in their richly furred robes of black velvet and satin with all their arms and equipment carried behind them in two coffers and gives a blow by blow account of each of the struggles between the three opponents. There is ample evidence that all the men who wrote of such knight errants, as well as many of the noble chroniclers, loved to describe tournaments and jousts in overwhelming and repetitive detail. Undoubtedly they knew that their readers were knowledgeable and passionately interested in such contests – their reports can truthfully be described as the sports pages of the Middle Ages. At least according to the French author, the French party got the best of the fighting and the Scottish king exercised his prerogative of stopping the contest, of admonishing them all to be good friends since they had accomplished their exercise of arms valiantly and honestly. Afterwards he gave a great feast and honourable gifts. They then left Scotland and went on to England where they were rather disappointed that the English king refused to give them any licence for tourneying nor were they very enthusiastically received. Lalaing and his companions returned to Flanders where a Welsh squire had already announced that he proposed to fight him at Bruges.

48. A fifteenth-century tournament

Lalaing was considered the flower of chivalry in the early fifteenth century. He was handsome, strong and vigorous, generally devout and virtuous (and 'chaste most of the time'), loyal and of noble spirit. According to a later description of him 'he bore the name of a knight but the courage of a king'.[29] Yet this doughty fighter and renowned champion was to die in 1453 at the age of thirty-two, hit by a stray cannon ball in a campaign at Ghent. The day of the knight with lance and sword, challenged but not totally overthrown by the skill of the archer, was to be eclipsed by the anonymous lower class artilleryman. Tournaments continued to exist as almost purely social occasions but they were no longer the path to renown and fortune.

CHAPTER TEN

THE ADVENTURERS

The adventurer hopes to escape from his confining circumstances by finding the road to honour and riches through his own exertions. In medieval terms that meant that anyone with even the slightest pretensions to noble birth generally sought the path of military success since it provided the most glittering rewards. Although merchant venturers were to be found in all the great port cities, gradually sending their ships to more and more distant places, they were not accepted as part of the upper-class world, nor shared its fascination with the social rituals of court, tournament and war. For young men on the fringes of such society success in actual wars or in some suitable military expedition was the best way to enhance their valour as well as their profits. Most adventurers in the twelfth and thirteenth century were drawn into the great crusading current which swept them off to the Holy Land and the surrounding territories where lordships might be acquired by a capable and fortunate knight. The fall of Acre (1291) put an end to this traffic though some erstwhile crusaders continued to lead the life of a wandering knight and, if fortunate, gained both riches and a chronicler to report their exploits with suitable flourishes.

Roger Flor was one of the most successful of such men in the late thirteenth century. The son of Emperor Frederick II's falconer, his family had been left penniless when his father was killed fighting for Conradin, Frederick's son. Roger came to the attention of a friendly Templar who arranged for him to become a sergeant in the Templars because of his abilities as a fighting seaman. The young man had several successes as a ship's commander for the

Templars and was in charge of the *Falcon*, the Templars' largest galley, at Acre at the time of the final Moslem attack. When it became obvious that Acre was doomed Roger turned his attention from continuing the fight to the profits to be reaped by charging the terrified noblewomen still in the besieged city exorbitant amounts for their passage to safety on his galley. After that profitable exploit the ex-Templar went on to a dashing career as a mercenary leader, fighting first for the Aragonese ruler of the island of Sicily and then for the Byzantine emperor at Constantinople. Muntaner, the Aragonese chronicler, who served as one of Roger's leading officials, describes in great detail the deeds of his master and the Catalan company he commanded. For a time Roger enjoyed enormous success, for he was given the daughter of the king of the Bulgarians as his wife, loaded with honorific titles and paid generously. But the wheel of Fortune, that favourite medieval symbol for the sudden rise and fall of men, spun swiftly in his case. The emperor's eldest son distrusted this ambitious mercenary and his rapacious followers and in 1306, during a week of feasting in Adrianople to which Roger and his retinue had been ceremoniously invited, arranged an ambush in which almost all the guests, including Roger, were murdered. Soon after the remaining members of the Catalan company were attacked and reduced to a straggle of mercenaries.[1]

The outbreak of the Hundred Years War, with its consequent need by both French and English kings for large numbers of military commanders, provided the adventurous and unemployed knight with golden opportunities, in the real as well as the figurative sense of that term. The best and most able, like Sir John Chandos and Bertrand du Guesclin, proved themselves in battle and then rose to greater responsibilities and rewards, having been discovered to have not only prowess but wisdom. At a more crassly opportunistic level there were the men who come to life as minor characters in Froissart, such as Sir John Hawkwood, the famous mercenary commander in Italy, and the Gascon, Bascot de Mauléon, who used their profits from pillage and levies from the terrified countryside to adopt aristocratic airs and the rich trappings of the great. Successful mercenary captains, despite Froissart's eulogistic remarks on their fighting abilities, were no more than enterprising adventurers whose swords were for hire to the highest bidder. They and their unruly companies devastated southern France, Spain and Italy during the second half of the fourteenth and the first half of the fifteenth century, leaving poverty and terror in their wake. Since most of these men had no established base, they can hardly be called travellers despite their footloose wanderings in search of a livelihood, although they added to the growing number of medieval men who had personally covered large expanses of Europe.

During this same period the level of geographic knowledge in Europe was rising dramatically. It was built up primarily by the sailors and merchants who were the natural spearhead of such an advance and whose reports were beginning to interest a wider public, including both rulers and intellectuals. The popularity of Marco Polo was particularly great, but there were also others. One of the better known was Nicolo Conti, a fifteenth-century Venetian trader who spent twenty-five years in the Far East. He had begun his career as a young merchant in Damascus where he learned Arabic and then travelled with a merchant caravan over the Arabian deserts to the Euphrates and Bagdad. He sailed down the Persian Gulf to India, travelled up such great rivers as the Ganges and the Irawaddy and went on to Siam, Java and southern Cathay before returning to the west. When he got back to Venice in 1441 he was ordered by Pope Eugenius IV, as a penance for his forced conversion to Mohammedanism, to tell the story of his travels to the pope's secretary. Poggio Bracciolini was a prominent humanist, passionately interested in news of unusual journeys, so he wrote down with enthusiasm all that Conti told him. The Venetian's reports included the current fabulous tales of Prester John but he also described for the first time for a western audience the practice of suttee in India and the existence of the white elephant of Siam who was worshipped as a god.[2] Conti was undoubtedly a spellbinding storyteller as Pero Tafur, a travelling Spanish noble, bears witness. He met the Venetian on his way back to Europe during a stay at the monastery of St Catherine at Mt Sinai and the two men travelled together across the desert to Cairo. Tafur remarked that the journey took fifteen days and was very hard 'but with the pleasure of hearing such good things from Nicolo de Conti I did not notice the labour'.[3]

Adventurers turned to the west as well as to the east and the Canary Islands were among the first places to be both explored and exploited. The position of this small archipelago of seven inhabited and six desert islands in the south Atlantic off the north-western coast of Africa attracted explorers. The Canaries had been described by the early geographers Strabo and Pliny, who glorified them with the optimistic titles of Islands of the Blest or the Fortunate Isles. Despite such attractive nomenclature the islands were little visited during the earlier Middle Ages for the southern Atlantic terrified both Christian and Moslem sailors for many centuries. The European fear of the Sea of Darkness where the sun set was shared by Moslem commentators who described it as 'the green sea of gloom'. Ibn Khaldun, the great Moslem historian of the fourteenth century, even regarded the Atlantic as the 'boundless impenetrable limit of the west'.[4] However, as the tools of navigation and the construction of ships became more sophisticated and serviceable, the seagoing Europeans, especially the Genoese, the Catalans and the Portuguese, ventured into the Atlantic to explore the western coast of Africa. By the mid-fourteenth century Cape Bojador on the edge of the Rio de Oro (now the Spanish Sahara) was already a well-known landmark. About this time an anonymous Spanish Franciscan in his *Book of the Knowledge of all the Kingdoms, Lands and Lordships that are in the world* – a grandiloquent title for a rather cursory treatise – gave the names of most of the Canaries, as well as of the islands of Madeira and those of the Azores, where the author claimed he had travelled with some Moors. In addition, the wandering Franciscan described the Guinea coast in fair detail, as well as part of Africa south of the Atlas mountains, for he appears to have had some acquaintance with members of Genoese and Venetian caravans who penetrated deep into the interior. The friar was sufficiently medieval to feel that it was important to illustrate his texts with the arms, flags or devices of all the nations or kingdoms he mentions and, in many cases, it was their earliest representation.[5]

The generally fertile Canaries with a pleasant climate which has endeared them to waves of more modern travellers proved particularly tempting to medieval noble adventurers in their early excursions into the southern Atlantic. The ambitious perceived the possibility of gaining a kingdom for themselves even if it was minute and remote. In the mid-fourteenth century Luis de la Cerda, the great-grandson of Alfonso the Wise of Castile, whose father had fled to the French court during a time of dynastic upheaval in Castile, decided to claim sovereignty over the islands. Luis's background was by this time primarily French: he had married a French wife, bore the French title of count of Talmont, had been named admiral of France and commanded French troops in the war over the Breton succession. His appointment to a French embassy sent to the pope at Avignon after the truce of Malestroit (1343) with the obligation to negotiate final peace terms between France and Brittany gave him the opportunity he coveted. He appears to have been far more active in petitioning the French pope, Clement VI, for the title of Prince of the Fortunate Isles than in his other more mundane negotiating duties. In November 1344 the pope granted Luis the lordship of the Fortunate Isles as a perpetual vassal of the Holy See with the obligation to pay an annual tribute of 400 florins. At a public consistory at Avignon the pope crowned Luis with a gold diadem set with precious stones, naming him *Prince de la Fortune* and the ceremony was followed by a formal procession on horseback. More practically the pope also wrote to the kings of France, Sicily, Aragon, Castile and Portugal encouraging them to help the Prince in attempts to gain his newly bestowed islands 'for the exaltation of the faith and the spread of Christianity'. Don Luis led an abortive expedition to the Canaries, despite Portuguese complaints to the pope that their exploration had given them a prior claim, but he returned without even catching a glimpse of his Fortunate Isles. One of his captains managed to land on Lanzarote but achieved nothing further.[6] The princely title may have fed Luis's pride but had no foundation in reality for during the rest of the fourteenth century the Canaries remained an occasional stopping point for Genoese or Portuguese sailors who found useful supplies of goats' meat there, but no riches.

In 1402 two French knights, Jean de Bethencourt from Normandy and Gadifer de La Salle from Poitou, set out on a serious attempt to conquer, convert and even colonise the Canaries, hoping to gain prestige and fortune for themselves. The accounts of their voyage were originally written by their respective chaplains, Jean de la Verriere and Pierre Bontier, and recognised the contributions of both men to the expedition. Later, when La Salle withdrew leaving Bethencourt in sole command, Verriere's text was rewritten to give all the glory to Bethencourt, ignoring or appropriating the achievements of the Poitevin. The two men, despite the later statement by Verriere that they met casually in La Rochelle when Bethencourt already had his expedition in hand, were actually companions in arms from the household of Duke Louis of Orléans, frequently serving as his gambling partners. Both men had also been given money by the duke to help them take part in the French-led expedition of 1390 against the Moslems of the Barbary coast of North Africa. It was perhaps that voyage and the stories learned from Bethencourt's uncle, Robert de Braquemont, who had heard of the Canaries while in Spain, which encouraged their adventure when a period of peace in France made life there seem less attractive and profitable. Bethencourt seems to have had the predominant financial interest, as well as the sharper eye for feathering his own nest. He had considerable holdings in Normandy and by 1401 was probably laying plans for the voyage since in that year he sold property he owned in Paris and borrowed 7,000 *livres* on the security of his Norman lands. Gadifer de la Salle on the other hand was an older man with a far more distinguished record as a knight and soldier.

When the two adventurers set out from La Rochelle at the beginning of May they had two well-stocked ships and La Salle had rounded up some eighty volunteers to sail with them, primarily acquaintances with whom he had fought during his service in Gascony and Bigorre. Their declared aim was 'to see and explore all the country' with a view to conquering the islands and bringing the people to the Christian faith,[7] but they were primarily concerned with their own profit and reputation. They sailed across the Bay of Biscay to Galicia and then down the coast of Spain to Cadiz, plagued by dissension between the Normans and La Salle's Gascons, by encounters with French pirates and Spanish distrust.

They finally succeeded in leaving Cadiz at the end of June and after an eight day voyage landed at Lanzarote, the most northerly island of the Canaries and the closest to the coast of Africa. At first all went smoothly, for the natives were friendly and allowed them to build a fort they called the Rubicon, but dissension again broke out after an unsuccessful raid on Fuerteventura. Revolt was imminent among the seamen who saw no obvious riches to be found on these islands so Bethencourt decided to return to Spain and departed with Gadifer's ship, promising to return by Christmas. La Salle was left in charge at their fort but his position became more and more precarious. A Norman malcontent fomented rebellion against the Poitevin, sacking the stronghold of the Rubicon which had been left in his charge while Gadifer was on a seal hunt in the neighbouring desert island of Lobos. The rebel leader then departed for Spain with his supporters, having struck an agreement with the captain of a newly arrived ship, carrying off the arms, provisions and even the books of his chief as well as two dozen natives whom the ship's captain could trade as slaves.

Unfortunately Bethencourt's promised return was much delayed, for he was preoccupied with his efforts to entrench his own position at the court of Castile. He succeeded in having King Henry grant him the lordship of the Canary Islands and in return Bethencourt did homage to the king and was granted a twenty per cent duty on all exports from the island to Spain. The king also granted him 20,000 *maravedis* for the purchase of provisions to take back to the other members of the expedition. The news of Bethencourt's personal success was brought to La Salle when the ship from Spain, bearing the needed provisions, arrived at Lanzarote in the summer of 1403. Bethencourt himself, with his proud new title of King of the Canary, did not return until April 1404. During the interval La Salle had occupied his time with exploration of the other islands of the archipelago which he found fertile and healthy as well as potentially useful as a base against the Moslems on the nearby African coast. Having achieved the surrender and baptism of the native king of Lanzarote, Gadifer was anxious to explore further along the coast of Africa, of which he had gained some knowledge through the earlier report of the Spanish

Franciscan. However, Bethencourt's self-serving insistence on appropriating all the lands and their profits under his direct rule broke up the partnership and La Salle left for Spain, hoping to improve his own position. When he could get no hearing at the Castilian court he abandoned any further connection with the Canaries and returned to France where, after the murder of the duke of Orléans in 1407, he took service with Jean Boucicaut until old age seems to have forced him into a retirement made more comfortable by a royal grant of 100 gold francs.[8] Despite his record of misadventure in the Canaries Gadifer had a chivalric reputation which allowed him to be put in the same class as Bertrand du Guesclin, the successful French commander under Charles V. The author of Le Jouvencel, a popular and very moral military romance of the mid-fifteenth century, bracketed the two men as the type of good knights who died poor but whose renown continued beyond their lifetime and who were honoured by all.[9]

Bethencourt gained more success, some financial reward and considerable prestige. With La Salle's departure he had taken over sole rule of the islands and in 1405 he returned to Normandy to collect colonists representing many trades. A fleet of three ships left Harfleur in early May 1405 and arrived at Fuerteventura where they were welcomed with so many trumpets, clarions, drums, harps and other instruments that 'God's thunder would have been drowned in the noise of the music that they made'.[10] Banners and standards were unfurled, Bethencourt gave a solemn feast attended by the native kings of the islands of Fuerteventura and Lanzarote at which minstrels played and all the company appeared in its best embroidered clothes, Jean de la Verriere, Bethencourt's chaplain who wrote this account, remarks with naive satisfaction that there were at least fifty-four wearing silver lace.[11] From then on the picture was less rosy. Despite determined attempts, Bethencourt had no success in conquering Grand Canary, the largest of the islands. In fact he was blown off his course by contrary winds and found himself on the African mainland near Cape Bojador where he indulged in a successful raid against the local Moslems and their camels, causing destruction and bringing away some captives. By this time the Norman lord was becoming tired of these continued efforts which were not providing him with any real riches. He named his nephew Macicot, who had come with the other Norman colonists in 1405, governor of the conquered islands (Lanzarote, Fuerteventura and Ferro) and in December 1406 Jean sailed off never to return. According to his chaplain who left with him, the scene was one of unmitigated grief with Canarians weeping and lamenting even more than the Normans, while some even threw themselves into the sea and held on to his vessel.[12] They may have had some cause for their lamentations as Macicot proved to be so tyrannical that eight years later the queen of Castile sent three warships to control him.

Bethencourt returned to Castile, finding the king at Valladolid, was warmly greeted and listened to with interest. He put forward the need for a bishop for the islands to ensure the proper spread of the Christian faith and the king agreed to write to the pope suggesting a suitable candidate who knew the natives' language. Carrying the king's letters, Bethencourt went on to Rome in style, as he had taken care to have new liveries made for all the ten people in his retinue and he had been given two Spanish horses and a handsome mule by the Castilian king. The pope received him with pleasure, agreed to appoint the proposed bishop and congratulated Bethencourt as 'a man worthy of honour' who could now have 'a place among other kings and be mentioned in their list'.[13] This was about as far as the ambitious Norman got in having his royal pretensions recognised in Europe among people of rank. It is obvious that the title of 'King of Canary' caused confusion and surprise and it was only rich merchants or the occasional municipal official who pandered to his sense of importance by giving him presents of meat and wine as a distinguished visitor.

The French conquest of the Canaries was to have no permanent effect, and only the name of the little town of Santa Maria de Bethencuria on Fuerteventura preserves the memory of the adventurous Norman. When Macicot de Bethencourt was in trouble with Castile he sold his rights in the islands to the commander of the Castilian warships, but then went on to make a second bargain with Prince Henry the Navigator of Portugal. Jean de Bethencourt died in 1422 and bequeathed his rights to his brother Regnault. The whole tangle took many years to unravel but the final judgment favoured Castile and even Jean de Bethencourt himself had received little profit from his exploration and grant of a tax on exports since his last trading vessels with a rich cargo were lost at sea. The story of the efforts of these two knights is an early abortive example of the growing interest in exploration fuelled by the profits that were expected to flow from it.[14] When results were meagre discouragement set in and the venture was often abandoned. It also illustrates the practice of capturing the indigenous inhabitants of non-Christian territories to be sold as slaves. The slave trade had been a profitable element in Venetian and Genoese operations in the east during the Middle Ages. In the age of exploration it was to be tragically extended by the European powers to wholesale use in Africa.

Adventure was also to be found when the traveller took a new and different approach to lands already known. Such was the case of Bertrandon de la Broquière, councillor and head carving squire of Duke Philip the Good of Burgundy. Like Ghillebert de Lannoy, envoy for the duke and King Henry V ten years before, Bertrandon was sent by the duke on 'a certain distant voyage'.[15] In the account he later wrote at the duke's request he explained that his report on his travels was meant to inform anyone who wished to undertake the conquest of Jerusalem and to take an army overland. It could also be used by any noble lord who wished to travel to Jerusalem and back and needed to know all about the cities and the main geographical features he would encounter. It seems likely that Duke Philip was still trying to build up a collection of reconnaissance reports which could serve as reference for a future crusade and gave de la Broquière the task of exploring the Turkish lands which Lannoy had been unable to enter because of the civil war then raging. The pattern of Bertrandon's travels also suggests the duke's interest in seeking alternative routes for a crusading army. The squire was probably in his early thirties when he left the Burgundian court at Ghent in February 1431, for he had already been in the duke's service for twelve years. Bertrandon travelled south-east through France, Burgundy and Savoy to cross the Alps by the Mont-Cenis pass and referred briefly to the difficulties of an Alpine

49. Bertrandon still dressed in Turkish costume presenting his report to the duke of Burgundy

crossing when the road was deep with snow and it was dangerous to speak in a loud voice since it might provoke an avalanche.[16] After a trip that took him through Italy to Rome and then north to Venice, he sailed to Jaffa with only brief stops at the usual ports. Bertrandon performed the usual pilgrimages in and around Jerusalem but his account does not give the wealth of detail on the shrines, as well as on the ports, which Lannoy had provided. The squire's decision to return home from Beirut by the unusual inland route from Damascus to Aleppo, through the Taurus mountains and across the harsh Anatolian plateau to Constantinople, meant that he would cover territory untouched by Lannoy. The long land journey from Constantinople through the Balkans, Hungary, Austria and Germany and thus back to France would also provide useful information on an alternative route, since the older knight had gone from Danzig (Gdansk) through what is now Poland and Russia to Caffa in the Crimea. With the combined reports of two able and exact observers Duke Philip had an up-to-date and extensive store of information on Turkish and Moslem lands and their inhabitants as well as of the military problems inherent in pitting an army against them.

Bertrandon, however, not only made his remarkable trip through Moslem and Turkish lands but, in a daring move which suggests the nineteenth-century figure of Sir Richard Burton, even joined a Moslem caravan coming from Mecca and travelled with it to Aleppo. He was an acute observer and careful to report as fully as possible all that he learned along the way, often providing many interesting sidelights. For example, he described the way in which the Moslems in Jerusalem carefully registered all the pilgrims proposing to go to Mount Sinai, listing not only their names and ages but also their facial appearance, height and such distinguishing marks as signs of wounds. They then provided a duplicate of this list for the chief dragoman of Cairo to which many of these pilgrims proceeded after the Sinai visit. This approximation of the modern passport was provided for the security of the pilgrims so that the desert Arabs would not be tempted to retain any of them or to make substitutions. Bertrandon himself only got as far as Gaza because of ill health, but he was able to provide a detailed picture of the desert Arabs, their clothes, arms and the fine horses they rode. In Beirut he observed celebrations which included the firing of cannon and of a kind of fire 'bigger than the biggest lantern I have ever seen lit'. This was the Greek fire well-known to crusaders, a combustible mixture of sulphur, pitch, charcoal, naphtha, incense and tow which could be packed in wooden vessels and thrown lighted against enemy ships or besieged cities. The squire was immediately struck by its military possibilities, especially for terrifying horses in battle. So Bertrandon bribed the servant of his host to teach him all he knew about it and was even given some of the wooden moulds and other equipment since it appeared easy to make for those who knew how. Such knowledge could prove a useful gift for the duke of Burgundy.[17]

The caravan which Bertrandon joined at Damascus must have been an incredible sight. It was said to contain 3,000 camels and took two days and two nights to enter the city. Because it was primarily a religious group returning from the great pilgrimage to Mecca, the Koran, wrapped in a silk cloth painted with Moorish letters, was solemnly carried on a lead camel which was also draped in silk. The procession was headed by four minstrels and a great number of drummers, all drumming furiously, while the lead camel with its precious burden was surrounded by thirty armed men equipped with swords, crossbows and little cannons which they frequently fired. Following the Koran and its bodyguard came eight old men on running camels and a Turkish lady related to the Grand Turk in a well-caparisoned litter carried by two camels and covered with cloth of gold. The great caravan included Moslems from many eastern countries – Moors, Turks, Tartars, Persians and other unspecified barbarians. Bertrandon got most of his information from a renegade slave of the great lady who had already been three times to Mecca. The slave spent considerable time with the Burgundian squire, telling him about Mecca and the port of Djedda as well as about the Moslem belief in the importance of the pilgrimage to Mecca. The trip across the desert had been long and painful for it took forty days for the over 800 miles from Mecca to Damascus, although camels could travel at the rate of thirty miles a day. Bertrandon was intent on getting accurate information to take back to Duke Philip and took the precaution of checking the information he had received with a priest who was the chaplain of the consul of the Venetians at Damascus. The priest knew the Koran well so the squire asked him to write out the Koran and the deeds of Mahomet in Latin. The chaplain complied and Bertrandon carefully carried the manuscript with him on his travels and duly presented it to the duke on his return to France.[18]

Bertrandon had worked out a cover story for his wish to join the caravan – the need to get to Brusa in western Anatolia where he claimed to have a brother and the current danger of the sea voyage because of constant fighting. He had also acquired a Moslem guide and servant, Baraq, who agreed to find him a place in the caravan and to protect him but insisted that, for safety's sake, the Burgundian must wear native clothes. Baraq led him to the bazaar to outfit himself and the squire bought two long white robes down to his feet, a headcovering of cloth, a cloth strap, breeches of fustian to stuff his robe into when riding and a white plush overcoat which he covered with cloth and used as a blanket. His white belt, or

50. Equipment which would have been familiar to Bertrandon as the Duke's chief carving squire

tarquois, was well adorned and from it were suspended his sword and knives, as well as a leather spoon and salt cellar. Finally he completed his outfit with red knee-high boots and spurs. His many purchases in the bazaar gave him the opportunity to watch the famous swordsmiths of Damascus and their processes of planing, tempering and polishing and he joined his voice in the general chorus of praise for the swords of Damascus as the most beautiful and the best in Syria. He even bought one secretly and remarked with pleasure that it 'cut better than any other sword I have seen'. He then purchased a horse for his trip, a small sturdy one he had shod in the Damascus fashion which he described in careful detail and which astonished him by holding up for the seven weeks it took to journey to Brusa. On matters like these where de la Broquière had professional competence he is very detailed in his comparisons of Moslem ways with European methods. He mentions that the Moors were not interested in trotting horses, for their own only walked and ran and had the stamina to run for a long time, even when fed only with a handful of barley and of hay in the evening. It surprised him too that the mounts were constantly kept bridled, even in the stables at night when their rear foot was nobbled. He was astonished, given the European preference for stallions, that the Moors liked mares and sold them for high prices, while a great lord there felt no shame in riding a mare with the foal following after. As a last finishing touch for his departure on horseback Bertrandon bought a *tabolzan*, a small cymbal to be put at his saddlebow. It was struck with a small flat stick of copper and used in battle or skirmish to assemble men, so it was the custom of 'all reputed men' to have such a piece.[19]

The caravan set off every morning at the hour when the caravan chief ordered the chief drummer to strike his drum three times. Without a word being said everyone got ready and lined up on the road. De la Broquière was astonished by their silence, 'ten of us make more noise than 1,000 of them' and to his equal surprise no one wished to sing any *chansons de geste* at nights during the trip.[20] He describes the Moslem call to prayers, the calls given at daybreak to approximate the call of the muezzin, and the Moslems' personal habits. He even details their careful ablutions and how the important Moslems carried handsome leather water bottles for this purpose, slinging them under the stomachs of their horses or camels. It was all very new and very different but Bertrandon seems to have spent his time well and looked at his new acquaintances with an open mind. He was particularly enthusiastic about the two assistants he had – Baraq, who was his protector in the caravan, and Mahomet, a Mameluke, who guided him as far as Konya through the Taurus Mountains where it snowed so hard that if it had not been for Mahomet's help both he and his horse would have died of cold and hunger. His praise of both men shows a fairness of judgment that western Christians did not often apply to the Moslems they met. Bertrandon wrote of Baraq that he had found more candour and loyalty in him than in many Christians although all he had given him was a jar of green ginger which he had to force upon him. In describing Mahomet's essential assistance Bertrandon declared: 'I write this so that I shall remember that a man outside our faith, for the honour of God, has done me so much good.'[21] Mahomet was generous in his alms to the poor, too, and equally unwilling to take any presents when they parted although he finally accepted a thin headcovering of western cloth. Bertrandon appears to have been a good travelling companion, curious and even suffi-ciently flexible to try and learn some of the language. In Damascus he had encountered a Jew from Caffa who spoke good Tartar and Italian and helped him to make a wordlist of everything he would need for himself and his horse on the road. On his first day with the caravan when they stopped before Baalbek he consulted his list to discover what to call the barley and hay he needed for his horse. He was immediately surrounded by ten or twelve Turks who laughed uproariously when they saw his list and decided to take his education in hand. He admits that they repeated a word so many times and in so many ways that he could not help but remember it and by the time he left the company he knew how to ask for most of the things he needed. Some items of food aroused his curiosity. At Iskander north of Antioch he encountered an encampment of Turcomans who shared their food with his party. The provisions included cheese, grapes and a large amount of curdled milk 'which they call yoghourt'. This was eaten with a flat, very thin bread folded into a cone. The making of this bread and its rapid baking on an iron grill balanced on a trivet over a small fire fascinated him sufficiently to prompt a complete description of the process. When introduced to caviar at Brusa, however, he merely remarked that he ate it because there was nothing else and did not find it enjoyable.[22]

After Bertrandon had left the caravan he travelled with whatever companions he met along the way. He arrived at Konya (Iconium), the seat of the Karamanian emirate, with ambassadors from the king of Cyprus, who bore presents of a remarkable variety – fine Cyprus cloths, forty sugar loaves, two crossbows with a dozen winders and a rare peregrine falcon. At Kutahya, a big city ruled by the eldest son of the sultan of Turkey, Bertrandon stopped at a Turkish caravanserai, or inn. The following morning he discovered that one of his saddlebags was missing and lodged a complaint. He was interviewed by a Turkish slave, a man around fifty and of some authority, who spoke to him in Italian. Bertrandon declared that he was French and had come from Damascus in Baraq's company. When he was accused of being a spy he fell back on his story that he was on his way to join his brother at Brusa but had been unable to go by sea because of the fighting between the Venetians and the Genoese. It emerged from the conversation that his interviewer had once been in Paris and Bertrandon decided that he had been among the captives taken at the great Christian defeat at Nicopolis. They both seem to have enjoyed the meeting for the slave was very good to him and helped him to get back his property.[23] Bertrandon then went on to his declared goal and found Brusa an important merchant city where markets for the different goods were in different parts of the city. Most of the merchandise consisted of luxury goods – silks, jewels, pearls, cottons – but there was also an extensive slave market where Christians, both men and women, were sold.

When he finally arrived in Pera, just across the harbour from Constantinople, de la Broquière met a Neapolitan who claimed to have been married in the land of Prester John and wanted Bertrandon to go there with him. The squire recorded that he asked him many questions and wrote down the answers but would not vouch for them, for 'if he told me the truth or not, I am only reporting'.[24] The information that he acquired was an interesting mix of fact and legend. The Neapolitan provided some accurate details about Ethiopia and mentioned such unusual African animals as lions, elephants, giraffes and gorillas. He included also such fabulous beasts as the unicorn (perhaps this was a rhinoceros?) and an extra-ordinary serpent the length of 150 greyhounds that could carry its head five fathoms high with a body like the mast of a great ship and a spur under its tail. This extraordinary fantasy, which reminds us of a medieval version of the Loch Ness monster, was balanced by the accurate description of the rainy winter season in those south-ern lands with wheat being sowed in December and harvested in February. When de la Broquière reached Constantinople the adventurous part of his voyage was over and he gives an unre-markable description of the imperial city only twenty years before its final fall to the Turks. The court still had contacts with Europe, however, for the Catalan merchants with whom he lodged took him to dinner at the emperor's palace. When one of the merchants told a courtier that Broquière was a representative from the duke of Burgundy the squire was immediately asked if it was true that the duke of Burgundy had taken *La Pucelle* (Joan of Arc), as that seemed to them impossible. The squire explained the course of events by which the Burgundian soldiers had captured the Maid but had then handed her over to the English, which astonished them.[25] Joan had been captured in May 1430 and burnt at Rouen in May 1431 so it is an interesting footnote that this locally important event, which went unmentioned by many European chroniclers, should seem a matter of concern in the far-off Byzantine capital.

By the end of January 1433 Bertrandon had left Constantinople for Adrianople in northern Thrace. The territory was under Turkish rule and the Burgundian witnessed and described the visit of the Grand Turk and his caliph. Bertrandon seems to have seen a good deal of the Turkish court for he was then travelling with the ambassador of the duke of Milan. When they started for home together their passage was made much easier by the sultan's dis-patch of a slave to serve as guide, for whatever the slave demanded was immediately done for them. They arrived in Belgrade, at this time the outpost of the kingdom of Hungary, where Bertrandon finally put down his opinions and judgments about the Turks.

Here are no mere traveller's tales but a factual report by a trained observer informing his master. The squire describes their horses, their arms, their method of fighting, their speed and silence on the road and the way they set their army up for battle. He estimated the number and kind of Christian men-at-arms needed to fight them and emphasised the necessity for light, not heavy, armour as the Turks were so mobile.[26]

From Belgrade Bertrandon's travels continued on a more commonplace itinerary and the observant squire could turn his attention to more familiar matters which still excited his interest. He commented on the great number of horse merchants to be found in Budapest, buying himself a horse there, and was intrigued by the Hungarian light chariots drawn by only one horse. These were a great contrast to the much more cumbersome variety in use in western Europe which needed several horses. Since he had now returned to countries ruled by European etiquette and customs he acquired a servant in order to demonstrate his social position for up until this time he had travelled alone or with temporary guides. The western amusement of the joust was a favoured entertainment in Hungary and Austria too and Bertrandon described the different varieties he attended in Budapest and Vienna. In the latter city he had some trouble in being recognised as a servitor of the duke of

51. The English method of shoeing a horse

Burgundy since he was still travelling in Turkish clothes but once this had been clarified he was warmly received and given generous presents. These included horses, richly embroidered hoods and even, in the Austrian fashion, a diamond to put on his head. His interest in military matters made him particularly curious about the wagons the Austrians used for fighting the Bohemians. The one he saw held only twenty men but he was assured that one had been built which could hold 300 men and required eighteen horses to pull it.[27] Such carts often had blades attached to their wheel hubs and seem to have been regarded as a medieval cross between an early tank and a troop-carrier. Bertrandon went on from Austria to Germany, Constance and down the Rhine to Basel, where the church council was still in session, and finally back to Burgundy. With some effort he found the duke who was staying in an abbey outside Châtillon and gave his report, dressed in the Moslem clothes in which he had joined the caravan in Damascus, leading the sturdy and faithful horse he had bought there and carrying the translation of the Koran and the deeds of Mahomet provided by the Venetian chaplain. Twenty years passed before the duke ordered his squire to write up his journey in full and by this time the victories of the Turks at Constantinople had almost extinguished European interest in any attempt at an overland crusade. Fortunately Bertrandon was able to rely on the diary he had kept in a small notebook during the trip to sharpen his memories. His nostalgia for his adventurous days in the Turkish caravan is suggested by the picture of himself in full Moslem dress reporting to the duke which served as the frontispiece to the presentation copy in 1457.

Duke Philip appears to have been pleased with the way in which his squire carried out his commission for he continued to show Bertrandon favour and to employ him in various special and responsible errands. In 1442 he was married to a rich Artois heiress and a few years later given the command of the castle of Rupelmonde in Flanders, a bastion of Burgundian power against the unruly townsmen of Ghent for it commanded the Escault river, Ghent's lifeline. Bertrandon de la Broquière died in 1459 in Lille, a quiet ending for a life which contained two years of extraordinary adventure. His envoi suggests that some of his fellows may have doubted his accuracy for he declares with some hauteur that his descriptions of his travels in obscure countries were not written from vainglory, pride or boasting, but merely to obey the duke's command. He added with some asperity, 'if any noble man wants to go there he can seek the road and find if I spoke truly'.[28] In fact, he left us a fascinating picture of life in the Moslem east twenty years before the fall of Constantinople when a disunited Europe could find no common will to withstand the onrush of the Turks.

The rather pompous prologue to the *Travels and Adventures* of Pero Tafur, a Spaniard who travelled extensively from 1435 to 1439, although always within the footsteps of previous travellers, hints at some of the motives which may have prompted these medieval adventurers:

> From the practice of travelling into foreign lands a man may reasonably hope to attain proficiency in that which prowess demands. Thus hidalgos may grow stout-hearted where, being unknown, they are beset by hardship and peril, striving to show themselves worthy of their ancestors, and by their own deeds to make their virtue known to strangers.[29]

Prowess and prestige were the publicly acceptable motives: there seems little doubt that profit and curiosity had an equal, if unacknowledged, part to play.

CHAPTER ELEVEN

FINAL JOURNEY

Since medieval courts and nobles were so often on the road death frequently surprised them far from home. The more important they were the more it was considered essential that their body, or at least their bones, should be returned to the mausoleum of their line. In such circumstances the final journey of their corpse to its place of burial could often be long and difficult. The inherent problems of distance and means of conveyance were magnified by the accepted belief that such a cortège – in death as visibly as in life – should mirror the importance and estate of the dead person, for it served as the last visual reminder of his place in the worldly hierarchy which he now had to relinquish. As surviving wills become more frequent in the fourteenth and fifteenth centuries those of the medieval establishment – kings, nobles and bishops – suggest the patterns within which such persons felt this final earthly act should be arranged in order to provide a fitting envoi. Frequently they specified with great care the place of burial, the number of followers in the cortège, the amount to be spent on lights and cloths for the coffin, the fees to be paid to the officiating clergy and religious as well as the robes and alms for the accompanying poor. Since chroniclers were often delighted to describe the elaborate funeral processions of kings and queens and also of important local lords, their more colourful reports add a general picture to the specific detail which can occasionally be found in the accounts and are interesting to compare with the instructions of the will itself.

For the early Plantagenets the abbey of Fontevrault in Anjou a little south of the Loire was considered as the 'cemetery of Kings'.[1]

Its *gisants* or tomb figures, of Henry II, Eleanor of Aquitaine, Richard the Lionheart and Isabella of Angoulême, the widow of John Lackland, are not only outstanding Romanesque sculptures but also tell us a great deal about the actual manner in which the kings and queens were carried to their burial. The Plantagenets began a fashion which was to spread among other royal families of using the funeral procession to emphasise the kingly nature of the sovereign. Henry II, for example, who died at Chinon in 1189, was reclothed in his official royal vestments with the crown on his head, the sceptre in his hand and slippers of gold tissue. It seems likely

52. The funeral procession of Charles V in 1380

that Henry thus clothed was displayed at Chinon before being carried the day after his death to Fontevrault for burial. By this time the science of embalming had progressed sufficiently far that Henry's face could be left uncovered for a short period. The Plantagenets were a new dynasty in England and this new elaborate funeral display was no doubt intended to reinforce its own legitimacy and to emphasise the sacred nature of the crowned and anointed king. The royal house of France adopted this type of display of the dead figure on an open litter both for the oldest son of Louis IX who died aged fifteen in 1260 and for Queen Blanche of Castile, who dressed as queen and with a gold crown, was carried through Paris by the noblemen of the country on a golden litter before she was buried at the abbey of Maubuisson near Pontoise.[2]

The course of events in the thirteenth century conspired to make royal funeral processions an elaborate adjunct to farflung travels. The dysentery and disease which afflicted the French crusading army in North Africa in the summer of 1270 decimated its ranks. The death of Louis IX himself on 25 August, which followed the earlier deaths of his son John Tristan and a leading official, Pierre le Chambellan, called for extraordinary measures. Louis' brother, Charles of Anjou king of Sicily, arrived at Carthage within a few hours of his brother's death and made the decisions about the procedure. The king's remains must be returned to St-Denis to lie with those of other French kings, but obviously the problems of transporting his body were insurmountable since the heat, the time required to cover the long distance, as well as the still not perfected state of embalming made it impossible to return the whole body. Charles took Louis's heart and entrails and buried them in his great monastery of Monreale outside Palermo, but the body itself was boiled in wine and water to strip the flesh from the bones, rendering them clean and resistant to decay. The same process was followed for the bodies of the king's son and his chamberlain. The French army only left North Africa in November, sailing to Trapani on the north-west tip of Sicily. The fleet encountered a serious autumn storm and had great difficulties in making land. The casualty list of the unfortunate expedition was not yet complete. In Trapani Philip III, the king of France, suffered the loss of Thibault, his sister's husband who was king of Navarre and count of Champagne, and his sister also died before the dispirited force returned to France. In a further stroke of misfortune Philip's queen, Isabella of Aragon, was thrown from her horse while fording a stream near Cosenza in Calabria. Since the queen was in an advanced stage of pregnancy the accident and the resultant stillbirth caused her death and her remains were added to the army's dismal burden. No wonder this returning host has been described as 'a body of mourners in a travelling necropolis'.[3]

It was not until May 1271 that the official burial at St-Denis could take place, although the king of Navarre and his wife had chosen to be buried in their county of Champagne at Provins. The chests containing the bones of Louis IX, his son John Tristan, Queen Isabella and Pierre le Chambellan were taken to Notre-Dame in Paris where the evening offices were sung, a great abundance of lights provided and a great company of nobles kept the night vigil. In the morning the funeral procession took the road to St-Denis with King Philip carrying on his shoulder the casket with his father's bones. A large cortege walked the ten miles from the cathedral to the abbey, for the king was accompanied by many nobles, followed by all the religious of Paris and the bishops, archbishops and abbots, wearing their mitres and carrying their croziers. The monks of St-Denis came out from the abbey to meet the solemn procession, whereupon a struggle over power and protocol disrupted the smooth performance of the ceremony. The archbishop of Sens and the bishop of Paris, within whose territory the abbey lay, had vested themselves to receive the bodies but the abbot and monks of St-Denis were jealously protective of their privileges as an abbey exempt from all episcopal jurisdiction. Not even for a royal funeral would they permit any suggestion of episcopal power in their church. The chronicle of Guillaume de Nangis clearly conveys the irritation and anger that gripped the chief mourners when they were confronted with the monastery's closed gates. The king stood before the shut door blocking his entrance to the church with his father's remains still on his shoulder, surrounded by barons and prelates. The king was determined to proceed but the monks would not give in so Philip finally ordered the archbishop and bishop to remove their vestments in order to allow the funeral rites to continue. Once the intransigent prelates had gone the monastery doors were opened and the funeral proceeded.[4] The unfortunate death of King Philip in 1285 while on an expedition against Aragon necessitated another long journey to bring his body back to St-Denis for burial. The striking nature of these unhappy processions may have made the French royal house even more conscious of the value of such ceremonies to reinforce the growing mystique of monarchy.

One of the most famous funeral journeys in English history has been that of Eleanor of Castile, the much-loved queen of Edward I. Queen Eleanor died at the end of November 1290 in Harby not far from Lincoln. Her entrails were buried in its cathedral and her heart at the Dominican church in London, but her embalmed body was ceremonially conveyed from Lincoln to Westminster. At each of its overnight stopping places the king erected a memorial cross – the famous Eleanor crosses – of which the best-known was at the little village of Charing then halfway between the city of London and Westminster. Edward himself, consistent with a life spent constantly on the move, died at Burgh-on-Sands north of Carlisle on 7 July 1307. He was immediately embalmed and wrapped in waxed cloth. After this the body was taken by stages to Waltham Abbey where it arrived 4 August. The final funeral ceremonies – the body spent one night at Holy Trinity London, one night at St Paul's and one night at Westminster before its burial in the abbey – did not take place until the end of October.[5]

During the fourteenth century most English and French kings died considerably closer to their capitals so that the funeral journey was primarily a ritual procession to St-Denis or Westminster. As ceremonies, both in England and in France, tended to become more and more elaborate, it gradually became common to have an effigy of a dead monarch, occasionally even of a dead queen, carried on the coffin. All this formality cost money. When King John II of France died a prisoner in England in 1364 the expenses incurred in bringing his body back to France, honourably and with the proper solemnity, as well as providing for his solemn obsequies and burial became a matter of diplomatic discussion. Charles V ordered his ambassadors to England in January 1369 to put forward these heavy charges as one of the reasons why his father's ransom had not yet been fully paid.[6] Nevertheless, the cost of funerals continued to rise over the next century.

Great lords, like their royal masters, often wished to be buried in a church which had a special place in their affections or the history of their line. Henry of Lancaster, Edward III's cousin and the greatest noble in England in the middle of the fourteenth century, ordered in his will that he should be buried in the collegiate church at Leicester near his father. Henry was not in favour of long-drawn-out rites for he specified that no matter where he died his body was only to remain unburied three weeks. The duke made no attempt to evade the usual amounts owed to the parish, providing that his body should rest overnight in the parish church, which was also to receive two cloths of gold and twelve torches, before it was taken to the collegiate church for burial. In addition, the parish priest was to have his best horse, or the price of it. Lancaster ordered that his funeral procession was to include nothing vain or extravagant such as armed men or draped horses, but it was to have a great sufficiency of candles and lights. Five candles of 100 pounds each, four great lamps and 100 torches were to burn around his body, the torches being carried by fifty poor men dressed at his expense in the Lancaster colours of blue and white.[7] Bartholomew Burghersh, who died eight years after Lancaster, had arranged for his body to be buried at the shrine of Walsingham. His body was to be taken there with speed after his death, but also with due recognition of his career and his importance. A torch was to be carried on either side of the coffin and lighted whenever the procession passed through a town. The chariot carrying the coffin was to be covered with a rich cloth of red cendal, adorned with the lion of his arms, and both the cloth and the torches were to be given to the church where the body rested at night. On the day of the funeral the usual torches were to be augmented by a candle at his head and feet while the body was to be covered only with the red cendal cloth. Burghersh was sufficiently proud of his knightly achievements to specify carefully that his helm should be transported on the top of the coffin and remain on it during his funeral for all to see.[8]

Count Amadeus VI of Savoy died in March 1383 in Apulia where he had led a fighting force at the request of the duke of Anjou. The Savoyards were attacked by plague and the count himself fell ill and died. In his will he asked for his funeral to be held in his own county, 'with the greatest pomp possible' and in the presence of all the archbishops, bishops, abbots and abbesses that could attend. His companions in Apulia took on the responsibility of fulfilling his last wishes. They had his body embalmed and began the long and arduous trip back to Savoy. They first travelled overland to the bay of Pozzuoli near Naples and there managed to load the coffin on a hired vessel. Unfortunately the boat also carried a number of sick men and many of them died during the voyage. As they sailed up the coast of Italy they were nearly shipwrecked by a dreadful storm off the tip of Elba, adding further discomfort to their unpleasant task. Their first landfall on the Ligurian coast aroused so much local hostility that they had to go on to Savona, where they were finally able to disembark the count's coffin and to find rooms in a couple of local inns. By this time their funds were exhausted and the healthiest members of the retinue explored every avenue to get enough money to continue their journey. They pawned their jewels, borrowed from the local usurers and were even reduced to stealing money from the pockets of the dying. After two weeks they were able to resume their journey, having acquired two horses and a litter to carry the coffin. The little procession crossed Piedmont, receiving homage from the Piedmontese vassals of Savoy, and took the Mont Cenis pass over the Alps. On their arrival in the Maurienne valley they were met by an escort of gentlemen and monks with candles who had sent by Amadeus VII to pay proper honour to his father. The journey across the mountainous Savoy countryside brought them finally to Chambery, Lake Bourget and the abbey of Hautecombe, the St-Denis of the house of Savoy. While the cortège slowly moved through the count's lands, ships had been kept busy travelling from Chambery to the abbey with officials and all the necessary provisions. Twenty-seven carpenters had been put to work at the abbey to build a suitable catafalque for the funeral ceremonies and there, in May 1383, the body of Count Amadeus was finally buried among his ancestors with the dignity and pomp he had requested.[9]

The contemporary funeral procession of Louis of Mâle, count of Flanders, was a far more imposing affair. The count had died at St-Omer on 28 January 1384 and the body was exposed in its abbey of St-Bertin for nineteen days. The delay may well have been caused by the complicated arrangements for the funeral and the added difficulty that Louis's will specified that his wife, who had died several years before, was to be buried with him in the same grave in the church of St-Pierre at Lille. Before the final journey could be begun her coffin had to be transported from its temporary resting-place in the county of Rethel. The funeral procession from St-Omer to Lille, a distance of about forty miles, took three days and on arrival the cortège stopped outside the city at the abbey of Loys, where the bodies once more laid in solemn state for another eight days. The formality was considerable. The bodies were laid out on biers covered first with a linen cloth and then by five cloths of gold, sewed one to the other, and they were surrounded by 120 torches held by squires and officials clad in black. Knights, squires and officials kept guard during the prayers and vigils in the banner-hung abbey. Finally, on 28 February the final procession began with all the solemnity and display possible. The bodies were each laid on a chariot and covered with a black cloth adorned with a crimson cross. The chariot bearing the count's body led the cortège, immediately followed by that bearing the countess. Behind them came the great body of mourners, led by Duke Philip the Bold of Burgundy, who had married the count's only daughter and heiress, and then, in proper order of rank, several important French lords, and great numbers of knights, squires and officials. Four hundred torches were carried by squires, officials and by the leading citizens of the Flemish and Artois towns, all clothed in black. When the great procession came to the Porte-St-Ladre, or Gate of the Sick, at the entrance to Lille, the bodies were taken off the chariots and placed on low carts, moved along by great officials and Flemish lords. From the city gate to the church the cortege was led by four knights holding the count's four tournament banners and four more knights with his four war banners. Behind them came four lords armed for the tournament and four others armed for war. After this display of power and chivalry came the carts with the two bodies. On arrival at the church, the procession of knights and banners was led apart into a great court belonging to one of the canons where the men and their horses could remain unseen until the next morning.

Within the church of St Pierre, in the choir before the high altar under a great black cross, a wooden chapel with five small towers had been constructed. On these towers were displayed the arms of the county's lands – the counties of Flanders, Artois, Burgundy, Nevers and Rethel. Both the turrets and the chapel were painted with the arms of Flanders on the right and the combined arms of Flanders and Brabant on the left. The bodies having been brought into the church, they were put on adjoining hurdles, the count's on the right hand place of honour and raised slightly above his wife's. As was to be expected, the choir of the church was filled with candles – about 700 each weighing a pound according to Froissart – while another 1,200 burned in the nave. The vigils then took place and on the following morning the funeral mass unrolled in all its solemn panoply. Delivered by the archbishop of Reims accompanied by four other bishops and a great number of prelates and ecclesiasties, it was attended by the duke of Burgundy as chief mourner, followed by princes and great lords in their proper order. During the offertory a great procession offered the count's escutcheons of war and tournament, four swords, four warhorses, four helms and his banners of tournament and war, with the duke of Burgundy making the first offering at the altar. After the funeral mass had been completed, the bodies were buried in the Lady chapel within the church. Then – probably with a sigh of relief – the whole entourage, including the great lords and the leading citizens of the Flemish and Artois towns, went off to a dinner given by the duke of Burgundy in the count's great hall. This was a solely masculine affair, except for the attendance of the wife of the governor of Lille. The elaborate ceremonies must have laid a heavy charge on the count's estate since all the guests had their lodging and meals given to them free of all cost, while knights and squires who had been part of the processions were all given the black clothes which they had worn. The descriptions of the count's funeral given by Froissart and the Sire d'Espierre, although exceedingly detailed on matters of protocol and prestige, make no mention of any alms to be given to the poor. It would not be out of character if such reporters were only interested in the parts played by the mighty.[10]

Duke Philip's own funeral twenty years later was equally ceremonious and the meticulous Burgundian accounts underline how expensive these long processions and delayed funerals actually were. The duke had died at Hal near Brussels on 27 April 1404 but he wanted his body to be taken for burial to the Chartreuse at

Champmol. Philip himself had founded this monastery just outside Dijon in order to provide a suitably splendid resting-place for the quasi-royal Burgundian line: his successors attracted the finest contemporary sculptors and artists from their own lands to beautify it and carve their memorials. The journey to Dijon was some 300 miles, mainly through Burgundian controlled territory, and careful preparations were made to ensure an adequate display of splendour. The body was embalmed, the entrails immediately buried in the church at Hal but the duke's heart was sent for burial at St-Denis, in recognition of his position as a king's son. These matters arranged, the body was clothed in a new white Cistercian habit, acquired from a Cistercian monk near Hal who was given eight *écus* for making it available. The body was then wrapped in leather and waxed cloth and put in a heavy leaden coffin weighing 700 pounds. The chariot carrying the body was drawn by six black horses and had banners with the duke's arms fixed at each of its four corners, while the coffin was covered with cloth of gold, bordered in black, and with a great red cross. Sixty hired mourners, dressed in the voluminous black robes and hoods recognisable from so many tomb sculptures, carried torches at the head of the procession, identified by the shield of the duke's arms on their sleeves. Behind them came the duke's son, his officials and all the members of his household. The accounts mention that more than 2,000 ells of black cloth were bought for the purpose of outfitting the whole procession at the duke's expense. Some effort was made to see that the clothes provided matched the people who wore them, for three tailors accompanied the cart full of robes from Brussels to Hal to make the necessary alterations. This may have been a wise precaution for it is recorded that the original houppelandes (long full overgarments with wide, flowing sleeves) made for the duke's two elder sons were not warm enough and the tailor had to make two long and two calf-length ones, lined with black lambskins for their greater comfort.

The itinerary of the cortège was carefully planned and all the necessities were anticipated. Twelve valuable cloths from Lucca were brought to be presented to the churches where the duke's body would rest on its journey. The duke's confessor was provided

53. Mourners around the tomb of Philippe Pot, characteristic of the funeral cortège around a king or great noble

with money for alms, offerings and masses. With all these expenses to meet the duke's heir was faced with a growing need for cash and borrowed 1,600 *livres* from a merchant of Bruges on the security of four baskets of gold and silver objects taken from the duke's ample treasury of plate. Once the cortège had arrived at the abbey of St-Seine in Burgundy it paused for two and a half weeks while the duke's eldest son paid off his father's household staff of some 180 people, including his barber and his clockmaker, and gave them money to defray their expenses on the road as they returned to their homes. On the last stage of their journey the solemn procession was met ten miles outside Dijon by the city's representatives, including not only the mayor and the aldermen but also 100 bourgeois and a further 100 poor men, all clothed in black. The clergy of Dijon joined the cortège once it had entered the city on its way to the duke's final resting-place at the Chartreuse of Champmol. The total cost of the long-drawn-out, elaborate journey was over 3,000 *livres*.[11]

As most wills made provision of alms to the poor corresponding to the wealth of the testator it would seem that the funeral of a great lord or lady might well have been a popular event. It could mean the opportunity of some money, and perhaps even the gift of a robe if one was lucky enough to be chosen as one of the mourners. Such rich possibilities of gain could even set the scene for a most undignified hubbub, as was evidenced at the funeral of the duke of Berry in 1416. Berry died on Monday 15 June 1416 at his Hôtel de Nesle in Paris and the first funeral took place at the nearby church of the Augustinians. On Friday evening the body was taken in solemn procession along the quay accompanied by the four mendicant orders of Paris and all the domestics of the duke's household. Mourning clothes were provided for these 380 servants by the executors of the duke's will at a cost of 2,840 *livres tournois*. The melancholy cortège was led by torchbearers carrying 100 torches to the sound of the constant ringing of little bells by paid bell-ringers. The spectacle caused so much interest among the Parisian populace that the crowd pressing into the church forced the thirteen royal sergeants, armed with white leather clubs, to struggle desperately to keep the unruly mob from impeding the chaplains in their functions. The pattern of a highly decorated chapel, massive provision of lights, torchbearers and standard-bearers at the services was much like that arranged for Berry's brother, the duke of Burgundy. After the usual prayers and vigils throughout the night the first funeral service took place in the morning after a great number of masses had been said. At its end the duke's almoner distributed the large sum of 500 *livres tournois* in small coins among the surging, almost riotous crowd.

Since Berry had wished to be buried at Bourges, the centre and capital of his duchy, the cortège left Paris immediately after the first funeral service. The coffin was placed in a covered wooden chariot, draped in black, and with a cross at each corner. It was drawn by five horses, also caparisoned in black and carrying shields of the duke's arms, harnessed between shafts painted in heraldic designs. The coffin was followed to the gates of Paris by the prelates and princes in attendance at the funeral. Once Paris had been left behind the 150 mile journey to Bourges was less ceremonious. The cortege included only the members of the duke's household, on foot or on horseback according to their station, and the accompanying mendicant friars, with no special display of banners or arms. The stops for the night were made at small villages as well as the larger towns in the duke's domains and the pattern was always the same. The inhabitants welcomed the procession and received the coffin in their church. It was not always easy, as in the small village of Chaumont-en-Sologne they had to break down part of the door of the parish church to enable the coffin to be carried in. The duke's executors later paid for the necessary repairs. Once the coffin had been installed in a church the local inhabitants joined the members of the procession in the daily offices by the light of the candles transported with the cortège in three great chests, while the bells tolled the knell. This progress took a week for it was not until the following Friday morning that they reached the duke's favourite castle of Mehun-sur-Yèvre where another funeral mass was cele- brated for all the members of the ducal household. From there the body went on to Bourges where it was taken to the cathedral to lie in state for the next two nights while the bells of all the local churches tolled. Before the body left the cathedral on Sunday there was another generous distribution of alms and, as the last move in this precisely planned pageant of mourning, the coffin was trans- ferred to the Ste-Chapelle founded by the duke in his palace at Bourges for the final vigil and burial service. The elaborate prep- arations of a temporary chapel under which to place the coffin and the draping of it and most of the church in black cendal had already been arranged. The precious cloth and the extraordinary amount of wax for candles – some 6,000 pounds – had been bought in Paris, packed in tuns and sent on to Bourges by cart. So many candles were lit and the heat they created was so great that the glaziers had been forced to remove some windows in the church to allow the air to circulate. On Monday 29 June the duke of Berry's final journey came to an end with the burial of his body in the crypt of his Ste-Chapelle.[12]

The funeral procession which returned the body of King Henry V to England in 1422 after his death at Vincennes just outside Paris can be compared with the long homeward journeys which brought the bodies of Louis IX and Philip III from North Africa and Aragon, although the passage of time had introduced further formalities. As in the earlier cases it was impossible to transport the whole body of the king so his bones were prepared for burial as Louis IX's had been, while Henry's entrails were buried at the abbey of St-Maur-des-Fossées near Vincennes. Because of the many arrangements required it was two weeks after Henry's death before the cortege could set forth on its homeward journey. Much of the detail sounds numbingly familiar with the black draped chariot and the lords and household members in their sober mourning clothes but there were also some differences. On the long, slow journey across northern France the king was represented by a lifelike effigy made of boiled leather, clothed in a mantle of royal purple, crowned with a diadem of gold and precious stones, holding the royal sceptre in one hand and the golden cross and ball in the other. This effigy was laid on a bed on the top of the chariot carrying the coffin and was sufficiently

54. Queens also might be represented by an effigy as in this case of Anne of Bohemia, Queen of Richard II

raised to make the royal figure easily visible to all the onlookers. The illusion of a living king's formal entry was re-enacted at each town on the slow journey to Rouen and north to Calais for the important men of each place solemnly carried a ceremonial canopy over the royal chariot during its passage. At every stopping-place the priests sang masses while men clothed in white held burning torches around the bier. Such solemn panoply was sufficiently impressive to attract many curious bystanders. One elderly Picard knight, suffering from gout, sought a first hand description from his herald who had seen the procession at Abbeville. The knight, who knew only too well about Henry's campaigns in France, asked with concerned interest if the king had his boots on. When his herald said no the knight cried out 'Never believe me if he has not left them in France.'[13] Once the long land trip had been completed, the cortege rested a few days before making the Channel crossing and finally arrived in London on 5 November, almost two and a half months after Henry's death. The mayor, aldermen and representatives of all the crafts of London joined in the slow sad march which, after a vigil and masses at St Paul's, moved ceremoniously towards Westminster Abbey. Each householder along the route had been ordered to have a servant at his door holding a torch to light the procession through the short November afternoon. The final ceremonies at Westminster seem reminiscent of those of the count of Flanders for the offerings included not only cloths of gold but four richly trapped horses, one of which was ridden by a knight dressed in the king's armour and crowned. It is not surprising that one of Henry's contemporary biographers could write that 'at which interment all things generally were done more honorablie and solemnely than had bin seene in England at the burying of anie Kinge or Prince at longe time before'.[14]

However, the general pattern of English funerals, even among the royal relatives was considerably less elaborate than those of the French dukes who were notorious for their love of splendour and display. Edward, duke of York and cousin of King Henry, who died at Agincourt, had made his will during the earlier siege at Harfleur. The duke wished to be buried at Fotheringay even if he died elsewhere and his body was duly carried from France to the church of the college which he had founded. Nevertheless, Edward had carefully specified that the procession carrying his corpse should not be an elaborate or overly ceremonious one. For such a great lord the retinue specified in the duke's will was very modest for his body was only to be accompanied by six squires, six valets and two chaplains, who were all to receive wages for fifteen days. The clerks and chaplains with the body were to have 13s 4d divided among them every night of the journey so long as they were present at the required prayers each day and they were also to have a daily 20s to distribute to the poor. York's interest in economy shows through in many of the items in his will for he specified that six torches were to burn around his body during the daily services and five candles each night, but these were not to cost more than 40s a day. He also ordered that one third of the cost of his funeral solemnities, which he restricted to £100, was to be distributed by half-groats to the poorest in attendance at the funeral services.[15]

Not only royal dukes but also some ecclesiastics felt the need of a ceremonious funeral. Bishop Hallum, who had been the highly respected leader of the English delegation at the Council of Constance died there in the summer of 1417. His will was made when he knew he was dying and its only request regarding his burial was that, if he died in Constance, he should be buried in its great church near the high altar and before the statue of the Blessed Virgin, whom he called 'my protectress and advocate'. The bishop took thought for those around him cast adrift by his death and ordered that his whole household should serve at his expense up to and including the day of his burial. His immediate retinue was to be sent back to England at his expense and in a suitable manner. Bishop Edmund Stafford, who died a year later, was rather more concerned about a properly dignified funeral. He specified that no matter where he died in England his body was to be carried to his diocese and buried in Exeter cathedral where he had recently built himself a monument. The funeral procession was to be relatively simple, although the body was to have 'decent' lights about it wherever it happened to spend the night. Once the bishop's corpse entered the diocese of Exeter, however, his coffin was to be surrounded by twenty-four poor, clothed in white and each carrying a burning torch. They were to receive 12d or more each from the bishop's executors, according to their labour. On the day of burial, besides a generous allowance for candles and torches and gifts made to the cathedral clergy, choristers and bell-ringers there were to be another 100 poor men sitting or standing around his bier, clothed in black or grey, and each rewarded with 4d.[16]

The last of these final journeys is, appropriately enough, that of Jacques de Lalaing, the redoubtable jouster and fighter who was killed by a random cannon shot during a siege in Flanders in 1453. The author of his life describes the extreme sorrow of the army on the news of their champion's death. The men were so sad and unhappy that the usual pandemonium of the camp, which could normally be heard for several miles, was suddenly stilled and only a bowshot away one would not have known anyone was there.[17] His body was suitably arranged by his mourning servants who brought it back to the castle of Lalaing on a black draped chariot. Lalaing's body lay in state in the great hall of the castle until it was carried to the nearby church of Ste-Aldegonde for the usual vigil, prayers and final burial service. The monument subsequently erected over his grave, which was described in the seventeenth century but destroyed during the French Revolution, represented the two opposing currents which had begun to run so strongly by the mid-fifteenth century. The tomb figure represented the typical medieval knight in full armour, bareheaded and with his hands joined in prayer, surrounded by thirty-two heralds in their coats of arms. Each carried a banner or a shield, displaying the arms of each of his noble ancestors for four generations. This conventional knight with his exaggerated insistence on his noble lineage and knightly status would seem to have his face firmly turned to the past, except for one telling detail that recognised the changing times. The feet of the tomb figure did not rest on the usual lion or dog but rather on a mortar or short cannon – the instrument of Lalaing's own death and the portent of a very different future.[18]

CONCLUSION

The company of rich and restless medieval travellers was a large and varied one, for the preceding chapters have merely provided a sampling of the noble men and women who spent much of their life on the road. Whether they were merely transferring themselves and the greater part of their households and belongings from one residence to another, travelled abroad as crusaders or pilgrims, pursued official business at the papal curia or the courts of Europe or the East, or sought adventure and riches, they travelled far more constantly and widely than has been generally acknowledged. Despite the many differences between individual travellers and the changing pattern of the centuries, certain similarities remain. Protocol became more elaborate and retinues larger between the thirteenth and the mid-fifteenth century but the acceptance of the inevitability of constant travel did not change. However, by the mid-fifteenth century the travellers' reports which have come down to us hint at a growing pleasure in travel. Many of these fifteenth-century travellers actively enjoyed their journeys and admitted to a heightened curiosity and fascination with the strange and the unfamiliar, an attitude which was encouraged by the growing emphasis on the individual response. All during this period the element of ceremony continued to be singularly pervasive and grew in complexity as even lesser nobles aped the formality and luxury of the royal and great noble households so far as their revenues permitted. For the medieval man or woman the maintenance of the proper ceremony, no matter how rough or rude the sur-roundings, was essential since it defined their place in the social hierarchy. Neither in life nor in death, as the great mourning pageants suggest, could most medieval lords and ladies bear to be separated from the external signs which both proved and displayed their status.

Nevertheless this underlying emphasis on prestige and their rightful place in the social hierarchy in no way restricted their activities nor kept an intent voyager from pursuing his curious adventures. Many of our travellers complained bitterly of the accidents of travel – the storms at sea, the horrors of mountain passes and the danger of brigands – but they did not allow such hardships and inconveniences to prevent them from continuing their journeys. Most of them seem to have thoroughly enjoyed the new and strange things they discovered on their travels and to have observed them with care and accuracy. St Bernard, travelling all day alongside Lake Geneva but oblivious to its existence, was not the typical medieval traveller, not even the typical peripatetic ecclesiastic. Despite the bare and often personally unrevealing comments made by many of these voyagers there is ample evidence of their curiosity and interest in the world around them and in the new experiences which their voyages offered. Generally the travellers of the upper class appear to have been intelligent, not intellectual, with a strong practical sense which lends credibility to their reports. Not surprisingly, upper-class men and women were neither philosophers nor scientists even in medieval terms. They reported what they saw very clearly but neither their acceptance of many fabulous tales about places or things of which they had no firsthand experience, nor their inability to go beyond appearances, is to be wondered at. The early sparsity of proven knowledge about far-off places and their inhabitants, both human and animal, was gradually overcome as more information was slowly absorbed into the common intellectual stock of the upper classes. They had, as the centuries went on, greater access to wide-ranging travel, more encounters with foreigners from far distant lands and were able to take advantage of the wider circulation of the written accounts of such great travellers as the missionary friars and the Venetian merchants.

Noble medieval travellers had one great advantage over their contemporaries for, during this period, the knightly class was an international body, recognising and respecting its fellow members wherever they were found. In a sense this favoured elite with its mutually shared patterns of life, customs, amusements and beliefs, often linked by ties of blood and marriage, sheltered many of our travellers from what would now be called culture shock. Their travels frequently took them among their social equals and they were generally greeted with warmth and genuine courtesy. After all, to be widely travelled was, in the Middle Ages, generally considered a mark of distinction, praised equally in such dissimilar situations as the great feasts of the Teutonic Knights in their frontier castles or in Christine de Pisan's refined poetry at the cultured French court of Charles V. Such men were able to make international friendships among their fellow crusaders and diplomats and could expect such courtly chroniclers as Froissart and Monstrelet to describe them approvingly if they lived up to the standard of Chaucer's 'parfit gentil knight' no matter for which side they fought. As well, they normally had the good fortune of being surrounded by a group of officials and servants on their journeys who could cushion their masters and mistresses from the inconveniences and complications that all travel necessarily involves. Brave, matter of fact, robust, generally good-tempered and curious about matters which aroused their interest – even in their fragmentary historical traces they have proved good travelling companions.

ABBREVIATIONS

BJRL   *Bulletin of the John Rylands Library*
BPH   *Bulletin philologique et historique (jusqu'au 1610) du comité des travaux historiques et scientifiques*
CLibR   *Calendar of Liberate Rolls*
CPR   *Calendar of Patent Rolls*
CS   *Camden Society*
EETS   *Early English Text Society*
EHR   *English Historical Review*
HS   *Hakluyt Society*
OHS   *Oxford Historical Society*
PPTS   *Palestine Pilgrims Text Society*
RS   *Rolls Series*
SHF   *Société pour l'histoire de France*
TRHS   *Transactions of the Royal Historical Society*

SELECT BIBLIOGRAPHY AND NOTES

This select bibliography has been designed for the inquiring general reader rather than the scholar and suggests chiefly introductory studies, many with extensive bibliographies, or other particularly interesting works not mentioned in the Notes. A book on medieval travellers draws from a wide range of sources and these have been listed with full bibliographical detail in Notes. Because of the diversity of the travellers it seemed most helpful to group relevant titles with the pertinent chapter notes for ease of reference.

Many books on geography, travel and discovery concentrate on the general history of their topic rather than on individuals but C. R. Beazley, *The Dawn of Modern Geography*, vols. 2 and 3 (New York 1949) provides excellent short studies of a wide range of medieval travellers. G. H. T. Kimble, *Geography in the Middle Ages* (New York 1938) and the first two chapters of B. Penrose, *Travel and Discovery in the Renaissance 1420–1620* (New York 1962) also discuss individuals though less comprehensively. J. J. Jusserand, *English Wayfaring Life in the Middle Ages*, rev. ed. (London 1921) and *Travel and Travellers in the Middle Ages*, ed. A. P. Newton (London 1926) have been basic works for over fifty years but much specialised work has been done since their appearance. Both the Hakluyt Society and the Palestine Pilgrims Text Society have made available in English translations many first-hand accounts of medieval travellers and pilgrims. A relatively recent book, I. de Rachewiltz, *Papal Envoys to the Great Khan* (London 1971) describes the extraordinary range of the friars whose poverty has put them outside the category of travellers portrayed here. J. Huizinga, *The Waning of the Middle Ages* (London

1924) remains influential in its view of the fourteenth and fifteenth centuries while P. Contamine, *La vie quotidienne pendant la guerre de Cent Ans: France et Angleterre* (Paris 1976) puts into popular form the work of one of the most respected French medievalists.

INTRODUCTION, pp. xi–xvii

1. *Materials for the History of Thomas Becket* (RS 67) 3, 29–31.

2. G. R. Owst, *Literature and Pulpit in Medieval England*, 2nd rev. ed. (Cambridge 1966), 134.

3. *The Art of Falconry* (being the *De Arte Venandi cum Avibus* of Frederick II of Hohenstaufen), trans. and ed. by C. A. Wood and F. M. Fyfe (Stanford 1961) 51–2.

4. *The Commentaries of Pius II*, trans. by F. A. Grogg, intro. and notes by L. C. Gabel (Smith College Studies in History, Northampton, Mass. 1937) 1; 18.

5. *The Travels of Leo of Rozmital*, ed. and trans. by M. Letts (HS 2nd ser. 108, 1957), 58, 62.

6. C. L. Kingsford, 'John de Benstede and his missions for Edward I' in *Essays in History presented to Reginald Lane Poole*, ed. H. W. C. Davis (Oxford 1929), 354.

Chapter 1   THE SHAPE OF THEIR WORLD, pp. 1–16

J. K. Wright, *The Geographical Lore of the Time of The Crusades* (New York, 1925, reprint 1965) as well as the works of Beazley and Kimble apply especially to this chapter as does R. V. Tooley, *Maps and Mapmakers*, 6th Eng. ed. (New York 1978)

1. *The Mongol Mission*, ed. with intro. by C. Dawson (London and New York 1955), 2–72.

2. Salimbene di Parma, *Cronica*, ed. F. Bernini (Bari 1942) 1; 304.

3. G. Peigniot, *Catalogue d'une partie des livres composant la bibliothèque des ducs de Bourgogne au XVe siècle*, 2e ed. (Dijon 1841), 32.

4. M. V. Clarke, *Fourteenth Century Studies*, ed. L. S. Sutherland and M. McKisack (Oxford 1937), 120.

5. R. F. Green, *Poets and Princepleasers* (Toronto 1980), 154.

6. Bartholomaeus Anglicus, *On the Properties of Things* (Oxford 1975) 2, Bk. XV, 823–4, 734, 812.

7. *The Book of Ser Marco Polo*, ed. and trans. by H. Yule, 3rd ed. rev. by A. Cordier (London reprint 1975), 2 v.

8. *Mandeville's Travels: Texts and Translations*, ed. and trans. M. Letts (HS 2nd ser. 101–2, 1953).

9. C. Deluz, 'La "géographie" dans le *Liber* de Guillaume de Boldensele, pèlerin de Terre Sainte, 1336' in *Voyage, Quête, Pèlerinage dans la Littérature et la Civilisation Mediévales* (Senefiance 2, Aix 1976), 25–38.

10. *Ludolph von Suchem's Description of the Holy Land* (PPTS 12 1895, reprint 1971), 2.

11. *The Autobiography of Giraldus Cambrensis*, ed. and trans. by H. E. Butler (London 1937), 97.

12. Gilles Le Bouvier, dit Berry, *Le Livre de la Description des Pays*, ed. E. T. Hamy (Paris 1908), 4–9.

13. Ibid., 29.

14. Ibid., 30–1, 51.

15. Ibid., 39–41; 46; 53; 54–5; 57; 61.

16. Ibid., 84, 58–9, 63.

17. Ibid., 78–9, 91–3, 74.

18. Ibid., 103, 116–17, 118–20.

19. Ibid., 123–4.

20. A. L. Moir, *The World Map in Hereford Cathedral*, 8th ed. (Hereford 1979).

21. R. Vaughan, *Matthew Paris* (Cambridge 1958), 237–44, 247–50.

22. E. J. S. Parsons, *The Map of Great Britain circa A.D. 1360 known as the Gough Map* (Oxford 1958).

23. Morgan Library catalogue (New York) re M877.

24. Kimble, *Geography*, 191; Tooley, *Maps and Mapmakers*, 15.

25. Tooley, 15; I. Origo, *The Merchant of Prato*, rev. ed. (London 1963), 99; J. Guiffrey, *Inventaires de Jean duc de Berry 1401–16*, 2 v (Paris 1894–6), 1; nos. 986–8; 2; p. 317, no. 1047.

Chapter 2 POINT OF DEPARTURE, pp. 17–37

General works on roads include C. Taylor, *Roads and Tracks of Britain* (London 1979), and J. Hubert, 'Les Routes de Moyen Age' in *Les Routes de France depuis les origines jusqu'à nos jours* (Colloque, Cahiers de Civilisation, Paris 1959). J. F. Tyler is informative in *The Alpine Passes: The Middle Ages* (London 1930). Two books on the sea and medieval ships and sailors are of particular interest: A. R. Lewis, *The Sea and Medieval Civilisation* (London 1978) and G. V. Scammell, *The World Encompassed* (Berkeley, California 1981).

1. M. Prestwich, *The Three Edwards* (London 1980), 25.

2. A. R. Myers, *The Household of Edward IV* (Manchester 1959), 85; M. McKisack, *The Fourteenth Century 1307–1399* (Oxford 1959), 436;

M. N. Boyer, 'A Day's Journey in Medieval France' in *Speculum* 26 (1951), 600.

3. C. Keen, 'The Traveller's Dial in the Late Middle Ages: The Chilinder' in *Technology and Culture* 18 (1977), 420–4.

4. J. Le Goff, *Pour un autre Moyen Age: Temps, travail et culture en Occident* (Paris 1977), 76; L. Douet d'Arcq, *Comptes de l'Argenterie des rois de France au XIVe siècle* (SHF Paris 1851, reprint 1966), 209, 228, 237; Peigniot, *Catalogue*, 83–4.

5. *English Historical Documents 1327–1485*, ed. A. R. Myers (London 1969), 422.

6. P. Meyer, 'La manière de langage qui enseigne à parler et à écrire le Français' in *Revue Critique d'Histoire et de Littérature* 10 (1870), 387–95.

7. *Bordeaux sous les rois d'Angleterre*, ed. Y. Renouard (Boirdeaux 1965), 224; G. A. J. Hodgett, *A Social and Economic History of Medieval Europe* (London 1972), 59.

8. *The Register of Henry Chichele, Archbishop of Canterbury, 1414–1443* 2: Wills, ed. E. F. Jacob (Canterbury and York Society 42, 1937), 242, 340; *Liber quotidianus contrarotulatoris garderobae: Anno regni Regis Edwardi I vigesimo octavo (1299–1300)* (London 1782), 28.

9. Raymond d'Aguilers, *Historia Francorum Qui Ceperunt Iherusalem*, trans. with intro. and notes by J. H. and L. L. Hill (*Memoirs American Philosophical Society* 71, Philadelphia 1968), 16; G. Fordham, *Les Routes de France* (Paris 1929), 10.

10. *Autobiography . . . Giraldus*, 201–2.

11. Salimbene, *Cronica* 1; 305.

12. H. David, 'L'hôtel ducal sous Philippe le Bon', *Annales de Bourgogne* 37 (1965), 254; *Le Livre de Seyntz Medicines*, ed. E. J. Arnould (Anglo-Norman Text Society 2, Oxford 1940), 99–102.

13. Ph. Wolff, 'L'hôtellerie, auxiliaire de la Route', in BPH 1960, 194–5; *Archives de l'Orient Latin* 2, Chartes I, 11, p. 249.

14. *The Itineraries of William Wey* (Roxburghe Club 1857), 155.

15. *CLibR 1251–1260*, 197, 245; B. F. and C. R. Byerly, *Records of the Wardrobe and Household 1285–1286* (HMSO 1977), nos. 442–60.

16. *Travels . . . Rozmital*, 62–4.

17. Dante, *Divina Commedia*, Purgatorio, canto 3, ll. 49–51.

18. *The Register of Eudes of Rouen*, trans. S. M. Brown, ed. J. F. O'Sullivan (Records of Civilisation 72, New York 1964), 196; *Chronicon Adae de Usk A.D. 1377–1421*, ed. with trans. and notes E. M. Thompson (London 1904), 242; P. Tafur, *Travels and Adventures 1435–1439*, trans. and ed. M. Letts (London 1926), 82–3.

19. *The Exempla of Jacques de Vitry*, ed. T. F. Crane (New York 1890, reprint

1971), 84–5, 126–7; J. Joinville, *The Life of St Louis*, trans. by R. Hague (London 1955), nos. 630–3; *Le Voyage d'Oultremer de Nompar, seigneur de Caumont*, ed. P. S. Noble (Medium Aevum monographs, new ser. 7, Oxford 1975), 56–9.

20. 'Narrative of the Voyage of Abd-er-Razzak', *India in the Fifteenth Century* (HS 1st ser. 22, reprint 1970), 45–8, 42.

21. *Autobiography . . . Giraldus*, 45; *Calendar of Papal Letters* 2 (1305–42), 484.

22. *Les chansons de Colin Muset*, ed. J. Bedier (Paris 1935), 27.

Chapter 3   ITINERANT KINGS AND QUEENS, pp. 38–60

Information about travelling courts is not easily isolated from the more general descriptions of royal households given in administrative histories. A sketch of the problems which faced both kings and nobles is provided in two articles by G. Stretton, 'The Travelling Household in the Middle Ages', *Journal of the British Archaeological Association* n.s. 40 (1935), 75–103 and 'Some Aspects of Medieval Travel', TRHS 4th ser. 7 (1924), 77–91. The introduction to A. R. Myers, *The Household of Edward IV* (Manchester 1959) is a brief but enlightening sketch of 15th century practice.

1. *Life in the Middle Ages*, selected, trans. and annotated by G. G. Coulton (Cambridge 1971) 3; 2–5.

2. T. F. Tout, *The Place of the Reign of Edward II in English History*, 2nd rev. ed. by H. Johnstone (Manchester 1936), 277–8.

3. *Liber . . . garderobae (1299–1300)*, 83.

4. M. N. Boyer, 'Medieval Suspended Carriages', *Speculum* 34 (1959), 360–3; T. Stapleton, 'Summary of Wardrobe Accounts of 10, 11, and 14 Edward II', *Archaeologia* 26 (1836), 342–3.

5. Byerly, *Records*, nos. 1699, 1704, 1709, 1711.

6. J. C. Parsons, *The Court and Household of Eleanor of Castile in 1290* (Toronto 1977), 32; 115 n. 177; 72 n. 68.

7. *The Household Book of Queen Isabella of England 1311–12*, ed. F. D. Blackley and G. Hermansen (Edmonton 1971), 121, 107.

8. *Liber . . . Garderobae (1299–1300)*, 98.

9. *The Chronicle of Muntaner*, trans. by Lady Goodenough (HS 2nd. ser. 47 and 50, 1920–1) 1; 353.

10. Joinville, nos. 93–7; *Recueil des Historiens des Gaules et de la France* 22; 616–22.

11. *Recueil* 24, 97, 259, 366; W. C. Jordan, *Louis IX and the Challenge of the Crusade* (Princeton 1979), 147.

12. Byerly, *Records*, nos. 573, 604; 526, 537; 536; 1699, 1704, 1700; 1694; 796:

J. P. Trabut-Cussac, 'Itinéraire d'Edouard Ier en France 1286–89', *Bulletin of the Institute of Historical Research* 25 (1952), 160–76.

13. J. R. H. Moorman, 'Edward I at Lanercost Priory 1306–7', EHR 67 (1952), 161–74.

14. Ibid., 173–74.

15. Ibid., 168–69.

16. Stapleton, 'Accounts . . . Edward II', 333.

17. Olivier de la Marche, *Mémoires*, ed. H. Beaune and J. d'Arbaumont (SHF Paris 1883) 1; 58–62.

18. Douet d'Arcq, *Comptes*, 239–41, 248.

19. Ibid., 241–4.

20. Ibid., 270–5.

21. *Chroniques des Règnes de Jean II et Charles V*, ed. R. Delachenal (SHF Paris 1910–16) 2; 236–44; L. A. Loomis, 'Secular Dramatics in the Royal Palace, Paris, 1378, 1389' in *Speculum* 33 (1958) 242–58.

22. La Marche 1; 270–82.

23. Ibid., 272.

24. Ibid., 280.

25. Ibid., 281.

Chapter 4 TRAVELLING HOUSEHOLDS, pp. 61–80

A more complete study of the countess of Leicester and her household can be found in M. W. Labarge, *A Baronial Household of the Thirteenth Century* (London 1965, reprint 1980) while N. Denholm-Young, *Seignorial Administration in England* (Oxford 1937) gives a useful introduction to the make-up of great households in the late thirteenth century. R. Vaughan, *Valois Burgundy* (London 1975) provides a general view of the life of the Valois dukes while Ch. Commeaux, *La vie quotidienne en Bourgogne au temps des ducs Valois (1364–1477)* (Paris 1979) is less scholarly but covers the whole range of society.

1. *Manners and Household Expenses of England in the Thirteenth and Fifteenth Centuries*, ed. H. T. Turner, intro. B. Botfield (Roxburghe Club 1841), 3–92.

2. Ibid., 3–5.

3. Ibid., 12–14.

4. Ibid., 42–8.

5. Ibid., 55, 9, 24, 8.

6. J.-M. Richard, *Une petite-nièce de Saint-Louis: Mahaut, comtesse d'Artois et de Bourgogne (1302–29)* (Paris 1887), 53.

7. Ibid., 55.

8. Ibid., 81.

9. Ibid., 123–9; *Manners*, 10.

10. Richard, op. cit., 130–2.

11. Ibid., 365–9.

12. Ibid., 368, 108–10.

13. Hoccleve, *Works: I, The Minor Poems* 2 (EETS ES 61, 1892), 14–15.

14. *Book of Ser Marco Polo* 1, 68–9; Richard, op. cit., 100–6.

15. F. Lehoux, *Jean de France, duc de Berri (1340–1416)* (Paris 1966–67) 2, 390–5.

16. R. Vaughan, *Philip the Bold* (London 1962), 190.

17. G. Salmon, 'Bateaux et Bateliers sur Rhone et Saône', *Voyage, Quête, Pèlerinage*, 146–7; Commeaux, *La vie quotidienne . . . Bourgogne*, 257–60.

18. J. Cordey, *Les contes de Savoie et les rois de France pendant la guerre de Cent Ans (1329–91)* (Paris 1911), 221–6.

19. Ibid., 348–9, 221–6.

20. F. R. H. Du Boulay, 'Henry of Derby's Expeditions to Prussia 1390 and 1392', *The Reign of Richard II*, ed. F. R. H. Du Boulay and C. Barron (London 1971), 155.

21. *Expeditions to Prussia and the Holy Land made by Henry, Earl of Derby*, ed. L. T. Smith with intro. and notes (CS new ser. 52, 1894), xxxv–xxxvii; lxxii–lxxix.

22. *The Travels of Leo of Rozmital*, ed. and trans. M. Letts (HS 2nd ser. 108, 1957).

23. Ibid., 100.

24. Ibid., 146–7.

Chapter 5   NOBLE PILGRIMS, pp. 81–113

It is difficult to give merely a brief list of books on pilgrimages but the following may serve as an introduction to the subject. J. Sumption, *Pilgrimage* (London 1975); R. Oursel, *Pèlerins du Moyen Age* (Paris 1978). For the Holy Land: R. J. Mitchell, *The Spring Voyage* (London 1964); H. L. Savage, 'Pilgrimages and Pilgrim Shrines in Palestine and Syria after 1095', *A History of the Crusades*, K. M. Setton general ed. 4 (Madison, Wis. 1977), 36–68; H. F. M. Prescott, *Jerusalem Journey* (London 1949; U.S. title, *Friar Felix at Large*, New Haven 1950) and *Once to Sinai* (London 1957, New York 1958). For Compostela: V. and H. Hell, *The Great Pilgrimage of the Middle Ages* (London 1964) E. Mullins, *The Pilgrimage to Santiago* (New York 1974); Y. Bottineau, *Les Chemins de Saint-Jacques* (Paris 1964). For Rome: G. B. Parks, *The English Traveller to Italy: 1, The Middle Ages* (Rome 1954). For local pilgrimages: D. J. Hall, *English Medieval Pilgrimage* (London 1965); J. Adair, *The Pilgrims' Way*

(London 1978); M. Méras, *Abbayes et Pèlerinages de France* (Paris 1964); L. Bély, *Le Mont Saint-Michel, monastère et citadelle* (Rennes 1978).

1. Ghillebert de Lannoy, *Oeuvres*, ed. Ch. Potvin (Louvain 1878), 9–178; see also M. W. Labarge, 'Ghillebert de Lannoy: Burgundian Traveller', *History Today* 26 (1976), 154–63 and R. Ariès, 'Un seigneur bourguignon en terre musulmane au XVe siècle: Ghillebert de Lannoy', *Moyen Age* 85 (1977), 283–302.

2. Etienne de Bourbon, *Anecdotes historiques, légendes et apologues*, (SHF Paris 1877), 389 n. 1.

3. Richard, *Petite-nièce*, 86–7.

4. H. Kraus, *Gold was the Mortar* (London 1979), 145–6.

5. R. Boutrouche, *La crise d'une société* (Paris 1947), Pièce justif. 21, 497.

6. PRO E315/42/246 (I owe this reference to M. M. Sheehan's index of early English wills); Chichele *Register* 2, 74, 488.

7. *Itineraries . . . Wey,* 5.

8. *Expeditions . . . Derby,* 220–4, 278.

9. *Pageant of the Birth Life and Death of Richard Beauchamp earl of Warwick K.G. 1389–1439,* facs. ed. H. A. Dillon and W. H. St. John Hope (London 1914).

10. Tafur, *Travels*, 56.

11. *Pageant*, 39–40.

12. 'Voyage en Terre Sainte d'un maire de Bordeaux au XIVe siècle', *Archives d'Orient Latin* 2 (1884), Documents, Voyages, 378–88.

13. Lannoy, 68.

14. J. Wellard, *Samarkand and Beyond* (London 1977), 142, 29.

15. J. Galey, *Sinai and the Monastery of St. Catherine* (New York 1980).

16. 'Voyage', *Archives*, 378 n. 3, 388.

17. *Voyages . . . Caumont*, 11.

18. Ibid., 32.

19. Ibid., 35.

20. *The Book of the Wanderings of Felix Fabri*, trans. A. Stewart (PPTS 7–10, 1887–97) 8, 607–8, 611ff.

21. *Voyage . . . Caumont*, 58–70.

22. Ibid., 80–2.

23. Ibid., 32.

24. *The Exempla, or Illustrative Stories from the Sermones Vulgares of Jacques de Vitry,* ed. T. F. Crane (London 1890) 217–18, 85–6.

25. *Le Guide du pèlerin de Saint-Jacques de Compostelle,* ed. J. Vielliard, 3e ed. (Macon 1963), 122–25.

26. *CPR 1321–24,* 15; Boutruche, *Crise,* Pièce justif. 21, 496; *Millénaire*

Monastique du Mont Saint-Michel: 3, Culte de Saint-Michel et pèlerinages au Mont, ed. M. Boudat (Paris 1971), 245.

27. *Travels . . . Rozmital*, 124–5.

28. *The Stacions of Rome*, ed. F. J. Furnivall (EETS old ser. 25). 37; Stapleton, 'Accounts . . . Edward II', 345; *Original Letters illustrative of English History*, ed. H. Ellis, 2nd ser. 1 (1827), 111.

29. *CPR 1391–96*, 537–8, 565–6, 568, 601–2, 572.

30. *Itineraries . . . Wey*, 156.

31. *The Register of the Common Seal*, ed. J. Greatrex (Hampshire Record Series 2), nos. 289–90.

32. R. Vaughan, *Philip the Good* (London 1970), 180–1.

33. J. Froissart, *Chroniques*, ed. Kervyn de Lettenhove, 26 vols. (Brussels 1870–7) 11, 339–49.

34. *Travels . . . Rozmital*, 100–3.

35. 'Pèlerinage du Seigneur de Caumont à Saint-Jacques de Compostelle' in *Guide*, ed. Vielliard, 132–40.

36. Tafur, *Travels*, 34–5.

37. *The English Hospice in Rome* (*The Venerabile*, Sexcentenary issue xi, Exeter 1962), 15–56.

38. Tafur, *Travels*, 36–43.

39. *CPR 1429–36*, 282, 471; *Original Letters*, 2nd ser. 1, 102; *The Register of Thomas Langley, Bishop of Durham, 1406–37*, ed. R. L. Storey (Surtees Society 166) 5; 101 *CPR 1388–92*, 171; *Pageant*, 25–6; Lannoy, 178.

40. Douet d'Arcq, *Comptes*, 272–3.

41. *Travels . . . Rozmital*, 43–4, 50–1.

42. L. F. Salzman, *Edward I* (London 1968), 82.

43. M. A. E. Green, *Livres of the Princesses of England* 2 (London 1849), 408–41.

44. Hall, *English Medieval Pilgrimage*, 114.

45. Froissart 6; 281–2.

46. Kingsford, 'Benstede', 352.

47. *Millénaire Monastique* 3, 244.

48. *Millénaire Monastique du Mont Saint-Michel; 1. Histoire et vie monastique*, ed. J. Laporte (Paris 1966), 303 n. 1.

49. *Register . . . Eudes*, 96–7; *Millénaire Monastique* 1; 333–4.

50. St. John D. Seymour, *St Patrick's Purgatory* (Dundalk 1918), 7.

51. *Chronique des quatres premiers Valois 1327–1393*, ed. S. Luce (SHF Paris 1862, reprint 1965), 22–3; Froissart 15; 145–6; *Travels . . . Rozmital*, 82.

52. Seymour, 37–43, 63–70; Lannoy, 170–3; Seymour, 79–81.

Chapter 6   KNIGHT CRUSADERS, pp. 114–135

Most easily accessible for an introduction to the Crusades are S. Runciman, *A History of the Crusades*, 3 v. (London 1951–4, paperback 1964); J. Prawer, *The World of the Crusaders* (New York 1972) and E. Christiansen, *The Northern Crusades* (New York 1980).

1. Joinville, *The Life of St Louis*, trans. R. Hague (New York 1955); see also references to Joinville in M. W. Labarge, *Saint Louis* (London and Boston 1968).
2. Joinville, no. 122.
3. Ibid., no. 159.
4. Ibid., nos. 399–400, 418, 583.
5. Ibid., nos. 332, 397.
6. Ibid., nos. 597–601.
7. *Rôles Gascons* 3, ed. C. Bemont (Paris 1906), xxxiii–xlvii.
8. E. R. Clifford, *A Knight of Great Renown* (Chicago 1961); C. L. Kingsford, 'Otho de Grandison', TRHS 3rd ser. 3 (1909), 125–95.
9. Ch. Kohler, 'Deux projets de croisade en Terre-Sainte', *Revue de l'Orient Latin* (1903–4), 406–20.
10. *Register Clement V* 6 (Rome 1885), no. 8205.
11. Clifford, *Knight*, 261–2.
12. Owst, *Literature and Pulpit*, 332–3.
13. P. Tucoo-Chala, *Gaston Fébus et la vicomté de Béarn 1343–1391* (Bordeaux 1959), 76.
14. *Archives de l'Orient Latin* 1 (Paris 1881), 418–22.
15. Christiansen, *Northern Crusades*, 149–50.
16. Tucoo-Chala, op. cit., 74–9.
17. *Medieval Hunting Scenes (The 'Hunting Book' by Gaston Phoebus)*, text by G. Bise (Miller Graphics n.d.), 17.
18. A. S. Cook, 'Beginning the Board in Prussia', *Journal of English and Germanic Philology* 14 (1915), 376–7, 380.
19. Christiansen, op. cit., 150; *Expeditions . . . Derby*, 142.
20. *Expeditions . . . Derby*, xcvi–xcvii, 106–12.
21. *Le Livre des faits du Bon Messire Jean Le Maingre, dit Boucicaut* in J. F. Michaud et J. F. Poujoulat, *Nouvelle Collection des Mémoires pour servir à l'histoire de France* 1^{cre} ser. 2 (1836), 214.
22. Ibid., 223, 224, 233.
23. Ibid., 229.
24. Ibid., 235–46; Runciman, *Crusades* 3, 455–61.
25. Froissart 2, 205–7.
26. Lannoy, 17–18.

27. Ibid., 20–7.

28. Ibid., 28–38.

29. Ibid., 44–9.

30. La Marche, *Mémoires* 2, 348–80.

Chapter 7   DIPLOMATS ON THE ROAD, pp. 136–162

The one full-fledged study of medieval ambassadors is D. E. Queller, *The Office of Ambassador in the Middle Ages* (Princeton 1967). There is a great deal of useful information on diplomatic activities in G. Cuttino, *English Diplomatic Administration*, 2nd rev. ed. (Oxford 1971) and on the nature of the educational treatises in B. Behrens, 'Treatises on the Ambassador in the Fifteenth and Sixteenth Centuries' EHR 51 (1936), 616–27.

1. G. Mattingly, *Renaissance Diplomacy* (London 1963), 28–49.

2. T. Rymer, *Foedera, conventiones, literae* 3rd ed. (Hague 1739–41, reprint 1967) 4, ii, 190–1.

3. Lannoy, 196; Rymer, *Foedera* 5; i, 118–19.

4. Froissart 2: 205.

5. Mattingly, op. cit., 38.

6. John Russell's *Boke of Nurture* in F. J. Furnivall ed., *The Babees Book* (EETS 32), 191.

7. G. Besse, *Recueil de diverses pièces servent à l'histoire de Charles VI* (Paris 1660), 94–111.

8. *Commentaries . . . Pius II* 1; 83; H. Bonet, *The Tree of Battles*, intro. and trans. by G. W. Coopland (Liverpool 1949), 186.

9. *Royal and Other Historical Letters illustrative of the Reign of Henry III*, ed. W. W. Shirley (RS 27, 1862) 1; 249–54.

10. Matthew Paris, *Chronica Majora*, ed. H. R. Luard (RS 57 1872–83), 7 vols (1872–83) 3; 318–25.

11. Paris, *Chronica Majora* 4, 145–7.

12. P. Chaplais, 'Some Private Letters of Edward I', EHR 77 (1962), 82, 85. (Also published in P. Chaplais, *Essays in Medieval Diplomacy and Administration*, London 1981, chap. XXI).

13. J. Stevenson, *Documents illustrative of the History of Scotland* (Edinburgh 1870) 1; 134–7.

14. Clifford, *Knight*, 184.

15. Cuttino, *English Diplomatic Administration*, 176.

16. Ibid., 175–6; L. F. Salzman, *Medieval Byways* (Boston 1913) 41–51.

17. *Chronicon Henrici Knighton*, ed. J. R. Lumby (RS 92, 1889–95) 2; 78–9; F. Bock, 'Some New Documents', BJRL 15 (1931), 94–7.

18. Froissart 14; 376–88.
19. *Narrative of the Embassy of Ruy Gonzalez de Clavijo to the Court of Timour at Samarkand, A.D. 1403–6*, trans. with notes by C. R. Markham (HS 1st ser. 26 1859, reprint 1970), 87.
20. Ibid., 31, 41–3; 35.
21. Ibid., 90.
22. Ibid., 158.
23. Lannoy, 378–9.
24. Ibid., 51–67, 99–162.
25. Ibid., 63.

Chapter 8   PERIPATETIC ECCLESIASTICS, pp. 163–184

W. A. Pantin, *The English Church in the Fourteenth Century* (Cambridge 1955) is an excellent introduction and E. F. Jacob, *Essays in the Conciliar Epoch*, 2nd ed. (Manchester 1953) and *Essays in Later Medieval History* (Manchester 1968) are particularly useful for the conciliar period.

1. *Snappe's Formulary* ed. H. E. Salter (OHS 80, 1924), 304–5.
2. *The Register of Eudes of Rouen*, trans. by S. M. Brown, ed. by J. F. O'Sullivan (Records of Civilisation 72, New York 1964); O. G. Darlington, *The Travels of Odo Rigaud, Archbishop of Rouen (1248–1275)* (Philadelphia 1940), 74–7.
3. *Register . . . Eudes*, 417, 460; 179, 543–4, 413.
4. Ibid., 382–3, 388, 397.
5. *Exempla . . . Vitry*, 2.
6. Salimbene, *Cronica* 2, 101–2.
7. Darlington, *Travels*, 75; Y. Renouard, *Etudes d'histoire médiévale* (Paris 1968) 2; 682–3; *Register . . . Eudes*, 382, 454.
8. *Roll of the Household Expenses of Richard de Swinfield, bishop of Hereford*, ed. J. Webb (CS old ser. 59, 1854).
9. Ibid., 34–42, 163; 214.
10. Ibid., 71.
11. Ibid., 163, 147, 149.
12. *Register of John de Grandisson, bishop of Exeter*, ed. F. C. Hingeston Randolph (London 1894–99) 1; 315–46.
13. Ibid., 331.
14. C. L. Kingsford, 'Otho de Grandison', TRHS 3rd ser. 3 (1909), 173–5.
15. *Register . . . Grandisson* 1, 242–44.
16. Clifford, *Knight*, 260–1; PRO Lists and Indexes 15, gives summary of Grandisson's letter in Ancient Correspondence LXVII, 14 and also lists similar letters from the Black Prince sent to other religious houses

and clergy in the west country. The date is assigned and perhaps questionable.

17. *Archives historiques de la Gironde* (Bordeaux) 21; 480–5.

18. J. Dahmus, *William of Courtenay, Archbishop of Canterbury 1381–1396* (University Park, Penn. 1966), 269.

19. J. H. Wylie, *The Reign of Henry V* (Cambridge 1914, 1919) 1; 417–18; Jean Juvenal des Ursins, *Histoire de Charles VI de France*, in *Mémoires*, ed. Michaud and Poujoulat 2; 500.

20. Wylie, *Henry V* 1; 498–500, 424–5.

21. Ibid., 1; 500–10; 2; 42–3; A. Coville, *Gontier et Pierre Col et l'humanisme en France* (Paris 1934), 51–2.

22. J. Amundesham, *Annales monasterii S. Albani*, ed. H. T. Riley (RS 28e, 1870–1) 1; 118–83.

23. Ibid., 147.

24. Ibid., 181–2.

25. *Commentaries . . . Pius II* 1; 16–21.

26. Ibid., 16–17.

27. Ibid., 18.

28. R. J. Mitchell, *The Laurels and the Tiara: Pope Pius II 1458–64* (London 1962), 53.

Chapter 9 THE SOCIAL ROUND, pp. 185–210

R. Barber, *The Knight and Chivalry* (London 1970) describes the social activities of knights, especially tournaments, and provides an extensive bibliography. D. A. Bullough, 'Games People Played; Drama and Ritual as Propaganda in Medieval Europe' TRHS 5th ser. 24 (1974) and G. Mathew, *The Court of Richard II* (London 1968) are particularly valuable for the fourteenth and early fifteenth century attitudes. N. Denholm-Young, 'The Tournament in the Thirteenth Century' in *Studies in Medieval History presented to F. M. Powicke*, ed. R. W. Hunt, W. A. Pantin, R. W. Southern (Oxford 1948) explains the early tournaments. O. Cartellieri, *The Court of Burgundy* (London 1929) gives a very full description of the magnificence of the Burgundian court and its social occasions. B. Henisch, *Fast and Feast: Food in Medieval Society* (University Park, Penn. 1976) is comprehensive and fascinating.

1. *Oeuvres poétiques de Christine de Pisan*, ed. M. Roy (Paris 1886, reprint 1965) 1; 65.

2. *L'Histoire de Guillaume le Maréchal*, ed. P. Meyer (SHF Paris 1891) 1; ll. 1201–1525, 2471–5094.

3. Ibid., ll. 1367–72.

4. *Livre de Seyntz Medicines*, 138.

5. *L'Histoire . . . Maréchal* I; ll. 2875–3164.

6. Ibid., ll. 3426–3520.

7. *Exempla . . . Vitry*, 62–3; Robert Mannyng of Brunne, *Handlyng Synne*, ed. F. J. Furnivall (EETS old ser. 123, 1901), ll. 4571–4620; Owst, *Literature and Pulpit*, 335.

8. S. Wenzel, 'The Joyous Art of Preaching', in *Anglia* 97 (1979), 314–15.

9. Bonet, *Tree of Battles*, 262.

10. T. Wykes, *Annales monastici* 4, ed. H. R. Luard (RS 36, 1869), 161–2.

11. 'Account of the expenses of John of Brabant and Thomas and Henry of Lancaster A.D. 1292–3', ed. J. Burtt, *Camden Miscellany* 2 (CS old ser. 55, 1853), iii–xiv, 1–15.

12. C. Bullock-Davies, *Menesttrellorum Multitudo* (Cardiff 1978), ix–xli.

13. *Le Livre de Chevalerie de Geoffroy de Charny*, publ. in Froissart, *Chroniques* 1, pt. 3, 463–533.

14. Ibid., 479–80.

15. Ibid., 529.

16. R. Barber, *Edward, Prince of Wales and Aquitaine* (London 1978) 42; Rymer, *Foedera* 2; iv, 57.

17. *Adae Murimuth continuatio chronicorum*, ed. E. M. Thompson (RS 93, 1889), 155–6.

18. *Livre . . . Boucicaut*, 219–20.

19. C. Green and A. B. Whittingham, 'Excavations at Walsingham Priory, Norfolk, 1961', in *The Archaeological Journal* 125 (1968), 285–8.

20. Froissart 14, 105–51.

21. *Livre . . . Boucicaut*, 230–2.

22. René d'Anjou, *Traité de la forme et devis d'un Tournoi* (Paris 1946).

23. A. Lecoy de La Marche, *Le Roi René* (Paris 1875) 2, 147–9; *Extraits des comptes et Mémoriaux du Roi René*, ed. A. Lecoy de La Marche (Paris 1873), nos. 731–34.

24. J. Ribard, *Un ménestrel du XIVe siècle, Jean de Condé* (Geneva 1969), 81–2.

25. *Livre des faits de Jacques de Lalaing*, publ. in G. Chastellain, *Oeuvres* 8, ed. Kervyn de Lettenhove (Brussels 1884, reprint 1971), 2.

26. Ibid., 63–4.

27. Ibid., 165–80.

28. Ibid., 170.

29. Ibid., 253, n. 1.

Chapter 10 · THE ADVENTURERS, pp. 211–231

The early sections of J. H. Parry, *The Age of Reconnaissance* (New York 1964) and Ch. de la Roncière, *Histoire de la marine française*, 2ᵉ vols. 1 and 2 (Paris 1909) both deal with some of these fifteenth-century adventurers.

1. *Chronicle . . . Muntaner* 2, 466–513.
2. 'The Travels of Nicolo Conti in the East' in *India in the Fifteenth Century*, ed. R. H. Major (HS 1st ser. 22, 1857), 3–39.
3. Tafur, *Travels*, 96.
4. Beazley, *Dawn* 3, 419.
5. *The Book of the Knowledge of all the Kingdoms, Lands and Lordships that are in the World*, trans. C. Markham (HS 2nd ser. 29, 1912).
6. *The Canarian*, trans. and ed. by R. H. Major (HS 1st ser. 46, 1872), x–xi; Ch. de la Roncière, *Histoire de la marine française* 2, 104–6.
7. *The Canarian*, 4.
8. P. Margry, *La Conquête et les Conquérants des Iles Canaries* (Paris 1896), 286–89.
9. Jean de Bueil, *Le Jouvencel*, intro. C. Favre, texte L. Lecestre (SHF Paris 1887) 1; 43.
10. *The Canarian*, 172.
11. Ibid., 177.
12. Ibid., 198.
13. Ibid., 204.
14. Margry, *La Conquête*; *The Canarian*; Beazley, *Dawn* 3; 444–54; La Roncière, *Histoire* 2, 112–19.
15. *Le Voyage d'Outremer de Bertrandon de la Broqueière*, ed. Ch. Schaefer (Paris 1892), xvii.
16. Ibid., 2–3.
17. Ibid., 15–16, 49–50, 38–9.
18. Ibid., 55–8, 261.
19. Ibid., 61–3.
20. Ibid., 73.
21. Ibid., 63, 121.
22. Ibid., 63–4, 89, 91–2.
23. Ibid., 111, 128–9.
24. Ibid., 143.
25. Ibid., 165.
26. ibid., 216–31.
27. Ibid., 244.
28. Ibid., 261.
29. Tafur, *Travels*, 19.

Chapter 11   FINAL JOURNEY, pp. 232–248

Upper-class attitudes to death and funeral pomp are discussed in T. S. R. Boase, *Death in the Middle Ages* (London 1972); J. T. Rosenthal, *The Purchase of Paradise* (London and Toronto 1972) and used as an introduction by R. Giesey, *The Royal Funeral Ceremony in Renaissance France* (Geneva 1960). The recent massive work by P. Ariès, *The Hour of Our Death* (New York 1981) is a quarry of material on every aspect of death through the ages but is very idiosyncratic.

1. A. Erlande-Brandenburg, 'La Sculpture Funéraire vers les Années 1200: Les Gisants de Fontrevault' in *The Year 1200: A Symposium* (New York 1975), 561.

2. R. Giesey, op. cit., 23.

3. F. M. Powicke, 'Guy de Montfort (1265–71)' in *Ways of Medieval Life and Thought* (London 1949), 86.

4. Guillaume de Nangis, *Philippe III in Recueil des Historiens des Gaules et de la France* 210; 486–9.

5. W. H. St John Hope, 'On Funeral Effigies of Kings and Queens of England', *Archaeologia* 60 (1907), 528–9.

6. *Chronique . . . Jean II et Charles V* 3; 124.

7. J. Nichols, *A Collection of the Wills of the Kings and Queens of England* (London 1780), 83–5.

8. Prestwich, *The Three Edwards*, 164 quoting *Testamenta Vetusta* 1; 77.

9. Cordey, *Comtes de Savoie*, 241–3.

10. Froissart 10, 278–85; 21, 261–8.

11. *Itinéraires de Philippe le Hardi et de Jean sans Peur, ducs de Bourgogne (1363–1419)*, ed. E. Petit (Paris 1888), 574–9; R. Vaughan, *John the Fearless* (London 1974), 1–2.

12. Lehoux, *Berri* 3; 406–18.

13. Enguerrand de Monstrelet, *The Chronicles*, trans. T. Johnes 2 vol. (London 1849) 1; 485.

14. *The First English Life of Henry V*, ed. C. L. Kingsford (Oxford 1911), 183–5; T. Walsingham, *Historia Anglicana*, ed. H. T. Riley 2 vol. (RS 28a, 1863–4) 2; 345–6; St John Hope, 'Effigies', 535–6; Monstrelet 1, 484–5.

15. *Register . . . Chichele* 2, 64.

16. Ibid., 126–8; 153–5.

17. *Livre . . . Lalaing*, 255.

18. Ibid., 256–7.

LIST OF ILLUSTRATIONS

15. Dover Castle. Keystone Press Agency.

16. Fourteenth-century rocking chariot, Rudolf von Ems, *Weltchronik c.* 1335. Zentralbibliothek Zurich, MS Rheinau 15, fol. 54r.

17. Mid-fourteenth century musicians MS Bodl. 264, fol. 180v. Bodleian Library, Oxford.

18. The Earl of Derby embarks for France. Froissart, Harl. MS 4380, f. 149. British Library.

19. The landing of Dame de Coucy and the unloading of her luggage. Froissart, Harl. MS 4380, f. 189b. British Library.

20. Fifteenth-century view of Jerusalem. MS Fr. 9087, fol. 85v, Bibliothèque Nationale, Paris.

21. Marco Polo setting out from Venice. MS Bodl. 264 f. 218. Bodleian Library, Oxford.

22. The Earl of Warwick going on pilgrimage. Cotton Julius E.IV f. 5. British Library.

23. The Earl of Warwick's feast for the Sultan's lieutenant at Jerusalem. Cotton Julius E.IV f. 10v. British Library.

24. Drawing of the precincts of the Church of the Holy Sepulchre from a thirteenth-century pilgrim's guide. MS 609 f. 4r. Bild-Archiv der Öster-reichischen Nationalbibliothek, Vienna.

25. The Earl of Warwick making an offering at the Holy Sepulchre in the hall where arms were hung. Cotton Julius E.IV f. 9. British Library.

26. Statue of St James holding a pilgrim's staff. Photograph by Dr H. Hell, Reutlingen.

27. Pilgrimage badge of Thomas Becket. By permission of the Comptroller of Her Majesty's Stationery office.

28. Departure of St Louis and his company on his first crusade in 1248. MS Roy. 16 G.VI, f. 404v. British Library.

29. St Louis, the best known crusader of the thirteenth century. Statue at Maineville (Eure). Archives Photographiques.

30. Individual combat between a Christian knight and a Saracen. MS Roy. 2. B. VII, fol. 150. British Library.

31. The castle of Marienburg, the headquarters of the Order of Teutonic Knights.

32. Gaston Fébus in his palace at Orthez. Froissart, MS Roy. 14 D.V., f. 8r. British Library.

33. Duke Philip the Good of Burgundy by Rogier van der Weyden. Institut Royal du Patrimoine Artistique. Copyright A. C. L. Brussels.

34. The marriage of Philip of Artois, Count of Eu to the daughter of the Duc de Berry. Froissart. MS Harl. 4380, f. 6. British Library.

INDEX